LOST NUKE

THE LAST FLIGHT OF BOMBER 075

DIRK SEPTER

VICTORIA | VANCOUVER | CALGARY

Heritage House Publishing Company Ltd.
heritagehouse.ca

Library and Archives Canada Cataloguing in Publication

Septer, D. (Dirk), 1949–
    Lost nuke: the last flight of Bomber 075 / Dirk Septer.

Includes bibliographical references and index.
Also issued in electronic format.
ISBN 978-1-926936-86-4

    1. Nuclear weapons—Accidents—British Columbia—Pacific
Coast—History. 2. Airplanes, Military—Accidents—British Columbia—Pacific Coast—
History. 3. Aircraft accidents—British Columbia—Pacific Coast—History. 4. Nuclear
weapons—Accidents—United States. 5. Airplanes, Military—Accidents—United States.
I. Title.

U264.3.S46 2011   363.17'990916433   C2011-905036-6

Cover design by Jacqui Thomas
Interior design by Frances Hunter
Front-cover photos by Doug Davidge (wreck) and John Rutherford (detail of aircraft);
back-cover photo by Michael Carroll/Myth Merchant Films

The author has made every effort to locate and obtain permission from the copyright holders of the photos in this book. If you find an error or omission, please contact the author via the publisher.

The information and views expressed within do not reflect the views of the publisher but remain solely those of the author.

 This book was produced using FSC®-certified, acid-free paper, processed chlorine free and printed with vegetable-based inks.

Heritage House acknowledges the financial support for its publishing program from the Government of Canada through the Canada Book Fund (CBF), Canada Council for the Arts and the province of British Columbia through the British Columbia Arts Council and the Book Publishing Tax Credit.

 Canadian Patrimoine
Heritage canadien
 Canada Council Conseil des Arts
for the Arts du Canada
 BRITISH COLUMBIA
ARTS COUNCIL

16 15 14 13 12   1 2 3 4 5

Printed in Canada

This book is dedicated to the crew of US Air Force
B-36B Serial 44-92075 and all the servicemen who lost their lives
during the Cold War, 1945-1991.

The Crew of Bomber 075

Name and Rank	Assignment on Last Flight
Survivors	
Barry, Harold L., Captain	Pilot/aircraft commander (front)
Cox, Ernest O. Jr., First Lieutenant	Flight engineer (front)
Darrah, Roy R., First Lieutenant	Observer (rear)
Ford, James R., Staff Sergeant	Radio operator (front)
Gerhart, Paul E., First Lieutenant	Navigator and radar operator (front)
MacDonald, Daniel V., Lieutenant Colonel	AFWSP Bomb commander (front)
Pooler, Charles G., First Lieutenant	Engineer (front)
Schuler, Richard J., Corporal	Radar mechanic (front)
Stephens, Martin B., Staff Sergeant	Gunner (rear)
Thrasher, Dick, Staff Sergeant	Gunner (rear)
Trippodi, Vitale, Staff Sergeant	Radio operator (front)
Whitfield, Raymond P. Jr., First Lieutenant	Co-pilot (front)
Missing and Declared Dead	
Ascol, Holiel T. (37), First Lieutenant	Bombardier (front)
Phillips, William M. (30), Captain	Navigator (front)
Pollard, Elbert W. (28), Staff Sergeant	Gunner (rear)
Schreier, Theodore F. (35), Captain	AFSWP Weaponeer/co-pilot (front)
Straley, Neal A., (30), Staff Sergeant	Gunner (rear)

Contents

This mission was to be as real as it gets, short of war.

—First Lieutenant Raymond P. Whitfield,
co-pilot Bomber 075

Prologue

During the Cold War years, between 1945 and 1991, the United States Air Force (USAF) accidentally lost several nuclear weapons; the first loss happened somewhere over northwestern British Columbia.

On February 13, 1950, while en route from Alaska to Texas, a huge six-engine USAF Convair B-36 "Peacemaker" (Bomber 075) disappeared along the north coast of British Columbia. The intercontinental bomber had been on a training mission to test the operational characteristics of the aircraft and its nuclear payload under severe winter conditions. Faced with multiple engine fires, the crew abandoned the aircraft over Princess Royal Island, about 320 miles north of Vancouver, BC.[1] Before the crew bailed out, they dropped a Mark IV nuclear bomb in the Inside Passage, not far from where BC Ferries' *Queen of the North* went down more than half a century later.

The accident led to a joint Canadian–American search and rescue operation, the largest of its kind ever conducted in this region. Unaware of the bomber's deadly load, Canadian Navy and Air Force personnel searched in appalling weather conditions for the missing crew. Though all but 5 of the 17 crew members were found, there was no sign of the bomber. For all intents and purposes, this giant aircraft had just vanished. Led to believe that it had flown out to sea and ditched there, officials made no attempt to locate it.

Right after the Peacemaker disappeared, the search for its crew received considerable media coverage on both sides of the border. However, a few months later a more pressing matter, the Korean War, captured the world's attention, and the missing-bomber incident was forgotten.

The accident was a source of great embarrassment and security concern to the USAF. Not only had one of their $4-million state-of-the-art bombers gone missing, but worse, they had also lost their first nuke, which was on loan for the exercise. Considering the potential for a nuclear disaster over the soil of a friendly neighbour and ally, who also happened to be their biggest supplier of uranium, how could the USAF admit to the loss of a nuclear bomb?

Almost three and a half years after it disappeared, the bomber miraculously reappeared where nobody expected to find it. On September 3, 1953, during an aerial search for another missing aircraft, the wreckage of the Peacemaker was found, not in the vicinity of Princess Royal Island where it had been abandoned, but in the opposite direction of the autopilot setting, some 200 miles north in the coastal mountains, at an elevation of about 6,000 feet.

Though the US Air Force immediately sent a salvage team, their attempts to reach the site by air and, later, overland proved unsuccessful. The following year, a USAF demolition team finally managed to reach the site. After securing and salvaging several unspecified, sensitive items from the wreckage, they destroyed the aircraft. Buried under snow and ice for most of the next 24 years, the remains were virtually forgotten.

An account of the incident released in 1977 under the US Freedom of Information Act revealed that the crew of Bomber 075 had dropped a nuclear bomb just prior to abandoning the aircraft. Official records confirm that there was a nuclear bomb aboard, but that it was unarmed. A declassified report of US military nuclear accidents released in the late 1970s provided only vague details, so it was unclear at the time whether the plutonium core (also called the plutonium or nuclear capsule), necessary for arming the bomb, was on the aircraft.

The USAF made a concerted effort to cover up the incident by changing "the facts." In a twist of misinformation, for example, all official reports stated that the wreckage was found on Vancouver Island.[2]

Having lived for years in the immediate area where the bomber went down, I was fascinated and inspired by the intriguing rumours and the recollections of residents. There were too many unanswered questions. How could the aircraft have continued to fly for about three hours in a direction exactly opposite to the aircraft's autopilot setting, gaining at least 3,000 feet in altitude? Did the man in charge of the bomb remain on board in an attempt to prevent a nuclear disaster?

In 1997, following a widely publicized visit by combined crews from Environment Canada and the Canadian Armed Forces, the exact location of the wreck site became known to the public. Though protected under the British Columbia Heritage Conservation Act and accessible only by helicopter, the site has since been ransacked and looted.

Having signed an oath of secrecy, the few surviving crew members remain tight-lipped about what actually happened. They do not dispute any of the several official versions of the incident. Today, the mystery surrounding Bomber 075 continues to fascinate aviation and history buffs alike.

Lost Nuke: The Last Flight of Bomber 075 is a compilation of all the facts and theories that I have gathered over a 20-year period. I have attempted to unravel the true facts behind more than 60 years of secrecy, misdirection and misinformation surrounding the world's first "Broken Arrow," as accidents involving nuclear weapons have come to be known.

Running the risk of being called a conspiracy theorist, I have included all possible scenarios, however unlikely. Ultimately, it will be up to you, the reader, to decide what most likely happened on Bomber 075's last flight.

PART 1 | Setting the Scene

CHAPTER 1

Dawn of the Nuclear Era and the Cold War

On August 6, 1945, a US Army Air Forces (USAAF) B-29 bomber, under the command of Colonel Paul Tibbets Jr. and named *Enola Gay* after his mother, dropped an atomic bomb named "Little Boy" on the Japanese city of Hiroshima. Three days later, another B-29 dropped a second, even more powerful atomic bomb named "Fat Man" on Nagasaki.

The usual casualty figures quoted are 66,000 killed in Hiroshima and 39,000 in Nagasaki. By the end of 1945, slower, agonizing deaths resulting from burns and radiation sickness would bring these totals to about 140,000 and 70,000 respectively. If the bomb that struck Nagasaki had not missed its intended target, Kokuran, with a larger population, the casualty count could have been even higher.[1]

The American people were left in the dark about the atomic bomb until it had actually been dropped, and even then, they were deceived about its target. On August 9, 1945, President Harry Truman announced on the radio, "The world will note that the first atomic bomb was dropped on Hiroshima, a *military* base [italics are mine]. That was because we wished in this first attack to avoid, insofar as possible, the killing of civilians."[2]

President Truman's claim that his final decision to use the atomic bomb saved the lives of half a million to a million American soldiers has been disputed. Many civilian and military leaders opposed the use of this new, powerful bomb against civilian targets. In his eye-opening book

The Decision to Use the Atomic Bomb and the Architecture of an American Myth, Gar Alperovitz clearly demonstrates that the American leaders were convinced that the end of the war was near because the Japanese, facing the prospect of Soviet entry into the war against them, were close to surrender.

Military leaders like Admiral William D. Leahy, General Henry H. "Hap" Arnold and General Dwight D. "Ike" Eisenhower saw no need to use the nuclear bomb, while most of President Truman's key cabinet members requested a clarification of Emperor Hirohito's views on surrendering.

Admiral Leahy, military chief of staff to presidents Franklin D. Roosevelt and Harry S. Truman, said, "It is my opinion that the use of this barbarous weapon at Hiroshima and Nagasaki was of no material assistance in our war against Japan."[3]

General Arnold, the commanding general of the US Army Air Forces, stated, "It always appeared to us that, atomic bomb or no atomic bomb, the Japanese were already on the verge of collapse."[4] Former president Herbert Hoover agreed. Two days after the bomb fell on Hiroshima, Hoover wrote to the publisher of the *Army and Navy Journal*: "The use of the atomic bomb, with its indiscriminate killing of women and children, revolts my soul."[5]

However, under influence of incoming Secretary of State James F. Byrnes, who thought that the use of the atomic bomb would send a strong message to the Soviets, the inexperienced president made this fatal decision.

The dropping of two nuclear bombs during the Second World War changed everything about warfare forever. In the confusion that prevailed in large parts of Europe in the months following the end of the war, the Cold War broke out, with the United States and its allies on one side, and the Soviet Union and its allies on the other. Although the United States and the Soviet Union had themselves been allies during the war, differences between the two over the occupation of Europe had led to growing mistrust.

On March 5, 1946, during a visit to the United States, Winston Churchill first used the phrase "Iron Curtain" to describe the political barrier that defined the eastern-European lands under the control of Russia.

The hardening of East–West relations in Germany after the war was accompanied by a growing tension in other parts of Europe and the Middle East. The situation worsened in January 1948 when the Soviet Union imposed restrictions on western traffic to Berlin. This and a dispute over the currencies to be used in the divided city resulted in a full-scale blockade of Berlin by the Soviet Union, in the summer of 1948.

The western powers thought that abandoning Berlin would mean losing all of western Europe, so they started supplying the city from the air. The western airlift was supplemented by a counter-blockade of the Russian zone by the West. The blockades lasted nearly 11 months, ending on May 12, 1949.

During the airlift, President Truman sent B-29 bombers to military bases in Europe. Although these aircraft were not armed with nuclear weapons, their deployment sent a signal to the Soviet Union that the US was capable of using them. By September 1948, American military planners were putting an increasing emphasis on nuclear weapons, both for use in war and as a deterrent to war. In fact, it seemed inevitable that the United States would start preparing for a war that might include the use of both nuclear and biological weapons.

In 1946 Congress had created the Atomic Energy Commission (AEC), transferring the responsibility for atomic energy from military to civilian hands. The AEC was put in charge of developing and maintaining custody of the US nuclear arsenal. From 1946 until the late 1960s, the commission was the sole US purchaser of uranium. Its authority also included the licensing of "source materials" containing uranium.

On September 24, 1949, President Truman announced that the United States had obtained evidence that the USSR had detonated its first atomic bomb. This did not leave any doubt about the need for a long-range retaliatory striking force. As America's primary deterrent to full-scale aggression, the United States Air Force's Strategic Air Command (SAC) would confront the Soviet Union with a massive airborne atomic retaliation if provoked or attacked.

Under SAC's commander, General Curtis E. LeMay, the B-36 became the heart of the United States' nuclear retaliatory system in the 1950s. LeMay, SAC commander since 1948, fought for obtaining more B-36 bomb groups and also instilled a sense of elitism among the members of his command.

By 1949, just over a year after he was put in charge of SAC, LeMay had acquired a whopping force that consisted of 868 aircraft, including 36 of the new intercontinental B-36 bombers, 390 B-29 and 99 B-50 bombers, 18 RB-17 and 62 RB-29 reconnaissance aircraft, and 67 KC-29 aerial tankers. The bombers were divided into 3 heavy-bomb groups and 11 medium-bomb groups, operating from 17 bases in the continental US.

Such a massive force required a large number of aircrews and support personnel, so many Second World War veterans were recalled for active duty. By December 1949, SAC employed 10,050 officers, 53,460 airmen and nearly 8,000 civilian personnel. Many more were required.

Later, when more and more B-36s had entered service with SAC and proved that the bomber's performance exceeded its original requirements, the B-36 became known as America's Big Stick.[6] In the early 1950s, the B-36 Peacemaker was the pride of SAC, reaching its operational peak in 1955. The aircraft would become the very symbol of SAC itself, as would General LeMay.

Although opinions about SAC boss LeMay differ, "Old Iron Pants" was generally perceived as a no-nonsense leader who expected perfection. "Though he was fairly small, 5 feet 5 inches, there was no doubt as to whom was in charge! He exuded a real aura of authority. [The] only time I ever saw him in person...he had so much 'fruit salad' on his chest that his wings were almost on his shoulder strap," former B-36 crew member Raleigh Watson recalled.[7]

"I always felt that as long as you did your job, he was not rough, but he was demanding," said another crew member, Walter Mitchell.[8]

One day, after landing at Carswell Air Force Base (AFB) in his C-54 and walking through base operations without being challenged, LeMay fired the whole command. Legend also has it that LeMay once approached a fully fuelled bomber with his ever-present cigar stuck firmly between his lips. When a guard asked him to put it out, as it might ignite the fuel, LeMay growled, "It wouldn't dare."

In early 1947, AEC assumed legal custody of 11 nuclear weapons, with the Air Force Special Weapons Project guarding and maintaining the bombs. Only by the order of the US president could a military organization take custody of a nuclear weapon. By late 1947, two assembly teams had been formed. However, nobody had ever practised assembly procedures prior to turning over the first AEC bomb to a bombing unit.

At the beginning of 1948, only six crews existed who were trained to drop an atomic bomb. Even though there were enough qualified personnel available to make up another 14 crews, SAC had a massive re-enlistment problem and severe manpower shortages in the trained positions. Atomic units had nearly 100 percent turnover of personnel in 1947. The most serious problem was the lack of weaponeers.

Late in 1948, SAC had a new war plan called Trojan, which emphasized a powerful first strike in an intense strategic air offensive. By then, through Herculean efforts, 70 crews had been trained for the atomic operations, more bomb commanders and weaponeers were expected, and a fourth atomic assembly team was forming, bringing the total number of assembly teams to four. However, in 1949 SAC rarely had more than 40 B-36 bombers on hand.

On January 31, 1950, a few months after the Russians detonated their first nuclear bomb and two weeks before the final flight of Bomber 075, President Truman authorized a program to develop thermonuclear, or fusion, bombs, popularly known as hydrogen bombs or H-bombs. The first country to acquire the H-bomb would gain an important psychological advantage in the Cold War.

LeMay believed a war between the United States and the Soviet Union was inevitable, and his strategy for such a conflict was simple. Instead of waiting for a Soviet nuclear attack, he believed in attacking the enemy where it would hurt most: in its cities. To prepare for such an attack, he had the B-36 crews constantly flying practice bombing runs over US cities at night, honing their ability to drop nuclear weapons.

LeMay established an unprecedented 24-hour-combat-readiness status with B-36 crews flying around the clock on global training missions and on-station airborne alerts, in full combat posture. "People were down there in their beds and they didn't know what was going on upstairs," he later wrote in his autobiography, *Mission with LeMay*. "San Francisco had been bombed over 600 times in a month."[9]

It was during such a bomb run, as the B-36 took its place as America's premier delivery vehicle for nuclear weapons, that Bomber 075 went down.[10]

CHAPTER 2

Birth of a Peacemaker

The story of the B-36 began nine years before the loss of Bomber 075. Early in 1941, while Germany renewed its air raids in the London Blitz and U-boat attacks intensified in the North Atlantic, General Henry H. Arnold, chief of the US Army Air Corps (which would later become the US Army Air Forces and finally the US Air Force), decided to move ahead with developing a bomber capable of travelling intercontinental distances.[1] The looming prospect of entering the war demanded a bomber capable of striking targets in Europe—a bomber that could carry the battle to Germany from the US mainland in case the Atlantic Ocean supply lines were broken.

On April 11, 1941, the Air Corps issued specifications to industry for the development of the strategic bomber. A number of companies grappled with the 10,000-mile-range requirement. Douglas Aircraft, which at the time was having major difficulties building a large long-range bomber under the B-19 program, expressed doubt that such an aircraft could even be developed, and declined to submit a design. On October 6, 1941, Consolidated Aircraft Corporation submitted its bid to design and construct two long-range, high-altitude bombardment airplanes, each equipped with six propeller engines.

The $15-million contract, under which Consolidated Aircraft would get a fixed fee of $800,000, was awarded on November 15, 1941 (a mere three weeks before the attack on Pearl Harbor). The contract covered the cost of building two aircraft, including the engineering, mock-up, fabrication and testing of the wind-tunnel models. Consolidated Aircraft was to build the aircraft at its plant in San Diego, California. The first was to be delivered within 30 months, and the second within 6 months of the first. The plan was to have the first B-36 take to the air in May 1944.[2]

Soon after Consolidated Aircraft's team of engineers began work, they faced a number of problems stemming from the large size of the aircraft. In order to fly the required 10,000-mile, two-day missions, the aircraft would require low aerodynamic drag, low fuel consumption and high engine durability. To get the smoothest possible airflow, the engineers decided to mount the propellers on the backs of the wings so that the propellers pushed rather than pulled the aircraft. By locating the engine housings in the rear portion of the wing, they minimized external drag and also improved directional stability.

In addition to aerodynamic smoothness, Consolidated Aircraft also had to pay particular attention to weight. To meet this challenge, engineers developed fabrication and manufacturing techniques specific to the B-36. Prior to the inception of the B-36, magnesium alloy had been used very little for aircraft construction, but Consolidated Aircraft incorporated this and other new alloys.

Measures were taken to minimize the aircraft's weight. For example, traditional carbon-dioxide fire extinguishers were replaced with methyl-bromide ones. Methyl bromide has a much lower boiling point than carbon dioxide so it can be stored as a liquid at a lower pressure, thus permitting lighter storage tanks and conducting lines, saving 250 pounds. A lightweight flap-operating system saved another 1,000 pounds, extending the B-36's range by 95 miles. Electrical motors to operate the flaps were installed directly in the flap surfaces, with electro-mechanical synchronizers coordinating the movement of the flaps on both sides of the aircraft.

Until almost the end of the war, the B-36 program was subject to shifting priorities, its development constantly being delayed to accommodate more urgent aircraft programs. After the United States entered the war in December 1941, the military was able to use bases in England for conventional bombers, notably the B-17 and B-24 heavy bombers.

Thus the B-36 intercontinental bomber project was put on the back burner until the summer of 1943.

Consolidated Aircraft itself had other priorities. At the time it started the B-36 development program, the company was also building the B-24 Liberator and the B-32 Dominator. For months, the firm put its primary emphasis on these two aircraft. Then, in September 1942, General Arnold ordered the "highest priority" for Consolidated's B-36, and for the B-35 Flying Wing being developed by Northrop Corporation. With the United States taking some heavy losses in the Pacific, Arnold believed that the North American-based bombers might be needed sooner than initially expected.

Meanwhile, to build its human resources, Consolidated Aircraft Corporation merged in March 1943 with Vultee Aircraft Corporation to form a new company that soon became known as Convair. Four months later, the US Army Air Forces placed an order with Convair for 100 production units of the B-36.[3]

The sense of urgency around this aircraft's development swayed with the winds of war. The B-36's high-priority status was short-lived as the Pacific momentum turned with the US Marines' victory at Guadalcanal and again in late 1944 after the US forces gained the Mariana Islands, which accommodated air bases within B-29 striking range of Japan. By then, the European tides had also turned in favour of the Allies and the long-range-bomber program seemed expensive and unnecessary. The priority of the B-36 program was lowered once again.

With decreased pressure to finish the B-36, Convair released personnel to more pressing projects. In 1943, the accelerated B-24 program siphoned off more and more experienced and qualified engineers, in spite of the July announcement that 100 B-36 bombers were needed. A year later, with the war surge progressing on both European and Pacific fronts, the future of the B-36 was solidified with a firm order made in August 1944. No priority was assigned to the project, and by the end of the year, the B-36 experimental shop was 18 months behind schedule.

The dropping of the first atomic bombs in August 1945 ushered in a new era in warfare and bombardment systems. With the war ending, warplane procurements were cut back and many contracts were re-examined. One day after Japan surrendered, the US government cancelled Convair's production of the B-32, and all unfinished bombers on the Fort Worth production line, along with their tooling, were cut up and relegated to the scrap heap.

Although the war was over, the requirement for a long-range bomber had not changed. For strategists in the Pentagon, the Cold War's nuclear-arms race was inevitable. The advent of the atomic bomb provided a new reason for the development of the intercontinental bomber.

The B-36 was the only bomber under development with the potential for intercontinental flight, and for the first time since the preliminary design days of 1941, the project could have the experienced engineering and production personnel that it required. An Air Staff Group conference, held a few days before Japan's surrender, recommended the continuation of the program.

On September 8, 1945, six days after the celebration of VJ Day, the B-36 was rolled out of the Experimental Building at Convair's Fort Worth plant. Eleven months later, on August 8, 1946, almost five years after the original order was placed, the prototype B-36 took to the air. In the warm morning hours, more than 7,000 Convair employees lined the fence along the runway to watch project test pilot Beryl Erickson, co-pilot Gus Green and their crew make two preliminary takeoff runs. Then, at 10:10 AM, the aircraft slowly and steadily rose from the runway and gained altitude for its 37-minute maiden flight. A second flight, 2 hours and 43 minutes long, followed a week later on August 14.

The flight-test program, which continued through the fall of 1946, experienced unprecedented difficulties resulting from the bomber's giant size. Its 100-inch-diameter wheels (later built at 110 inches in diameter) supporting nearly 300,000 pounds of gross weight limited the aircraft to using only three airports in the United States: its home base at Fort Worth, the Air Force Proving Grounds at Eglin Field in Florida, and Fairfield-Suisun Army Air Field (later called Travis AFB) in California.[4] As well, the aircraft's single-wheel landing gear brought up the possibility of a blowout on takeoff or landing. Special runways with concrete 22 inches thick would need to be constructed to accommodate the huge bomber. Work continued on the single-wheel design with Goodyear Tire and Rubber Co. as the subcontractor. The 110-inch-diameter wheel (9 feet 2 inches) was the largest aircraft tire ever developed, weighing in at 1,475 pounds.

For more than a year, the XB-36 and a second prototype, the YB-36 (Serial 42-13571), were flown with single-wheel landing gear. The B-36A prototype was the first production model to use multi-wheel landing gear. For better weight distribution, Convair mounted two four-wheel bogies on a single strut. Though it was tested, the bogie design was later dropped, due to the development of aircraft brakes that allowed for a conventional multi-wheel undercarriage. The four-wheel landing gear required runways only 13.5 inches thick and shaved 2,600 pounds from the aircraft in the process.

Of the remaining problems, two of the most troublesome were engine overheating and stress from propeller vibration. The overheating problem, which almost caused the USAAF to cut back the B-36 contract in 1946, made it difficult for the aircraft to maintain high-altitude (above 30,000 feet) operations for extended periods. There were also numerous electrical system failures caused by fatigue in aluminum wiring.

Stress from propeller vibration became evident during one of the early flights when a propeller broke loose, taking a piece of wing flap with it. Falling 10,000 feet, it landed in a farmer's field, with one blade holding it upright. On another test flight, vibration stress on the electrical and other supporting systems caused all three engines on one wing to quit. On a third flight, stress caused the inboard wing flaps to come off.

The B-36 almost came to a premature end on its 16th test flight, on March 26, 1947, when the right main-gear retracting cylinder burst and the landing-gear brace broke loose from its fitting in the wing spar. This in turn caused the right wheel to swing down past its normal position and crash into the right inboard nacelle, crushing fuel, oil and hydraulic lines. Test pilots Erickson and Green remained at the controls and the rest of the crew bailed out. The pilots dumped ballast water, but since there was no provision for dumping fuel, it took six hours of flight to burn off some 7,015 gallons of fuel. They finally made a bicycle-type landing on the remaining undamaged wheel, a feat that saved the B-36 program.

On another occasion, while an airspeed indicator suspended from the B-36 by a 75-foot cable was being calibrated, the 50-pound instrument fell after the cable snapped. It smashed through a skylight in a Fort Worth elementary school washroom. Seven children suffered cuts and abrasions, none of them serious, but the instrument gouged a seven-inch hole in the concrete floor. A fragment broke a nearby commode, putting it out of commission—all in all, a rather unsophisticated target for the world's largest and most expensive bomber.

The Convair test pilots had some difficulty adapting to the unique traits of the massive aircraft as they were getting it off the ground. Its 230-foot wing was set just forward of the midpoint of its 162-foot fuselage. As the six engines drove the aircraft forward along the runway in a rush of enormous power, its long, slender nose would steadily lift upward, and the pilots would find the cockpit 30 feet above the runway before the landing gear even left the ground. Once in the air, however, pilots praised the aircraft, finding it easier to fly than the old B-29.

For three years, the project engineers at Convair had struggled to solve many seemingly unsolvable problems. Eventually they managed to overcome the challenges, and many of their solutions would set future industry standards. However, just as the B-36 was about to enter service in 1946, it became the subject of political controversy. The concept of an intercontinental bomber was not popular in some circles. Critics raised questions about its intercontinental capability. They conceded that progress was being made in building such a large aircraft, but questioned its military effectiveness and necessity. With the unit price of each B-36 climbing at an alarming rate, people began to wonder whether it would become a milestone or a millstone.

Despite all the naysayers, on August 14, 1947, the B-36 reached a critical goal, climbing to 37,000 feet, the highest official altitude for the aircraft. Its top speed was 346 miles per hour, with a cruise speed of only 212 miles per hour after weight had gradually been added to the prototype to increase strength.

With the B-36 test flights coming to an end, an unarmed version of the aircraft, the B-36A, was put into service in 1948. It included several modifications from the prototype aircraft, including a multi-wheel landing gear system and a redesigned forward crew compartment that had an improved canopy "greenhouse," which provided better visibility for the pilots. The B-36A was not equipped with defensive armament because the early remotely controlled gun turrets and the 20-mm cannon were complex and prone to frequent failures. Defects in both the gun and turret postponed the system's installation in the B-36. Once the guns were installed, a lack of 20-mm ammunition delayed testing until mid-1949. As late as February 1950, the commander of the Eighth Air Force was complaining that there was little point in driving a B-36 around with guns that did not work.

As a result of the gun-installation problems, the B-36A aircraft were used exclusively for training and type familiarization. Between 1949 and 1951 they were modified into reconnaissance aircraft.

A philosophical clash between the navy and the air force had continued throughout these setbacks. What the navy really wanted, of course, was more funding for its new fleet of super aircraft carriers. It went so far as to accuse its rival of financial impropriety with Convair.

In August 1949, the navy's charges against the procurement policies and combat effectiveness of the B-36 led to high-profile congressional hearings on the B-36 program, with air force, navy and Department of Defense officials all testifying. Admiral Arthur W. Radford, Pacific Fleet Commander, called the B-36 a "billion-dollar blunder," charging that the air force had commissioned an aircraft that could not perform its mission because it was vulnerable to jet-fighter interception—it was a sitting duck. In the end, however, Congress decided that there was no wrongdoing and not enough evidence to warrant the cancellation of the B-36 program. It was a triumph for both the B-36 and the theory of strategic bombardment in the nuclear age.[5]

The B-36B was the first model put into front-line service with Strategic Air Command. It was based initially at Carswell AFB, close to the Convair plant. Among those early B-36Bs was an aircraft known as Bomber 075.

The B-36 was the largest bomber ever built. Its wingspan was 10 feet longer than that of a Boeing 747 jumbo jet. Its enormous single tail, altered from the original twin-tailed version, rose nearly 47 feet off the ground. With the capacity to hold four railcars' worth of fuel, the B-36 could remain airborne for more than 50 hours. By comparison, a B-17 Flying Fortress had a combat radius of 750 miles and could carry 6,000 pounds, while a B-29 could carry 20,000 pounds over a combat range of 1,219 miles. The combat range of the later B-36J (III) version, with a bomb load of 72,000 pounds, was 2,495 miles, or 12 times the bomb load of the B-17G and 3 times the combat range.[6]

Convair B-36 Specifications

POWERPLANT
- Six 3,500-horsepower R4360-41 Major air-cooled radial engines
- Four 5,200-pound J47-GE-19 turbojets

PERFORMANCE
- Maximum speed: 381 miles per hour at 34,500 feet
- Cruising speed: 202 miles per hour
- Initial climb rate: 1,510 feet per minute
- Service ceiling: 42,500 feet
- Combat ceiling: 38,800 feet
- Combat radius: 3,740 miles
- Total mission time: 42.43 hours
- Range: 8,175 miles

WEIGHT
- Empty: 140,640 pounds
- Combat: 227,700 pounds
- Maximum takeoff: 311,000 pounds

DIMENSIONS
- Wingspan: 230 feet
- Length: 162 feet 1 inch
- Height: 46 feet 8 inches
- Wing area: 4,772 square feet

ARMAMENT
- Two 20-mm M24A1 cannons, each in retractable, remotely controlled fuselage turrets and nose mounting with 9,200 rounds of ammunition
- Maximum bomb payload: two 48,000-pound Grand Slam bombs; normal bomb load up to 72,000 pounds

FUEL TANKS
- Nine tanks total
- Three tanks in each wing
  – inboard (Nos. 3 and 4): 4,212 gallons each
  – centre (Nos. 2 and 5): 4,084 gallons each
  – outboard (Nos. 1 and 6): 2,262 gallons each
- Left and right wing auxilliary tanks – 4,800 gallons each
- Bomb-bay tank: 3,000 gallons
- Total useable fuel: 33,716 gallons

CONSTRUCTION COST
- $3.63 million (1950 dollars) each

Getting the 150-ton B-36 into the air required six Pratt & Whitney R4360-25 pusher-prop engines, with more than 3,000 horsepower each, and propellers 19 feet in diameter. With a crew of 16, the aircraft's forward and rear crew compartments were separated by a bomb bay more than 80 feet long. In full attack configuration, the B-36 could carry two atomic bombs.

The B-36's distinctive droning roar was the result of manually synchronizing the speed of each engine to within a few revolutions of the others. The slight differences in speed produced harmonics of the individual engines' and propellers' audio-spectral outputs, and the 19-foot props would "slap" the slipstream trailing from the wings. The aircraft's roar actually rattled windows on the ground as it flew overhead at 30,000 feet. During takeoffs, its vibrations certainly would have rattled china in quite a few Fort Worth cabinets.

"No other plane made the sound that a B-36 did, especially when taking off," said Steve Henderson, who has fond childhood memories of the B-36. Before being transferred to Alaska, Henderson's father, First Sergeant Virgil R. Henderson, worked at the Headquarters Squadron of the Eighth Air Force, from 1950 to 1955. "I often watch *Strategic Air Command* [the 1955 Paramount motion picture] just to listen to the thundering drone of those six engines."[7] The movie, starring Jimmy Stewart and June Allyson, includes some of the best footage ever shot of the aircraft. B-36H Serial 51-5734 itself deserved star billing, and the movie won a special citation from the National Board of Review for its aerial photography.[8] The crash scene in snow-covered mountains was similar to Bomber 075's demise.

Due to its enormous size and development cost, the B-36 acquired more nicknames than any other aircraft in aviation history, ranging from complimentary to outright derogatory. In the late 1940s and early 1950s, newspapers often referred to it as the "Giant Superbomber" or the "Atomic Bomber." Around 1948, because of excessive time spent on the ground due to maintenance problems and mechanical difficulties, the first B-36A and B models were tagged with the name "Ramp Booster." Fortunately, because the early operational problems were soon overcome, this not-so-complimentary nickname was short-lived. The large amount of aluminum used in the B-36 and its large size led to the nickname "Aluminum Overcast," because while flying overhead it blotted out the sun. Other nicknames included "Magnesium Monster," "Flying Apartment House," "Mailing Tube with Wings," "Magnificent Beast" and "Flying Cigar Humidor."

During development, Convair held a contest among its Texas-based employees to name the new bomber. Almost 10 percent of the 624 entries suggested Peacemaker. Similar names suggested were "Peacebinder," "Peaceeagle," "Peacekeeper" and "Peacemaster." "B-36 Colt" also earned some support because of the role the Colt .44 pistol had played in keeping the peace in the early days of Texas. B-36 "Earthshaker" was one of the more humorous suggestions.

The winning name, Peacemaker, was never submitted to the US Air Force for official adoption because Fort Worth clergymen deemed it sacrilegious to apply the name to a weapon of war. Regardless, the name stuck and the aircraft was forever known as the Peacemaker.

Bringing the B-36 up to fully operational status and combat effectiveness was a team effort. However, if one individual were to be credited with being primarily responsible for that accomplishment, it would probably be Brigadier General Clarence S. "Bill" Irvine.

When Irvine became commander of the Seventh Bomb Wing on January 3, 1950, a new era began at Carswell AFB for the B-36. Until then, many of the aircraft had been grounded due to maintenance and mechanical difficulties. Irvine's extensive engineering experience, aircraft-development background and operational combat experience made him the most qualified man for turning the B-36 into an effective combat aircraft.

Irvine issued an order that every B-36 training flight be scheduled to last 24 hours. Takeoff was set for 10 AM on the appointed day, with the return at the same time the next day. Failure to properly accomplish the training mission would result in its commander appearing "on the carpet" in Irvine's office. The second time an officer appeared there, he would be transferred.[9]

General Hoyt S. Vandenberg, the USAF chief of staff from 1948 to 1953, stated that the development of the B-36 as an intercontinental bomber had changed the entire concept of strategic air warfare. On February 22, 1949, during a luncheon talk in Fort Worth, Vandenberg said the USAF was not disturbed by "clever, underhanded cracks" that continued to be made about the B-36, mostly by anonymous writers of published stories who did not quote sources.[10]

The Convair B-36 was considered an interim bomber because it was in service after the Boeing B-29 Superfortress and before the Boeing B-52 Stratofortress. Only operational for a decade, the Peacemaker, like most temporary aircraft, never received the credit it deserved. While a new generation of jet bombers was being built, this aircraft helped to maintain America's security during the Cold War.

At close to $4 million USD apiece in 1950 dollars, the Peacemaker was the symbol of America's might and its ability to deliver nuclear bombs almost anywhere. Equipped with a revolutionary K-bombing navigation system, and with American air bases abroad, the global-ranging B-36 could navigate to virtually any spot in the world and put its bomb on target from any altitude. By today's standards, this may not sound impressive. But this came at the end of a time when bombers were lucky to *find* their targets and even luckier to hit them.

The Soviet Union produced approximately 6,000 MiG-15 fighters to fight against the B-36. Although tensions with the Soviet Union and communist China in the 1950s made the aircraft's presence comforting to US military officials, the Peacemaker never dropped a bomb in combat. During the B-36's term of operational service, the threat of nuclear retaliation posed by its existence, supplemented by the use of medium-sized bombers, likely prevented a major world conflict.

During the height of and through most of the Cold War, the US deployed some 12,000 nuclear weapons and components outside the continental US. These were stored in at least 23 countries and 5 US territories. Because many of these foreign countries either disavowed nuclear weapons or did not allow them on their territory (at least publicly), the weapons were stored in secrecy. During the mid-1950s, for example, the US deployed nukes in Morocco without telling the French government then ruling Morocco. During the Cuban Missile Crisis of 1962, the US stored nuclear-capable depth charges at its Guantanamo base.

From 1950 to 1984, Canada hosted a range of US nukes. Starting in 1950, Mark IV nukes were deployed at Goose Bay, Labrador, and sometime between 1968 and 1970 the US Navy deployed anti-submarine depth charges at Argentia, Newfoundland.

At the height of Canada's involvement with nuclear weapons, an estimated 250-450 warheads were available to the Canadian military. In the mid-1960s, Bomarc surface-to air missiles were equipped with nuclear warheads. Next, the RCAF installed Genie air-to-air missiles on its CF-101 VooDoo fighter aircraft based in BC and Quebec, and Falcon air-to air missiles on other fighters.[11]

CHAPTER 3

The Mark IV Nuclear Bomb

The Mark IV bomb's design was completed in 1949. The first nuclear warhead to be made using mass-produced components, it was a fairly advanced weapon. It was about 10 feet 8 inches in length and almost 5 feet in diameter. The bomb's outer casing was streamlined to avoid the aerodynamic wobble that plagued Nagasaki's Mark III "Fat Man" bomb. With 49 kilotons of explosive power, more than twice the explosive power of the Mark III bomb dropped on Nagasaki, the Mark IV had been proof tested in a three-explosion series in 1948.

"I do remember having nukes on hand at Ellsworth [AFB] during the early '50s," said a former electrician gunner. "A separate compound was constructed to the north of the base and manned by army personnel. The bombs were transported to the flight line and turned over to the crew for loading. My crew only [practised] the operation a time or two and I think in a real wartime situation the loading would have been done by experts for reasons of expediency."[1]

The nuclear bombs were loaded in total secrecy behind a black, four-sided bomb-security curtain. The nuke would be brought out to the aircraft on a bomb cart covered with a tarp. A jeep with a machine gun would lead the procession, and another jeep with a machine gun would follow. The bomb would be pushed into the curtained enclosure and uncovered.

Personnel with a specific job were not allowed in the bomb-bay area until it was time to perform their task, and when they were done, they were ordered to leave. During the process, two airmen would be operating some sort of black box that was hooked to the bomb. Crew members did not know what this was and did not question or discuss it. "Talk about being security brainwashed," one crewman later observed. "Or was it fear?"[2]

A crew member who was one of the guards recalls having a quick look under the curtain to see what was going on and seeing a large shape that some of the officers were working on. "Another crew member, also a guard, 'got all bent out of shape' and said he would have to shoot me because I wasn't cleared to be under the curtain. We were both armed with loaded .38s. He appeared to be serious, but never said any more."[3]

Because this happened at Ramey AFB near Aguadilla, Puerto Rico, in early 1955, the bomb was most likely a dummy. The incident shows not only the trouble the US Air Force went through to make it all seem real, but also the degree of paranoia and fear at the time. As it was, the Soviet Union may have known more about those bombs than the crew members did. Maybe the secrecy was for their benefit, just to make them more security-conscious.

"As I remember it was the Flight Engineer that installed the trigger mechanism, and as the Electrician Gunner, it was my job to exchange the safety plugs with ones that would allow the circuit to be completed. I believe the ones we carried weighed in the neighbourhood of 11,000 pounds, roughly 10,000 of which was chemical explosive designed to create maximum compression of the uranium prior to nuclear detonation."[4]

Most of the Mark IV's weight was made up of an inner and an outer sphere of high explosives, weighing nearly three tons. The bomb's destructive nuclear punch came from a plutonium core levitated within a hollow sphere of natural uranium known as the tamper. The tamper was designed to boost the yield of the nuclear bomb by creating a surface for neutrons to deflect off and back into the core. Near the rear of the weapon, a cylindrical electrical package known as the X-unit held the bomb's sophisticated arming, fusing and firing system.

Unlike the pure plutonium cores used in earlier nuclear weapons, the Mark IV's composite core consisted of layers of both plutonium and uranium encased in a thin nickel coating, and it weighed only about 13 pounds. In the heart of the core was the "urchin," or initiator, a tiny sphere composed of beryllium and polonium. At the moment of compression, the core was transformed into a liquid state. The urchin began releasing the neutrons required to initiate the nuclear chain reaction. Any neutrons escaping the core were reflected by the tamper back into the core, further feeding the fission process and producing a nuclear explosion.

Until early 1949, atomic weapons were required to be completely loaded with their fissionable material prior to the aircraft taking off. Given the ever-present possibility of a crash on takeoff, followed by a fire reaching the bomb bay, this requirement caused great concern. A fire in the bomb bay would probably cause a small nuclear explosion, possibly the equivalent of a few hundred tons of TNT.

Such an explosion would likely not have been too serious with regard to physically damaging airport infrastructure. However, it could have a catastrophic effect with regard to contaminating the immediate area with both fission products from the explosion and unconsumed nuclear material. Downwind conditions might subject base personnel to serious radioactivity levels and psychological hazards that would preclude further use of the base for a period of time.

Thus methods and equipment had to be developed whereby the active material could be kept separate from the actual weapon on takeoff. Only after the bomber had taken off successfully and was over either enemy territory or open space such as the ocean would the core be inserted into the weapon.

The early manual in-flight-insertion/in-flight-extraction (IFI/IFE) procedure often required special tools or equipment and access to an unpressurized aircraft bomb bay. Aircraft like Bomber 075 carried the Mark IV in bomb bay No. 1, the forward bomb bay, which was the most accessible for in-flight arming. Manual IFI/IFE was usually a difficult, inconvenient and sometimes dangerous process, which could take anywhere from 10 to 30 minutes to complete. It required special training, and lengthy, precise and delicate handiwork in cramped, cold, noisy and shaking aircraft bomb bays.

During flight, access to the interior of the weapon could be obtained by removing the antenna nose plate, exposing the large duralumin sphere that held the device together inside the bomb's aerodynamic shell. After removing the detonator mounted on the trap door, the weaponeer would use the specially designed IFI tool to assist him in removing two 88-pound lenses from the concentric spheres of high explosives. IFI, if done manually, was a process rather than a device. In the early years, the weaponeer did it by hand. In a self-contained automatic weapon, IFI was usually mechanical, as it would change the geometry of the core and explosives into a sphere for arming.

In the years immediately following the end of the Second World War, new techniques and equipment were developed, allowing both manual and automatic motor-driven insertion and extraction of active material after the aircraft was in flight.

A development program to produce manual IFI/IFE equipment was first proposed in May 1948, with the initial work beginning in October of that year. Seven prototype sets were manufactured late in 1949, and the first 50 tools had been produced by January 1950.

The IFI/IFE tool consisted of a vacuum suction cup, on a rod about 30 inches long, that attached to the high-explosive lenses that formed a lightweight "trap door" into the core. Once removed, these lenses were stored in baskets beside the weaponeer at the front of the bomb bay.

The problem with the vacuum system was that under extremely cold conditions frost would form on the lenses, preventing the suction cup from attaching to the surface of the lens. This required the development of a rod with a threaded end that could be screwed into a receptacle on the face of the lens.

"On the Mark IV there's something like a tailgate to stand on in front of the bomb and below it," B-36 researcher Jim Laird explained. "It's got all the plug-ins of oxygen and a tie-down spot for the 'birdcage' [the lead-lined container used specifically to carry the bomb's nuclear core], and some other things like baskets to put the [high-explosive] lenses in."[5]

Last to be removed was the "pit plug," a seven-inch cylinder of aluminum and depleted uranium. Finally the radioactive core would be carefully inserted. Once the bomb's missing components were replaced, the Mark IV would be an armed nuclear weapon and ready for war.

In the early days of the US atomic weapons program, manual IFI/IFE had some important advantages. For example, if during an emergency the bomb had to be jettisoned, the nuclear core could be removed before the weapon was dropped.

At the time, the entire US nuclear stockpile consisted of only a few dozen or so nuclear cores, so each one was worth more than its weight in gold. To ensure safety and retention of the nuclear core during and after in-flight emergencies, extreme measures were taken. If a nuclear core was being transported over water in its carrying case, for example, the case would be attached to a self-inflating dinghy.

The Atomic Energy Commission, by contract with the Bendix Company, produced the equipment to facilitate the manual IFI and IFE of nuclear cores. Of the IFI equipment, known as the H-1, some 460 sets were produced. The first sets, delivered in January 1950, were in service for about a year and were used only on the Mark IV and the early Mark V bombs. By January 1951, when all in-flight insertions of the core were automated, the H-1 became redundant.

Using the IFI device, the high-explosive lenses could be grasped and deposited in two different baskets provided in the bomb bay for this purpose. Because of the formation of oxide, the core could not be touched by hand. The IFI device was made out of a non-sparking material, possibly aluminum. The device was threaded into the centre of the tamper. After removing the tool, the lenses could be put back in.

"We were aware that the weapons and capsules emitted radiation, but we were told the levels were acceptable and most of us gave it no thought," says former nuclear specialist Jim Oskins. "In the beginning, we each carried a film badge that was read once a week to see how much radiation we had been receiving. After a few months the film badges were replaced by dosimeters that we read every six months. We were never told how much radiation we were receiving."[6]

PART 2 : Lost Nuke

CHAPTER 4

"Abandon Ship!"

Shortly before midnight on Monday, February 13, 1950, radio operators at the United States Air Force's Strategic Air Command headquarters at Offutt Air Force Base in Nebraska received distress calls from B-36 Bomber 075, which was flying off the north coast of British Columbia. The giant aircraft belonging to 436 Squadron, Eighth Air Force, Seventh Bomb Wing, Seventh Bomb Group of SAC, was en route from Eielson AFB near Fairbanks, Alaska, to its home base at Carswell AFB, Fort Worth, Texas. The bomber had taken off two days earlier from Carswell AFB for a training mission to Alaska and back, to test the operational characteristics of the aircraft and its payload under severe winter conditions.

Although Bomber 075's mission was to test all wartime operations, the mission's real purpose was most likely to carry out a test for arming the Mark IV nuclear bomb that was on board. By this time, the Mark IV bomb had been part of the US military's inventory for a year or more, but the arming procedure, known as in-flight insertion of the core (IFI), had only been practised on the ground. The first sets of specially designed tools for the IFI had been delivered to the aircraft just the month before. The ultimate test of the arming procedure would require the presence of an operational bomb on board.

Captain Harold L. Barry, a 30-year-old pilot from Hillsborough, Illinois, was in command of Bomber 075, with First Lieutenant Ray

Whitfield Jr., 25, serving as co-pilot. Barry had a total flying time of 1,403 hours, of which some 900 hours had been spent on B-36 aircraft. Whitfield had volunteered to be one of the co-pilots so he could look after "his aircraft," since Bomber 075 was permanently assigned to him. The regular 16-member crew of Bomber 075 included a 5-man relief shift for the B-36's long-haul, non-stop capability. In addition to the regular crew, there was also an observer on board, Lieutenant Colonel Daniel V. MacDonald.

Two specially trained crew members were involved with the delivery of an atomic bomb: the weaponeer, who armed the bomb, and the bomb commander, who supervised the weaponeer and certified that the bomb was "ready." The bomb commander usually held the rank of colonel; in the case of Bomber 075 it was the observer, MacDonald, who was attached to the Office of Plans and Operations at USAF headquarters. MacDonald was not a regular member of the 075 crew, so his presence suggests that practising the arming procedure on the Mark IV was part of the mission.

Captain Barry and his crew had been briefed at Carswell AFB on February 1. They'd also been given physical exams that showed no evidence of illness or fatigue, except for the radar operator, First Lieutenant Paul Gerhart, who had had a slight head cold for a couple of days. Although the crew arrived at Eielson AFB on February 3, the return flight to Texas was delayed for more than a week because of extremely cold temperatures in Alaska. This delay gave Barry's crew ample time to rest. Except for preparing their operational plans, the crew had no additional duties while they waited out the delay.

Colonel John D. Bartlett, commanding officer of 436 Squadron at Fort Worth, headed the crew that ferried Bomber 075 up to Eielson from Carswell. Bartlett was the Eighth Air Force's original B-36 project officer and the Seventh Wing's chief pilot for transition training from B-29s to B-36s.

It was still extremely cold when the bomber landed at Eielson. One of the crew members described the conditions as "minus 40 degrees, snow and wind, miserable! De-icing was impossible in those conditions. The engines remained running at all times to provide de-icing heat for the aircraft. If the engines were stopped, the oil would solidify."[1]

Lieutenant Stacker, flight engineer on Bomber 081, described another problem. "The big difficulty on the ground at Eielson AFB was the reservicing. The gas trucks had broken down, and because the aircraft arrived without dipsticks, the calculations for the amount of gasoline on board were merely guesses. At the time, a dipstick was used to check the fluid levels in the fuel tanks. This square wood pole, approximately 7 feet long, was marked in increments of 100 or 200 gallons.

"As the fuel gauges were indicating just an estimate, the ground crew would manually dip the fuel tanks. To double-check, the third pilot would also dip the fuel tanks. They would use these figures for weight and balance charts, and takeoff weight. Oil tanks also had to be dipped while the water injection tanks were visually inspected."[2]

With temperatures ranging from −51°F to −29°F, the crew shuffled refuelling units in and out of a heated shed often enough to provide 075 with 17,385 gallons of added fuel. About 80 maintenance people in two crews gave the aircraft a complete check-over before it was cleared to take off again. Some minor repairs were done, including torquing the hose clamps on the No. 3 and No. 4 engines to stop fuel leaks. Crews also worked for about an hour and a half on the aircraft's radar tilt antenna, which was stuck. They did not complete the antenna repair, but placed the necessary parts aboard the aircraft. The problem was to be fixed later in the air.

While the maintenance crews worked, Barry's combat crew performed pre-flight checks on the aircraft. Staff Sergeant Dick Thrasher, tail gunner and mechanic, would later report that while he was walking up to 075, he spoke with one of the gunners who had brought the aircraft up from Texas. When Thrasher asked what kind of shape the aircraft was in, the gunner said, "Well, it's okay, but it will never make it back."[3]

The flight from Alaska to Texas would be lengthy, estimated at 16 to 24 hours. The aircraft carried enough fuel for 28 hours in the air.[4] Besides carrying 252 pounds of 20-mm aircraft cannon ammunition, Bomber 075 also carried an 11,000-pound Mark IV atomic fission bomb.

The Alaska training exercise involved 10 B-36 aircraft and was described as a "developmental" flight for perfecting operational procedures for nuclear-armed bombers operating out of forward bases

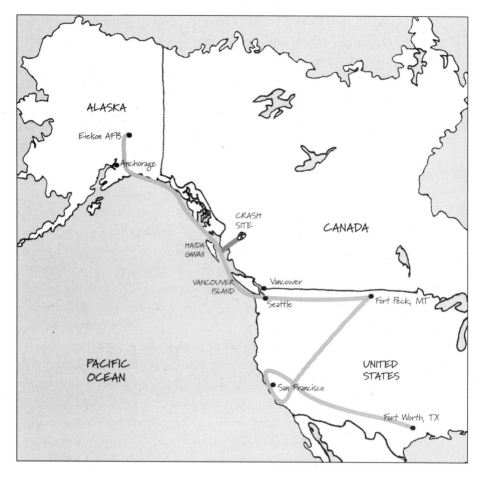

This map shows the intended flight path of Bomber 075 and the location of its final resting place. SANDRA BASKETT

in the Arctic. Research conducted by the privately funded Center for Defense Information in Washington, DC, revealed that the fleet of bombers was actually on a "simulated combat profile" exercise, originating in Alaska, to perform a mass attack on the west coast of the United States.

The plan was to fly from Carswell AFB to the forward staging area at Eielson AFB in Alaska, where the aircraft would refuel and take on supplies. After the ferry crews who had flown the bombers to Alaska were replaced by combat crews, the aircraft would then be able to fly its mission and return to home base. The three-day mission was to see four B-36 Peacemakers take off on the first day, followed by three aircraft per day for the next two days. Before the exercise was called off during the third segment of the mission because of 075's crash, eight aircraft had taken off.

About three hours prior to takeoff, the task force commander, Lieutenant Colonel George T. Chadwell of the Seventh Wing, conducted the operations briefing. He also held a briefing for the flight engineers and airplane commanders. The flight engineer, Major McWilliams, did the observers' briefing, and Lieutenant John H. Jones gave the weather forecast, which called for a deep low-pressure system in the flight path over the southeastern coast of Alaska, with severe icing conditions present at certain levels. Frontal activity and clouds were expected for nearly the whole distance from Anchorage to Cape Flattery. The weather office recommended that if the aircraft ran into icing conditions, it should climb above them. Chadwell mentioned this to all the crews he briefed.

After taking off from Eielson AFB, Bomber 075, the ninth aircraft in the schedule, was to head toward Fairbanks, climbing to 12,000 feet before adjusting direction to follow the coast along the code-named "Amber Route" to Washington State and Montana. Over Cape Flattery, Washington, on the US mainland's most northwesterly corner, the bomber, then at an altitude of 14,000 feet, would turn east and head for Fort Peck, Montana, climbing to an altitude of 40,000 feet—3,000 feet higher than the official maximum altitude. This altitude was considered out of the reach of any possible Russian interceptors. From there, Bomber 075 would begin its simulated bombing run to southern California and its target, San Francisco, which was chosen because it was about the same distance from the Alaska deployment site as the potential target of Leningrad, USSR. Once the simulated bombing run reached the Golden Gate bridge, the B-36 would turn east again and continue its non-stop flight to Fort Worth.

At 4:27 PM, Bomber 075 left the ground at a speed of between 135 and 140 miles per hour. As was later revealed in USAF records, the weight and balance form retrieved from Alaska asserted that the bomber was 51,570 pounds over its recommended maximum takeoff weight of

278,000 pounds. Although this may seem dramatic, this discrepancy was not considered unusual.

Colonel Bartlett, who was in the tower, asked Captain Barry how the flight was going in its early moments and reported, "He said the inboard flaps had stuck, which seems to be something that sticks with this great differential in temperature because it happened on the other aircraft."[5]

Except for its radar, Bomber 075 was reported to be in good mechanical condition as it flew away from Eielson AFB. While some crew members worked on the radar, the rest performed tasks related to the training exercise, such as testing the defensive systems and gun handling. There is no record of mechanical difficulty prior to 11:14 PM, about seven hours into the flight, when VHF contact was made with Bomber 083, which was in approximately the same location.[6] In fact, Bomber 075 was virtually brand new, with less than 200 hours of flying time on the airframe at the time of the mission. Total time on engines No. 1, 2, 4 and 6 was also less than 200 hours, while engines No. 3 and 5 had flown only 4 hours prior to the flight north from Texas.

After having undergone a 120-hour inspection on November 26, 1949, Bomber 075 had flown only 15 hours and 45 minutes before starting this mission. The flight to Eielson AFB had added approximately 19 hours, putting the aircraft's total flight time at just over 200 hours.

Crew members would later recount that they had difficulty making voice-position reports on the flight. As a result, they had to relay their position at required checkpoints through their accompanying sister aircraft, Bomber 083.

South of Sitka, Alaska, Bomber 075 ran into cloudy conditions and started to climb. At that moment, the airplane's gross weight was estimated at 278,000 pounds.

Before entering the clouds, all engines had been operating satisfactorily, but after the climb, the propellers began surging while in automatic position. One of Bomber 075's flight engineers, Lieutenant Ernest O. Cox Jr., of Pampa, Texas, switched the engines to manual control. Cox discovered that to hold the propellers at the desired 2,300 revolutions per minute, he would have to adjust them continually, which he was unable to do. He thought the aircraft was picking up considerable propeller ice.[7]

Around 11 PM, Bomber 075 requested that Bomber 083 relay a message informing air traffic control that it was 80 miles northeast of Sandspit, BC, on Moresby Island in the Queen Charlotte Islands (now known as Haida Gwaii). The first distress signal was issued by Captain Barry, who said the aircraft was in difficulty while flying at 12,000 feet. "We started picking up some ice," Staff Sergeant Dick Thrasher recalled.[8]

"At 0725Z [11:25 PM Pacific Standard Time] they said they lost an engine and started to let down about 0730," recalled an 083 crew member.[9]

At the official inquiry into the incident, Cox described the weather as "raining and sleet, snow, very little snow and rain, freezing rain." When specifically questioned by Colonel Salvatore E. Manzo, "Freezing rain?" Cox answered, "Yes, Sir."[10] The outside temperature during Bomber 075's final flight varied from –17°F to –19°F at 12,000 feet. Earlier, the crew had heard what they thought was hail beating against the aircraft. Although the propellers were surging erratically, no one heard any ice coming off the props. Barry decided that they had encountered icing conditions and gave the order to climb to 15,000 feet.

Then, from the rear of the bomber, a crew member reported that engine No. 1 was on fire. Barry immediately feathered the engine to reduce drag, but when the propeller started turning backward, the

The "Mae West"

Named in honour of the Hollywood actress and comedienne of the 1930s, "Mae West" is the nickname for an automatically inflating life preserver developed during the Second World War. The front of the life preserver vest incorporates two large bladders that are inflated with compressed carbon dioxide. Allied aircrews soon called them Mae Wests for their resemblance to their favourite star's curvaceous torso—and the rhyming of "breasts" with "life vests." The Mae West was a great improvement over older life preservers, which were made out of kapok, making them rather bulky to wear inside an aircraft. Other life preservers were inflatable, but the wearer had to inflate it himself using lung power, a difficult task in a rough sea, especially for wounded survivors. The Mae West, which was quickly inflated using a small bottle of compressed gas, would keep the survivor's nose and mouth above water, even when he was unconscious.

engine stopped.[11] The aircraft levelled off at 15,000 feet because it could not climb higher. Then the same crew member reported a fire in No. 2 engine. Approximately one and a half minutes after No. 2 engine was feathered, No. 5 engine caught fire and also had to be feathered. The aircraft started losing altitude rapidly.

Amidst the severe on-board conditions of 075, its crew had tried to stay in contact with 083. As the aircraft approached the coast of British Columbia, Barry radioed: "One engine is feathered. Two others are losing power. We are descending." The weather in the area during the time of the distress call, as recorded at Cape St. James on the southern tip of the Queen Charlotte Islands, was overcast skies with a 500-foot ceiling, visibility 3 miles in light rain, wind southeast at 52 miles per hour.

A second message from Bomber 075 reported: "One engine on fire. Contemplate ditching in Queen Charlotte Sound between Queen Charlotte Island and Vancouver Island. Keep a careful lookout for flares or wreckage."[12]

Bomber 083 called back and asked for 075's position and current heading. Though 075 gave its position, it did not report its heading. The 083 radio operator later reported to investigators: "About five minutes later they called back and said they lost two more engines due to engine fire. They never did specify anything else. I called them for approximately one hour and 45 minutes at 5-minute intervals trying to pick them up on VHF."

The fires eventually went out on all three burning engines. Emergency power was applied to the remaining three engines, but the torque pressure did not increase. The rate of descent was slowed down to about 100 feet per minute; the airspeed was about 135 miles per hour. At 11:41 PM, Bomber 083 received a message from the stricken 075 that the aircraft was letting down over water. At 11:55 PM, the US Civil Aeronautics Administration (CAA)[13] reported that the aircraft's last known position was 53°00'N, 129°29'W on a heading of 30 degrees.[14] This put the aircraft just west of Princess Royal Island.

As the *official* report on the loss of Bomber 075 put it, "the last call was at 0740 Zebra [11:40 PM PST]. They said [they had] lost engines and they might have to bail out. They might have been going out to sea and coming back."[15]

The crew of Bomber 075 never knew whether their last transmission was heard because they received no response. All they knew was that Bomber 083 was in range of their VHF radio. Only later did they learn that the other aircraft had actually received their messages.

After the third of the six engines died and they started their rapid descent, Barry made the decision to jump and ditch the aircraft in Queen Charlotte Sound.

From his position in the cockpit, co-pilot Lieutenant Whitfield observed the crew functioning normally while making preparations to leave the aircraft. "They had been trained to follow procedures for this and were doing their jobs."[16] The crewmen were checking their parachutes and putting on their Mae West life preservers. Up front, Whitfield checked the men to confirm that they were placing the life-preserver straps under, not over, their parachute straps. Staff Sergeant Martin Stephens similarly instructed those in the rear compartment. According to Staff Sergeant Dick Thrasher, Stephens was rushing them. Thrasher found it just "too difficult to get the damned Mae West straps under," and he put them over everything.[17]

During the flight from Alaska down the BC coast, crew members would normally wear Mae Wests and parachutes. However, once they were in trouble, it would be prudent to remove their parachutes and Mae Wests, put on their exposure suits and then their Mae Wests and parachutes again.

Three crew members from other bombers have commented on the 075 survivors' testimony. The first suggested that standard regulations were not always followed. "This was time consuming, in the dark with [in later flights] eight guys in the aft compartment with all their personal gear strewn around," B-36 veteran Bob Preising explained. "Crews did not wear their Mae West and parachute when flying over cold water because you can only survive a few minutes without your exposure suit."[18]

In bomb bay No. 1, weaponeer Captain Ted Schreier was busy disarming the Mark IV nuclear bomb. Once a weaponeer got some practice and was good at it, loading and unloading the nuclear core could be done in 20 minutes. Since this was probably the first time Schreier had disarmed a nuclear bomb in flight, he may have been unable to complete this task.

On the order of the bomb commander, the Mark IV bomb was dropped from the aircraft with the intent that it be destroyed over Queen

Charlotte Sound at an altitude of 3,000 feet. Flight engineer Cox reported observing a bright flash, followed by a loud sound and a shockwave.

Lieutenant Paul Gerhart, the navigator and radar operator, reported in succession that the aircraft was over land, then over water, then land again, then more water and more land. The many small islands below the aircraft and the larger Aristazabal Island to the west of their sudden crash target would explain this sequence. When the bomber was over the much-larger Princess Royal Island and flying at an altitude of about 5,000 feet, Barry gave the order over the intercom: "Abandon ship."

To save his crew from drowning in the frigid Pacific Ocean, and with the bomb now destroyed, Barry had violated standing orders and turned the giant bomber east toward the Canadian mainland, according to Cox. Just before he ditched, Barry turned off the aircraft's radar signals to prevent disclosure of its position and set the automatic pilot to accomplish a gentle turn back out toward the open Pacific.

Later, the flight engineer stated that after he hit the ground, he saw the bomber in a gentle bank to the left.[19] The position of the aircraft at that time was 53°00'N, 129°29'W, west of Princess Royal Island between the Estevan Group and Campania Islands. The aircraft's speed on two or three engines was estimated at 145–165 miles per hour, and the rate of descent was likely to have been between 200 and 500 feet per minute.

Before jumping, radio operator Staff Sergeant James Ford tied down the transmitter key to produce a steady signal. This would enable rescue units to get a "quick fix" on the bomber's last position. After removing the escape hatches at the front and back of the aircraft, the crew started jumping, reportedly bailing out in about 10 to 12 seconds. Fifty years later, Thrasher said that the bailout actually took much longer than the time indicated by Captain Barry. When Cox bailed out, he noted that Barry was still in his seat, busy putting the aircraft on autopilot to fly southwest, out to sea.

Just after 12:00 AM on Valentine's Day, the men had completed their leap into a dark night with a 55-miles-per-hour gale and driving rain.

Sister aircraft Bomber 083 stayed in the vicinity for nearly an hour, trying in vain to locate the aircraft or reach it by radio. It was minutes into Valentine's Day and the US Air Force had just lost one of their most sophisticated intercontinental bombers, carrying a real atomic bomb.

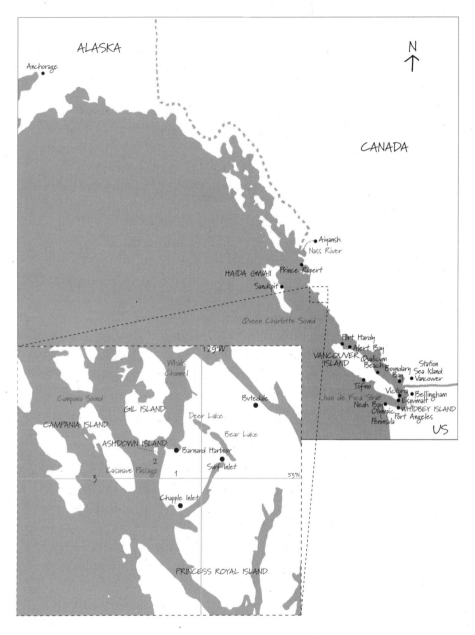

An overview of the areas covered during Operation Brix. The inset shows the Princess Royal Island area where 12 survivors were found. 1 marks the location where Staff Sergeant Trippodi and Lieutenant Pooler were found. 2 marks where US Coast Guard vessels and the HMCS *Cayuga* were anchored. 3 marks the location where the bomb was jettisoned. PETE KOHUT

CHAPTER 5

Operation Brix

When Bomber 075 radioed "letting down over water" close to midnight on February 13, it triggered a flurry of activity at both the US Civil Aeronautics Administration (CAA) and at Strategic Air Command. Within minutes the CAA alerted Flight "C," Fourth Rescue Squadron, Air Rescue Service-Military Air Transport Service (ARS-MATS) at McChord AFB near Tacoma, Washington, reporting the aircraft in serious trouble. Two minutes later, operations personnel and the alert crew were notified.

Quickly the US Air Force, Navy and Coast Guard and the Royal Canadian Air Force (RCAF) were alerted, and an extensive Canadian–American air-sea search was set in motion.[1] RCAF headquarters at Vancouver took the lead on what became known as Operation Brix.

Early on Tuesday, February 14, the Royal Canadian Navy base near Victoria, BC, and search master Wing Commander RCAF (Ret.) D.G. Bell-Irving were called into action, along with American forces in the Pacific Northwest. Aircraft closest to the crash site were dispatched from 123 Search and Rescue Flight of the RCAF Station Sea Island near Vancouver, as were surface craft from 122 Marine Squadron at Patricia Bay on Vancouver Island.

In Washington State, both the US Coast Guard and US Navy stations dispatched all available search aircraft. At 12:12 AM, the US Coast Guard

Air Station at Port Angeles, Washington, reported that it would have a Catalina flying boat ready to go in a short time. Whidbey Island Naval Air Station reported that 12 P2V Neptune patrol aircraft were available. It contacted the RCAF in Vancouver to establish its role in the search patterns.

At 12:10 AM, crews were briefed to proceed to the last known position of the distressed aircraft and conduct an expanding-square search from that position. There were no known ships in the area, and the closest search and rescue base was almost 370 miles to the southeast.

The CAA reported that the last known heading of Bomber 075 was 30 degrees, recorded when the aircraft was in contact with Sandspit Radio only minutes before disappearing. Because a second B-36, Bomber 083, was flying in the same direction at the same heading, there was some confusion.

Observations were received from several locations along the coastal route to Alaska, but the only stations reporting contact with Bomber 075 were radio-receiving stations at Sandspit and, earlier, at Anchorage and Annette, Alaska. Anchorage reported that its last contact with 075 was at 6:20 PM, when the B-36 had reported leaving Anchorage and estimated arriving in the Seattle area at 11 PM. Annette Radio reported intercepting contacts between 075, Sandspit Radio and Bomber 083 at 11:48 PM, when 083 relayed 075's reported position of 53°00'N, 129°49'W.

Bell-Irving later recalled the search for the bomber and its 17 missing men. "As search master, shortly after the [CAA] distress call I telephoned the Royal Canadian Navy (RCN) operations centre at Esquimalt in the middle of the night." As soon as she could get up steam, the Esquimalt-based Tribal-class destroyer HMCS *Cayuga* (DDE 218) was at sea. "Apart from the position report given with the distress call, we had little to go on, so the area to search was vast. We decided to concentrate initially on a sea search; low cloud precluded a search over the mountainous area of the coast."[2]

The year 1950 had not started out very well for the US Air Force. Within the first seven weeks of 1950, it had lost six aircraft. The worst incident, which happened only 18 days before 075 went down, involved a Douglas C-54 Skymaster transport carrying 44 persons, which disappeared somewhere between Anchorage, Alaska, and Great Falls, Montana, while en route to Texas.

Douglas C-54D-DC (DC-4), Serial 42-72469

When this Douglas military transport disappeared on January 26, 1950, it was 2 hours into an 8.5-hour trip from Alaska's Elmendorf AFB to Great Falls, Montana, by way of Amber Airway 02 over Canada. There were 8 crew members and 36 passengers on board. All were military personnel except for one civilian and her infant. The transport's last radio report was made at 5:09 PM from a location near Snag, Yukon, just east of the Alaska border.

At the time, it was the worst aviation accident in Canadian history. The crew had filed an 1,800-mile flight plan that showed they would enter Canada about two hours into the flight to fly over Whitehorse, Yukon, track the Alaska Highway to British Columbia near Fort Nelson and then parallel the BC–Alberta border over the Rockies to Montana.

The ensuing search involved 7,000 people and 85 aircraft. Although the aircraft is commonly believed to have gone down in the Watson Lake, Yukon, area, other possible crash locations include Greenwood in the Kootenays and the Puntzi Lake area near Quesnel. Yet in more than 60 years, no trace of the aircraft or its passengers has been found. Thus this accident remains one of the great aviation mysteries of North America.[3]

Most available US search aircraft were still searching for the Douglas C-54, when the new search and rescue initiative to find Bomber 075 was begun. As a result, a US Coast Guard PBY Catalina, Serial AF3956 out of Port Angeles, Washington, was the only Coast Guard aircraft immediately available to join the Canadian naval vessel *Cayuga* and available Canadian aircraft for the search for 075. On short notice, Air Force command directed all Air Rescue Squadrons still involved in the C-54 search to McChord AFB to join the search for 075.

Around 1:20 AM, the RCAF reported that it was dispatching a high-speed launch to the area and would dispatch aircraft shortly. When the US Coast Guard Air Station at Annette Island in the Alaska Panhandle reported an hour later that it had two PBY Catalina flying boats ready to go, they were asked to dispatch the two immediately.

Soon after Bomber 075's last report, a large aircraft had been observed as far south as the Juan de Fuca Strait, which lies between Vancouver Island and the Olympic Peninsula in Washington. Therefore, the searchers decided that aircraft and surface vessels were to search in the vicinity of Vancouver Island en route to the area where they thought 075 had been lost. The observations were later assumed to have been about Bomber 083.

Shortly before 4:00 AM, the US Coast Guard Air Station at Port Angeles announced that their PBY Catalina aircraft, which was carrying a lifeboat, had departed McChord AFB. But 15 minutes later, the aircraft was forced to return to the base because of heavy ice and both engines cutting out.

By daylight on February 14, all surface vessels in the rescue area were alerted to be on the lookout. The RCAF motor launches, M234 *Montagnais* and M235 *Huron*, had left Patricia Bay just north of Victoria at 1:30 AM and 2:30 AM respectively. They proceeded slowly through the Gulf Islands in the darkness, but at daylight increased to a top speed of 39-45 miles per hour. En route, the RCAF launches searched the Inside Passage, while the Navy vessel covered the west coast of Vancouver Island.

At 8:10 AM, headquarters of the Fourth Rescue Squadron at McChord AFB was asked to obtain additional aircraft from the Fifth Rescue Squadron for the B-36 search. About half an hour later, Catalina flying boat AF3956 departed on its second attempt to join the search. Whidbey Island Naval Air Station also dispatched four P2V Neptunes.

Under the command of Captain M.A. Medland, the *Cayuga* left her Esquimalt base at 8:15 AM and proceeded "with all dispatch" to the search area. Doug B. Dickson of Sundre, Alberta, one of the radiomen on the *Cayuga*, clearly remembered the search and rescue operation. "On the early morning of February 14, the communications staff of *Cayuga* was informed that an American aircraft had crashed north of Vancouver Island. We were to help in the rescue of survivors. Leave would be up and all hands would be on board. Our staff had to ensure that our communications system was ready and watches on 'broadcast' and all other frequencies were operating and manned."[4]

Dickson was given the task of operating the HF/DF (high-frequency direction finding, nicknamed "Huff-Duff") office and searching the aircraft distress signals. When he initially arrived on *Cayuga*, the vessel was "in something of a mess with a skeleton crew. I was, in fact, the only communications person in a radio room that had cable lying all over the place. In no time flat, dockyard mateys had restored the radio room and other areas of the ship. And, of course, we suddenly had a flood of new crew. I went from running my own show to being on the bottom of a heap of some 12 or so communications personnel with Chiefs, a P.O. [Petty Officer], etc."[5]

Another crew member, Percy Lotzer, remembered "the weather that day was pretty bad with rain and wind, rough seas and visibility poor. It did not improve during the night."[6]

The RCAF deployed a Sikorsky H-5 helicopter to search for the missing aircraft, and the supply vessel M-468 *Songhee* left her Patricia Bay base at 6:30 AM with a barge in tow to be used as a mobile landing and refuelling platform for the helicopter. It is believed this was the first time a helicopter was used in Canadian air-sea rescue activities.[7]

Because it was too dangerous to fly a helicopter at night without proper instruments and training, the helicopter made the first leg of the journey secured on the barge so it could continue making headway until daybreak, when it would be possible to take off and fly safely.

The Sikorskys in 1950 had a small hauling capacity and a short range, so they were not an ideal search and rescue aircraft. Fixed-wing aircraft such as Lancasters, Cansos and Norsemans would fly the actual search patterns. But once the wreck or survivors were located, helicopters could become a useful tool for rescue operations by shuttling personnel short distances.

Hours into the flight, the helicopter experienced engine trouble. Flight Lieutenant Hugh Campbell was forced to land on the golf course at Qualicum Beach on Vancouver Island. Once repaired, the helicopter proceeded to the forward search base at Port Hardy.[8]

By noon, 17 surface craft and 34 aircraft had officially joined the search for 075, but poor weather was against them. A 500-foot cloud ceiling and light rain did not help, while surface visibility was fair at three miles. Winds blew from the southeast at 52 miles per hour and seas in Queen Charlotte Sound were running so high that it was impossible to launch boats. Fog later in the day forced RCAF aircraft back to the closest air terminal at Port Hardy. US Coast Guard airplanes returned to Annette Island, Alaska, and Port Angeles, Washington.

On the first day of the search, the water probability area was the priority because survivors could not last long in cold water. There was little to see. At 1:48 PM, the B-29 search aircraft AF1830 reported observing what appeared to be a one-man life raft due west of Tofino, on the west coast of Vancouver Island. Later, it was confirmed not to be aircraft wreckage.

RCAF Douglas Dakota 650 searched 150 square miles southwest of Calvert Island using square search at 300 feet with half a mile visibility. Dakota 676 searched the area north of Port Hardy with indefinite results because of heavy rain.

The heavy rain made forward observation impossible, so RCAF Beechcraft 105 made no search beyond Port Hardy. RCAF Norseman 370 searched the coastline from Comox to Port Hardy. Unfortunately, all of these searchers were too far to the southeast of the actual crash site.

An aircraft farther north reported an oil slick about a mile long and 50 to 70 feet wide located roughly southwest of Princess Royal Island and due west of the south tip of Aristazabal Island. Newspapers then reported that an oil slick had been spotted off Princess Royal Island and that it was assumed the bomber had crashed into the sea.

Though by all known accounts Bomber 075 was supposed to have crashed somewhere in the Pacific Ocean, it is interesting to note that on the very first day of the air search, the US Air Force had at least one of its Alaska-based aircraft searching well north of Prince Rupert, flying up the Nass River as far as Aiyansh. The search was flown at an altitude of between 500 and 1,000 feet with one- to three-mile visibility in all areas except north of the Nass River, where they flew at altitudes of 1,000 to 7,500 feet.[9]

Bad weather again hampered the aerial search on Wednesday, February 15, the second day of Operation Brix. The search area was expanded to include all of Vancouver Island and the over-water area 50 miles west of it. Since the weather Wednesday was predicted to prohibit searching north of Vancouver Island, the B-29s could adequately cover the over-water area assigned to ARS, and the ARS aircraft could be released to assist the US Coast Guard in completing their search area, even though the weather prevented dropping a para-rescue man.[10]

As military rescuers from the 129th Heavy Anti-Aircraft Battery, Royal Canadian Artillery, Victoria, assembled, so did civilians. Five members of the Vancouver chapter of the Alpine Club of Canada flew into the area on an RCAF Lancaster. They were led by Fred Parkes, an insurance adjuster and expert mountaineer. His team included Herman

Genshorek, a painting contractor and a former Canadian army mountain troops instructor; Charles Jenkins, an insurance broker; Alan Melville, a duplicator; and Eric Brooks, a teacher at Lord Byng High School in Vancouver. Reporter Tom Hazlitt and photographer Bill Cunningham from the *Vancouver Sun* accompanied the team.

In the meantime, HMCS *Cayuga* had assumed control of the ground and surface-vessel search along the west coast of Vancouver Island. On Wednesday, the US Coast Guard had two cutters, *Winona* (WPG65) and *Cahoone* (WSC131), standing by the Canadian vessel. Other vessels nearby included the US Coast Guard *Citrus* and *White Holly*, plus the 70-foot Canadian federal fisheries patrol boats *Babine Post* and *Chilko Post*.

In the early afternoon on February 15, the crew of the fishing vessel *Cape Perry* sighted a wisp of smoke among the trees on Princess Royal Island. Captain Vance King dispatched a small rowboat and found the first two survivors, Lieutenants Ernest Cox and Roy Darrah.

The *Cape Perry* had been on its way from Butedale to Helmcken Inlet to pick up a load of herring for delivery to Vancouver. Having been informed of the crash, like all other vessels passing along the coast, it had been keeping a lookout.

When the rescued airmen came aboard, the first thing King asked was how they had parachuted. "They said they had dropped as number three and number seven, so I knew I was in the circle where the others should have landed. About one-half mile down the beach, we picked up a third man." The third man was radar mechanic Corporal Richard J. Schuler.[11]

Then, as King was turning to leave, he saw another wisp of smoke. When he investigated, he found seven men huddled on the shore, waiting for rescue, having left behind an eighth, Staff Sergeant Trippodi, who was later saved.

While the *Cape Perry* was picking up the survivors, the *Cayuga* had continued its journey into Queen Charlotte Sound and was only 70 miles away when, at 1:45 PM, it received a radio message to head toward the *Cape Perry* to pick up the 10 survivors who had been rescued. Making 25 knots, the destroyer reached the southern entrance to Squally Channel to the west of Princess Royal Island in 2 hours and 45 minutes.

King described the dramatic rescue of the men he saved to International News Service by radio telephone. All were in poor condition, he said, although not actually in dire straits. "All were wet, weak and hungry. They were too tired to talk. Some tried to smile their thanks but they could only make a sour face. They were just too tired to lift their lips in a smile. Mostly, they were wet, soaking wet, for 24 hours."[12]

It was pitch dark when the crew jumped and they did not know exactly where the aircraft was, except that it was over land. "They had no idea where the eventual crash of the plane may have been," said Reuben Schenk, a *Cape Perry* mate.

In a short radio-telephone interview before he and the other survivors on the *Cape Perry* were flown to McChord AFB, Captain Barry described some of their harrowing experiences. "We are all in good shape. We were over the island when we bailed out. I was the only one to land in the water. It was the toughest country I have ever seen. I landed in the water in the middle of a lake but struggled ashore. With the exception of Staff Sergeant Trippodi, all the men are in good shape but are very tired. All of them have been soaking wet since the crash . . . We were heading 165 degrees at 5,000 feet when the men bailed out."[13]

Speaking for his nine shivering and unshaven buddies, Lieutenant Darrah told his rescuers, "It was the most horrible night in my life." But the crew of the *Cape Perry* did not get much chance to talk with the survivors.

Almost three hours after they came aboard the *Cape Perry*, the 10 men were turned over to the US Coast Guard cutter *White Holly* and subsequently picked up by a US Coast Guard Catalina flying boat.

The RCAF dispatched three aircraft—Dakota 676 and Cansos 11067 and 11015—to pick up the survivors and airlift them to Port Hardy, only to find the US aircraft whisking the 10 rescued airmen away.

The first thing *Cayuga's* crew saw was a Catalina flying boat taking off. They learned from an intercepted radio transmission that it had the first 10 survivors on board. Even though there appeared to be a lot of confusion, some would later find the lack of communication by the US rescue team baffling and suspicious.

Percy Lotzer, a crew member on the *Cayuga,* thought that the Canadian teams could have done an excellent job of looking after the survivors. But the US authorities had them flown to Tacoma as soon as possible for security reasons.[14]

The Catalina flew to Port Hardy, where it met a US Air Force C-82 Flying Boxcar that had been dispatched to fly the survivors from Port Hardy to McChord AFB. The next day, a Douglas C-54 Skymaster flew nine of the survivors to their home base at Fort Worth, Texas. During the flight, they were subjected to yet another engine failure over Albuquerque, New Mexico. "That's when some of us seriously thought, 'To hell with it,'" First Lieutenant Paul Gerhart said. They managed to land safely at Carswell.

Back at Princess Royal Island, HMCS *Cayuga* put search personnel ashore as darkness set in, knowing that at least one other crewman was still on the island. The 25-man landing party from the *Cayuga* fanned out over the rugged terrain.

Lieutenant William Kidd of Vancouver and Chief Petty Officer Ernest Woolley of Langley Prairie, BC, led the *Cayuga's* rescue team to injured airman Staff Sergeant Vitale Trippodi. By the time the detail from HMCS *Cayuga* found him, he was delirious, suffering from shock and frostbitten feet. Lieutenant Commander Andrew B. Weir and his medical assistant, Petty Officer Alex Matte, gave Trippodi a sedative, placed him on a stretcher and made him as comfortable as possible. In almost complete darkness, he was carried down the hillside and transferred to the *Cayuga*.

"I lay there in that ice and snow for a day or two until I was found by a Canadian rescue team who got me to a ship," Trippodi recalled. "Those Canadians who picked me up were the swellest people I ever met. The first thing they did was to give me morphine to kill the pain in my foot. Then I drank all their cocoa."

The rescue team also included Petty Officers James Brahan and Roderick Bolt, Leading Seaman Ernest Partridge and Able Seamen Rupert Brodeur, William Cull, Frederick Hughes, Donald Evans and Glenn Clemmett. Leading Seaman Douglas Dickson and Able Seaman Lloyd Hilton maintained contact with the ship with walkie-talkies.[15]

Dickson gave a first-hand account of the rescue operation:

> The fishermen [on the *Cape Perry*] gave information that another man had spent the night of the 14th tangled in his parachute upside down hanging from a tree. His buddies had found him and cut him down. He was in very bad shape and

could not walk, so they rolled him in his parachute and left him on a hillside. He was supposed to be three miles in from the shore.

Our Captain asked the US vessel [*Winona*] if they were sending in a search party. The reply was, because of the foul weather, they would wait till first light on the 16th. A search party was organized and radiomen Lloyd Hilton and myself were to accompany the search party with portable radios so we could keep in touch with *Cayuga*. Our only information was [that] Staff Sergeant Trippodi was on the side of a cliff, three miles in. Our party was taken to the beach. Because of [the] rough water and rocky beach we had to jump into the water; we did not want to damage our boat.

As we worked our way inland the terrain was unbelievable. No snow in this area but the deadfall of very large trees that you could not climb over or go under. The green moss is very thick and slippery. This made our navigating very difficult. After a time we were losing our communications with the ship. Lloyd and I flipped a coin; I lost and had to stay put. It was not very long before I heard a voice off to my left between the search party and myself. We all headed to that area where the voice was heard.

We found Trippodi; he was wrapped in the parachute and was in pretty bad shape. Not much could be done in the way of first aid. He was placed on a stretcher, wrapped in warm wool blankets and given hot chocolate. He said: "I didn't think that hot chocolate could taste so good!"

The trip out was very tough. We all took turns carrying the stretcher. Lloyd and I had the parachute. If I was on the stretcher, Lloyd carried the parachute and vice versa. We made it back to the ship and Staff Sergeant Trippodi was taken to sick bay. The rescue party was all given a tot. I was very proud of being a small part in the rescue of Staff Sergeant Trippodi and how we all worked together to make it happen.

We never heard where he was taken after he left *Cayuga* or what happened to him. There were many things that were going on during the complete operation that we were not aware of in regard to all of the search parties, number of men and equipment.

Oh yes, the parachute: Lloyd and I kept it. We split it in half. I don't know what he did with his, but my half was put away. My wife Cherie and I were married in July 1950 and our first son was born in May 1951. We had his christening gown made from the parachute. Our son, now 49, still has it and it will be passed down for many generations to come.[16]

After the rescue of Staff Sergeant Trippodi ended at 9 PM on February 15, searchlights from HMCS *Cayuga* and the US Coast Guard cutter *Winona* probed the skies overnight, rescue personnel hoping that the beams would act as beacons for the missing airmen.

The *Cayuga* requested an aircraft with medical staff be sent at dawn on February 16, when the search for survivors would resume. That morning, accompanied by Lieutenant Commander Weir and Petty Officer Matte, a motorboat from the *Cayuga* transported Trippodi to a waiting US flying boat.

That day, the third of the search, Operation Brix was able to modify the search plan with the arrival of new resources. By day's end, there was a total of 13 aircraft combing land and sea around Queen Charlotte Sound.

A US Navy PBY Catalina searched Gil Island and Whale Sound while another navy Catalina and an RCAF Douglas Dakota searched the coastline of Princess Royal Island. Earlier that morning, the RCAF's Canso flying boat 11067 had arrived from Vancouver with 15 army personnel for a ground-search party.

❂

One of the most determined efforts to get to the rescue site was made by Lieutenant Richard C. Kirkland, the duty officer in the alerts room at Flight "C" of the Eighth Air Rescue Squadron (ARS) at McChord AFB. Kirkland had flown 103 combat missions in the Second World War with the famed Flying Knights Squadron in the Pacific theatre. He described his role in the search and rescue mission in his memoir *Tales of a War Pilot*. With the war coming to an end, the veteran pilot signed on for another term, wishing to attend helicopter school rather than train in the latest fighter jets. Once he was assigned to an air-rescue unit, Kirkland enjoyed not only flying big choppers, but also the associated rescue work. It was a job "which involved saving lives, the antithesis of what I'd done as a fighter pilot."[17]

The Great Imposter

Although the Canadian destroyer HMCS *Cayuga* played a critical role in the search and rescue efforts for Bomber 075, the ship's place in history has been etched by the infamy of a man who joined the crew before the *Cayuga* sailed into the Korean War as part of the Canadian military commitment to the United Nations. Ferdinand "Waldo" Demara, Jr. (December 21, 1921–June 7, 1982) was 29 when he joined the crew of HMCS *Cayuga*, masquerading as his former mentor, trauma surgeon Dr. Joseph Cyr.

Demara, a man of many names, was fresh off a stint as Brother John Payne of the Christian Brothers in Alfred, Maine, where he had founded a college on behalf of the order. In 1957 *Time* magazine wrote:

> Perhaps his most impressive impersonation came during the Korean War while impersonating a doctor on the Royal Canadian Navy destroyer. When several Korean combat casualties were brought on board, the responsibility of saving their lives fell to Demara, the ship's sole "surgeon." Demara, who allegedly possessed a photographic memory and unusually high IQ, ducked into his quarters with a medical textbook and emerged to save the lives of every single man, including one who required major chest surgery.

When Demara's exploits were covered by Canadian newspapers, contact was made with the real Dr. Cyr in New Brunswick. Only when he saw a picture of the *Cayuga*'s "doctor" was Cyr able to identify Demara as his good friend Brother Payne. The Canadian navy opted not to press charges.

The *Cayuga* went on to complete three tours of duty in Korea, and the story of HMCS *Cayuga* being the last home of "the Great Imposter" lived on, well after the ship was paid off in February 1964.

Valentine's Day had hardly begun when Brigadier General John D. Montgomery from SAC headquarters entered the alerts room and ordered Kirkland to immediately call his commanding officer and bring his rescue outfit to duty. The lieutenant quickly dialled Major Bush Smith, who wasn't home. "I tracked him down at a Valentine's Day party, along with most of our crew members." Kirkland rounded up every pilot and crewman he could locate and had them all assemble in the briefing room.

After Montgomery explained the mission, Kirkland suggested using his Sikorsky H-5 helicopter, the same model the RCAF had mobilized the previous morning.[18] It took a day to ready the equipment, so just before noon on February 15, Kirkland and co-pilot Captain Lawrence Clayton, who usually flew B-36 bombers, departed McChord AFB and headed to RCAF Station Sea Island, just south of Vancouver. Because of the poor weather, Kirkland was forced to "scud run," which was not very safe. The goal of scud running is to stay clear of foul weather by flying with visual rather than instrumental references. To avoid clouds, pilots lower their flying altitude and, in Kirkland's case, follow the coastline or roads and railways north. He headed toward Seattle, flying just above the main highway and "frightening motorists and dodging power lines." Kirkland made his way past Seattle, then Bellingham and then across Boundary Bay at the border, finally landing in front of the base operations building at Station Sea Island. Kirkland and Clayton were greeted in the ops office by the squadron leader. "They tell me this is a top priority mission, but the bloomin' ducks aren't even flyin' today. I don't know how you got that crazy windmill up here," he said.

Kirkland was told that an RCAF rescue boat was already en route to Princess Royal Island with a landing barge and fuel. At dawn on the third day of the search, February 16, the weather had not changed much. "It was still 'stinko' with the clouds hanging down to the treetops. But it wasn't any worse than the day before," Kirkland recalled.[19] Kirkland was able to follow the shoreline up the Strait of Georgia with more scud running, and a little over two hours later, quite unaware of what was transpiring around him, he landed his helicopter at the RCAF communications outpost at Port Hardy for refuelling.

"We started searching as soon as we departed Port Hardy and entered the Queen Charlotte Sound," Kirkland explained. His helicopter hugged the heavily wooded coastline, where many inlets meandered into the mountains. Luckily the tide was out, creating an area between the water's edge and the treeline where he could hover, dodging the boulders and tree stumps that loomed out of the mist. Kirkland believed he had enough fuel to reach his destination near the north end of Princess Royal Island, "But I hadn't allowed for winding around the inlets, so it was a close squeeze on fuel. But we made it and I landed at a rickety pier at an old mine in Surf Inlet."[20]

Unable to search the island's mountainous terrain in this kind of weather, Kirkland decided he could shuttle ground-search personnel. Hovering along an old railroad bed, he could save them a lot of time. Kirkland refuelled his helicopter and, as soon as the ground-search crew arrived in the motor launch, ferried them back into the mountains.[21]

By this time, he had received word that Bomber 075 survivors had already been found on the island's shoreline, even before the aerial search was well underway. He also knew that a second US military helicopter scheduled to join the search, Sikorsky H-5A AF6636, had been delayed due to mechanical trouble.

The *Daily Colonist* newspaper in Victoria described the ground search as "reduced to a laborious, dangerous, inch-by-inch scrutiny of huge areas of Princess Royal and adjoining islands." But six members of Bomber 075's crew remained missing, so the search went on. At first light on that third day of the operation, search and rescue teams that had joined the *Cayuga* rescuers landed on Princess Royal Island to look for the missing crewmen. There were 55 men in total, including the RCAF rescue team, two Canadian Army teams and the five civilian mountaineers from the Vancouver Alpine Club. It was a race against time, as the men still missing were likely suffering from injuries and exposure, unable to assist in their own rescue.

Before heading out, the men in charge of each land-search party were briefed in *Cayuga*'s operations room. The executive officer, Lieutenant Commander C.R. Parker went over all aspects of the search, pointing out areas already covered, assigning new territory to each party and informing them all of any clues that had turned up since the previous evening.[22]

That day, the searchers from the *Cayuga* found a 12th survivor of Bomber 075, Lieutenant Charles Pooler. A six-man team led by Lieutenant Glen M. deRosenroll found Pooler approximately one mile inland, at the southeast corner of an uncharted lake.

"We started out searching at 8:30 that morning," deRosenroll explained, "and found the airman about two hours later. He was on the

Princess Royal Island

About 370 miles north of Vancouver, Princess Royal Island is home of the white kermode, or spirit, bear (*Ursus americanus kermodei*). This 1,404-square-mile island is cut with rivers and pocked with lakes. A 1.2-mile channel separates it from the BC mainland. It is part of First Nation Tsimshian Territory, home of the Gitga'at people. The island is part of the Great Bear Rainforest, spectacularly beautiful with inlets, hills, endless swaths of deep green forest, grizzlies, eagles, wolves and black bears.

far side of a small lake. All of us had been yelling. We heard his call for help, and we shouted that we would soon be with him. We reached him all right… his left ankle had been broken, and we took him out on a stretcher." When the rescue party reached him, Pooler was surprised to learn they were Canadians.

The terrain was so rugged and inhospitable that it took Pooler's rescuers seven hours to travel the one and three-quarter miles to shore to get him out. "It was pretty tough going…getting him out of the bush," deRosenroll continued. "Those woods are really thick, and the slushy snow was up to our waists most of the time. We didn't get to the shoreline until around 6:30 that evening."[23]

The motor launch returned the party to the *Cayuga*, where Pooler was given immediate medical attention from surgeon Andrew Weir. Though he had a broken right ankle, multiple abrasions and was surffering from exposure, Pooler's general condition was favourable. Pooler said he had been greatly heartened by the sight of the searchlights displayed by HMCS *Cayuga* during the night of February 15.

A *Cayuga* team led by Lieutenant G.C. McMorris landed two miles farther south and hiked for 10 hours. A third *Cayuga* team, led by Commander Edwards, landed just north of the first team. That day they slogged through heavy snow, searching the mountainsides to the north and east for 15 hours. This group, too, found Pooler, according to Percy Lotzer, a member of the team. "As radio operator, I carried a 35-pound 'collection of electronic junk' and battery, called a portable radio set," Lotzer explained. "I came near not going because the stores were unable to outfit me with suitable wet gear. With the shortage of radio operators for the number of search parties proposed, I and the Chief were cajoled into believing I would be okay with double sweaters, dungarees, etc.

"As I recall, we were out a total of 15 to 16 hours, during 12 of which I was soaking wet to my belt. This happened shortly after getting ashore in a low and flat area, which stayed that way for a fair distance. We then started off into the woods over rough ground, deadfalls, etc. It was drizzling and there was a light cover of snow on the open patches with a greater build up in the small ravines." Lotzer maintained contact with the *Cayuga* until the radio got wet when he fell. Despite the radio's failure, Lotzer carried it for the rest of the day.

"We had a Webley revolver, which was fired from time to time. At some point we heard a gunshot reply. We responded to it by gunshots from ourselves and zeroed in on him [Lieutenant Pooler] and found him walking with difficulty in a clearing. When we got to him, he was standing in the middle of this small frozen-over lake about five miles long.

"And then this other group came out of the woods. Much to my chagrin, Commander Edwards instructed them to take this crewman back to the ship. Commander Edwards set it up then that deRosenroll took this guy back."[24]

"We seem to have covered very little ground during the next several hours," Lotzer later recalled. "In any event, with the advent of darkness came the admission that we were 'slightly misplaced.' I chose to follow the Chief and the rest chose to follow Lotzer and his dead radio. At this point the Commander decided that we should consider camping for the night and be better able to get our bearings in daylight. But the Chief pointed out that it would be unlikely that I would last until morning. As a fortunate result, we took off again following the Chief. [25]

"As darkness settled in, we were able to see the search lights from *Cayuga* going vertical and then laying down over the island to indicate the way." The rescue team had to climb down a cliff and jump a few feet to reach a cutter sent to shore by the *Cayuga*.[26]

Search teams from the US Coast Guard vessels *Cahoone*, *Citrus*, *White Holly* and *Winona* did not find any trace of the missing men. A search team from *Winona* landed four miles to the south and covered about five miles, while a rescue team from the *Cahoone* proceeded south. The team from the *Citrus*, which landed at the head of Chapple Inlet, covered about five miles in a northerly direction.

Teams from the RCAF and the Alpine Club of Canada covered a nearby mountainside. A team of both army and navy men tried to reach an abandoned parachute reported by an aircraft but didn't succeed because of oncoming darkness.[27]

Though a helicopter located four parachutes, it was not known if they belonged to the men already rescued.

A helicopter spotted some footprints in the snow at the head of Deer Lake that led to the west coast of Princess Royal Island. But a dwindling fuel supply forced the aircraft to turn back without investigating. Two parachutes were located in trees between three lakes south of Port Belmont. Ground-search parties reached one empty parachute hanging from a tree and sighted another.[28]

Royal Canadian Navy officials at the scene tersely warned: "This is no 24-hour operation. We expect it will be a long search."[29] As it turned out, Pooler was the last crewman to be found. He remained aboard the *Cayuga* off Princess Royal Island for four days after his rescue, until February 20, then was flown to Port Hardy and subsequently transferred to McChord AFB. Three days later, Pooler and Trippodi remained hospitalized, by then in Madigan General Hospital in Seattle.

A few days into the search, a US Coast Guard Catalina flying boat equipped with high-powered loudspeakers had swept over Princess Royal and Ashdown Islands, its crew shouting directions on how to reach the beach. They told any survivors who might be injured to "sit tight" while searchers came to their rescue. They broadcast the American national anthem and a message to the five missing airmen: "Don't give up hope; we are still looking for you."[30]

Around noon on February 16, a man's cry for help and a volley of gunshots heard by rescuers from the *Cayuga* kept up hope that the remaining crew members would be found alive. Later that day, RCAF officials said that even though they were "fairly sure" the missing men were somewhere on the island, they would not abandon the search in the surrounding waters.[31] For the duration of the search, the helicopters operated out of Surf Inlet on the west side of Princess Royal Island.

The *Cayuga* continued to direct all land and sea rescue operations from its anchorage about a mile south of Ashdown Island. Much of the responsibility for providing food and sleeping quarters for all the other rescue workers also fell to the *Cayuga*. By Friday, February 17, with gale-force winds blowing over Queen Charlotte Sound, the *Cayuga* had become a veritable hotel. The ship's complement of approximately 215 officers and men had grown by almost 20 percent.

In addition to the members of the Vancouver Alpine Club and five para-rescue troops from the RCAF's Air-Sea Rescue Station near Vancouver, 30 men from Work Point Barracks in Victoria had flown up on February 15 to assist in the ground search. The first group of 15 men, commanded by Captain Mark Holmes, went straight to the scene of operations on Princess Royal Island aboard an RCAF Canso aircraft and boarded the *Cayuga*. The second group, under Lieutenant Michael Kearney, was flown to Port Hardy and later taken to the *Cayuga*.

Among the ship's crew, a group of about 45 ordinary seamen was always among the first to volunteer for the day-by-day searches. Other ground searchers came from the US Coast Guard cutter *Winona*. A group of Gitga'at woodsmen from the Hartley Bay First Nation, familiar with the area, conducted a search of their own near Barnard Harbour, inland to the northwest of Surf Inlet.[32]

Sparked by a report from a US Air Force aircraft of a blood-spattered patch in the snow where a man had apparently fallen and stamped SOS in the snow, the search for survivors continued despite the gale. Seven ground-search parties disembarked from the *Cayuga*, although high winds prevented search aircraft from flying. One search party did not return to the destroyer until nearly midnight. The island's thick growth forced the men to crawl a "considerable distance" on their hands and knees, delaying them for hours. Snow had begun to fall on the island, and was now up to 18 inches deep in some places.[33]

A Royal Canadian Navy spokesman at Esquimalt called that day's search efforts "completely fruitless." Captain Medland noted, "The weather was in full control and showed little indication of relaxing its grip." The strong winds forced *Cayuga* to hoist her anchor and ride out under power on the night of February 17.[34]

The weather also delayed the arrival of a party of six experienced prospectors familiar with the terrain of Princess Royal Island. Search master Bell-Irving had assembled this hardened team from the Station Sea Island and as soon as the weather allowed the RCAF planned to fly the sextet in to join the search.

High winds on Saturday, February 18 forced search aircraft to be grounded for the second day in a row. After a 70-miles-per-hour morning gale beat them to shelter, the weather eased, allowing ground parties to continue combing the snow-covered landscape of Princess Royal Island that afternoon. One of the helicopters took off for a short time and checked the Deer Lake and Bear Lake shorelines.

The ground-search parties found some survival articles, presumably discarded by rescued survivors, two parachute logbooks and a lifejacket. In the late afternoon, a search party from the *Winona* found some debris believed to be a box of supplies dropped from Bomber 075. Darkness prevented further investigation.

Early the next day, Sunday, February 19, the previous day's debris was identified as a wooden box containing "oddments of radio equipment" that had burst on landing and created a 15-foot track down the middle of the lake. The aircraft's flight path and bailout location could finally be determined from this track.

With already poor weather conditions worsening, time was running out for finding the last of the missing airmen alive. Ground-search parties returned to Princess Royal Island, landing the greatest number of teams to date. Some 65 men resumed the search, 25 from *Cayuga* and 10 from each of the US Coast Guard cutters anchored off the island.

Later that day, an aircraft carrying two members of the press arrived over the *Cayuga,* circling in the clouds overhead. Meanwhile, an RCAF Lancaster bomber arrived from the photo reconnaissance detachment in Whitehorse, Yukon, to photograph the search area.

A naval message gave a vivid description of the search operation: "At dawn each day the rugged shore of Princess Royal Island takes on an air of wartime invasion. Search parties strike out in the still dark forests of the island while motorboats bring equipment and more rescue squads from HMCS *Cayuga* and USCG *Winona*, which are anchored a few hundred yards offshore."[35]

Also on February 19, Colonel John D. Bartlett, commanding officer of 436 Squadron at Fort Worth, visited 12 Group RCAF in Vancouver.

As commander of the crew that had ferried Bomber 075 to Alaska, he had obtained permission from his own commanding officer to fly north and confer with Canadian officials at Sea Island. Three of the survivors, Captain Barry, Lieutenant Gerhart and Staff Sergeant Stephens, accompanied him. They worked with RCAF search and rescue officials to pinpoint on aerial photographs the area where they had jumped and where the missing men might have landed.

The search and rescue specialists on the *Cayuga* determined that "the four missing airmen who were known to have jumped first had probably landed in the water between Princess Royal Island and Gil Island. The fifth missing airman, assuming survival and that he had jumped later, was thought to have made his way to south and inland [of Princess Royal Island] because of the terrain."[36]

Barry, Gerhart and Stephens, however, hoped that the first four jumpers might actually have landed on tiny Ashdown Island, due west of the Port Barnard Gitga'at village, rather than on Princess Royal Island. They supplied information about the course, position and altitude of the aircraft, and reconfirmed the bailout order.

The survivors said the crew bailed out at 11:50 PM on February 13 over a span of 12 seconds, from a point about 5,000 feet above sea level and 2.5 miles inland from the west coast of Princess Royal Island. Although their comments seemed mildly different from those gathered soon after rescue, they all believed that everyone had left the aircraft over land. The fact that some survivors were found close to the island's western shoreline suggested that all of the men had been pushed northwest by the prevailing winds once their parachutes opened.

From this knowledge about the jumps of the five missing men, it was determined that the four who were the first to leave the aircraft—Captain Phillips, Lieutenant Ascol and Staff Sergeants Straley and Pollard—likely landed in the water somewhere in the vicinity of Casanave Passage, between Ashdown and Princess Royal Islands, or farther north in Whale Channel. The wind had probably carried them back out to sea, since they may have bailed out too close to shore.[37]

The coldness of the water precluded the possibility of a human surviving immersion for more than two hours. There was also a strong possibility that the men had drowned in the turbulent waters. Lashed by a 58-miles-per-hour wind on the night of the accident, a 19-foot ebbing tide had created extremely large waves. It seemed more and more likely that the men had been lost at sea.

Barry, Gerhart and Stephens also confirmed that a wooden box had been pushed out of the rear escape hatch during bailout, right after Straley and Pollard had exited the aircraft. As this box had no parachute, a free fall was assumed, thus establishing a point on the aircraft's track and placing the missing Straley and Pollard some distance north of the position where the box was found.[38]

With this input from Sea Island, search officials aboard the *Cayuga* decided that the missing men had likely landed in Campania Sound or Whale Channel. Still, the search continued south of the "box-on-the-lake" location and on Ashdown Island. They retrieved a Mae West, a radar reflector and another parachute. Four days earlier, this parachute had been sighted from the air "with what appeared to be a man hanging from it," according to a message sent from a search aircraft.[39]

The *Cayuga* was running short of supplies when it welcomed the 175-foot Canadian Navy Auxiliary tanker HMCS *Dundurn* on Sunday, February 19. This marked the first major job for *Dundurn* since she had been brought to Esquimalt from the east coast in 1946. Serving on the vessel commanded by Captain James Patterson of Victoria were officers and men of the coastal harbour tug HMCS *Heatherton*. The *Cayuga* took on about 400 tons of fuel oil, medical supplies and general stores.

Early the next day, the recently refitted and modernized destroyer HMCS *Sioux* arrived alongside the *Cayuga* to deliver additional supplies and a motor-launch propeller. She left the scene within an hour to return to Esquimalt.

Though hampered by the adverse weather conditions, the search continued into a second week as eight search parties, totalling 150 searchers, landed on Princess Royal Island and smaller islands nearby. They found some articles believed to be from the missing B-36, but still no survivors. Three teams from the *Cayuga* and a joint team from *Winona* and *Cayuga* searched the western side of Chapple Inlet. Another joint *Cayuga-Winona* team remained ashore for two days, roughing it in the bush and working their way to the southern tip of the island, where they were picked up.

Two teams from *White Holly* searched a half-mile-wide area near

Barnard Harbour. Four army teams concentrated on an area a mile long and half a mile wide along the Princess Royal Island shoreline of Casanave Passage, searching an area where tracks had been reported the previous day and on February 21 by RCAF Noorduyn Norseman 789.

One helicopter managed a few flying hours searching the south shore of Gil Island, the east shore of Ashdown Island and the east side of Casanave Passage. Meanwhile, Norseman 789 investigated a reported oil slick in Laredo Channel, which had disappeared and was believed to have been caused by a fishing boat.

On February 22, *Citrus* searched the east and west shores of Chapple Inlet with a small boat while the *Cayuga* did the same on the east side of Campania Sound. A *Cayuga* team sighted what appeared to be two parachutes in the mountains approximately a mile south of Barnard Harbour. Aircraft under *Winona*'s control searched the shores of Whale Channel and Douglas Channel. The same day, searchers found a partially inflated one-man life raft in the water between Gil and Princess Royal Islands. Nothing indicated that the raft might have been used by any of the still-missing men. Its supply of provisions had not been opened, and the raft had not taken on any water.[40]

Four search teams who had camped on the island overnight investigated three new clues in the northern area of Princess Royal Island. However, a reliable naval source called the new leads slim. In a terse radio message late on February 21, *Cayuga* reported: "No survivors found. Water container and other items located. Helicopter reported tracks in [northern] area."

At the end of February 21, the US Coast Guard cutters *Winona*, *White Holly*, *Citrus* and *Cahoone* were advised that the ground search had been discontinued. Finding the life raft had been taken as "reasonable definite indication" that the five missing crew members had probably perished in the sea. HMCS *Cayuga* was instructed to co-ordinate the evacuation of all ground personnel. This included the civilian contingent, which had grown in number throughout the search.

After arriving at Surf Inlet, the six prospectors had been transported by the motor launch *Montagnais* to take on terrain that was impossible to access by sea. They were equipped with snowshoes, walkie-talkie radios, pup tents and field rations. Team leader Andy Hay was accompanied by

Stanley "Stan" Lothrop, Vic Tilley, J.B. "Bish" Thurber, Tom McQuillan and Peter McNee, all from Vancouver.

Most of the Alpine Club mountaineers were involved in the search for eight days. Nine crew members of the fishing boats *Collinson* and *Qwatsu* were employed on Operation Brix for four days. The Canadian Fishing Company Ltd. contributed the services of men and boats on the company payroll without charge to the RCAF. The number of Port Barnard villagers who helped with the search was uncounted. In addition, at the request of the search master, additional boats were chartered, men hired and supplies purchased as necessary.

The evacuation of ground personnel was completed on February 22, and in full darkness, at nine o'clock that evening, the *Cayuga* weighed anchor and returned to Esquimalt, fighting a gale the entire way home.

The *Montagnais* and aircraft were instructed to remain in the area and continue the search. The RCN coastal tug HMCS *Clifton* was diverted to the area to provide further assistance.

Other aircraft and ships, mainly from the US, looked for signs of the five missing men on a reduced level using a high-speed launch, a Norseman aircraft, three helicopters and seaplanes from the US Coast Guard. Bad weather continued to interfere with the operations, but on February 26 a USAF helicopter scanned the shorelines of Princess Royal Island, Gil Island and parts of Campania Island. The next day, the helicopter continued searching more shoreline in the area.

On February 28, the *Montagnais* landed two parties on the south shore of Gil Island. They searched the shoreline and beaches west of York Point to Fawcett Point, and the north shores of Ashdown and Princess Royal Islands from Redfern Point to Aitken Passage. A helicopter searched at treetop level. Neither search obtained any results.

Norseman 370 continued searching until March 5, officially the last day of the search mission. The search was then reduced to a casual status for "following up of possible clues." The Canadian fishing fleet operating in the area would still keep a sharp lookout for possible survivors along the various shorelines. The aerial and ground searches were finally suspended on March 10. They had failed to recover the last five missing crew members or their remains.

Operation Brix had covered approximately 25,000 square miles. A total of 40 aircraft had been involved in the search, including 7 Consolidated PBY Catalinas, 2 Douglas C-47 Dakotas, a Noorduyn Norseman, a Beech 18 Expediter, 2 Sikorsky S-51 helicopters and an Avro Lancaster from the RCAF.[41] During this operation, the RCAF motor launches *Huron* and *Montagnais* were employed for 21 and 17 days respectively. Supply vessel *Songhee* clocked 253 hours during 30 days on Operation Brix.

Indirectly, the search also claimed eight more lives, far from the search area. On February 15 at about 7:30 AM, a Boeing B-29 Superfortress carrying 15 people crashed shortly after taking off from Great Falls, Montana, to rejoin the search. The big four-engine aircraft went down about three miles southwest of Great Falls AFB, bursting into flames after it hit the side of a highway and careened across the road. The aircraft had spent much of the previous day searching Queen Charlotte Sound before being rerouted to Great Falls when weather prevented a return to the B-29's home field near Spokane, Washington. Seven crew members survived the crash.

Both the Canadian and US militaries did extensive reviews of the search and rescue operation for Bomber 075. What lessons were learned? How could similar operations be improved in the future?

The accident brought home the deadly serious business of military training flights, especially those taking place in extreme climates. Bomber 075's transcontinental flight transported its crew within a few hours between climate extremes, from the relatively warm south to one of the most inhospitable and remote areas on earth. During cold-weather operations, metal shrinkage occurred, and fuel and lubrication behaved in unexpected ways.

As a result, flight surgeons began studying the effects of fatigue on crew members during long missions of 24 to 40 hours, as well as in-flight feeding and adjustment strategies for the transition from temperate-zone bases to extremely high altitudes above 40,000 feet. It was also recognized that survival training would need to be improved for extreme environments such as that of Alaska, as would the recommended gear, clothing and general health requirements for the crew. For example, the parachutes used by the B-36 crew were all white with no coloured panels. They proved extremely difficult to spot and many false reports originated because they resembled snow on trees.

Operation Brix involved personnel and resources from two different nations, both military and civilian. It was carried out in a remote area with limited resources, most of the time under unfavourable circumstances. Although an intensive air-and-ground search was carried out simultaneously over a fairly small area, in only two cases did aircraft actually spot people on the ground, and these were search and rescue personnel, not survivors. This illustrated well the tremendous problem of finding *survivors* in heavily wooded terrain.[42]

On February 27, 1950, a meeting chaired by Captain M.A. Medland was held on HMCS *Cayuga* to discuss Operation Brix. The whole operation had been carried out with little coordination and poor communications, forcing the Canadian *Cayuga* crew to "make do on their own." Captain Medland said it was evident that *Cayuga* had not received all the information, particularly regarding search plans and intelligence.[43] For example, only by intercepting US radio transmissions did the *Cayuga* learn of the position of the 10 airmen rescued and aboard the *Cape Perry*.

Receiving Trippodi on board was the *Cayuga*'s first lucky break, because he was able to provide first-hand details of the bailout. It was this hard information that would "set the pattern for the whole subsequent search, and though at odds with information received from interrogation of the 10 [survivors] who had been evacuated, it was used throughout [the search] and was gradually corroborated as the days went by."[44]

Captain Medland noted, "During the interval [February 14–16] some doubt existed as to how neighbourly this mission was going to be." In the end, *Cayuga* took command of 13 aircraft and, despite radio difficulties, kept constant control of the direction and pattern of the ongoing search.[45]

It wasn't until the third day of the search, after 12 survivors had been rescued, that *Cayuga* was officially informed that it was directing the ground search for the remaining missing crew members. *Cayuga* was also notified that the air search was to be coordinated with the ground search. However, this contradicted an intercepted radio message from Seattle two days earlier that had directed a US commander to take total charge of all operations.

Not until February 17, the fourth day of the search, did the Canadian search and rescue staff finally determine the true location of the bailout.

The two rescued survivors, the odds and ends of equipment found by the search teams, and the position where the first survivors were picked up indicated that the priority search area was the three-by-five-mile corner of Princess Royal Island adjacent to the *Cayuga's* anchorage.

Captain Medland described the conditions for rescue parties on the island as grim. After his review, he praised the co-operation and efforts of the Canadian navy, army and air force personnel, US Coast Guardsmen, members of the Vancouver Alpine Club, prospectors, fishermen and trappers who participated in the search. Captain Medland did not include the US Air Force on his list.

"The boat crews did a magnificent job in getting landing parties ashore and back aboard. There were few beaches and most landings were made on rocky cliffs," he said. Sailors from the *Cayuga* who volunteered to go ashore said it was impossible to keep dry, wading through snow up to their waists in many places, fighting their way through dense, damp underbrush and climbing over fallen trees and snags and rocky terrain. Ground-search personnel suffered much discomfort because of high winds and extremely heavy rainfall at near-freezing temperatures. Often ground-search parties did not return until 10:00 PM.

In the initial stages of the search, navy personnel were adequately provided for from the ship's resources. Additional personnel depleted these resources, as would a prolonged operation. Army personnel appeared to have little idea what clothing would be required for Princess Royal Island. "It's incredible how many things went wrong," *Cayuga* radio operator Percy Lotzer noted. "Putting all those amateurs loose out there, and I am one of them, they were damn lucky they didn't lose some more."[46]

Various combinations of personnel had been tried during the ground search. After some experimentation, it was found that the most effective method of carrying out a large-scale ground search was to employ teams of five or six men in allotted areas. Standby crews were based centrally to facilitate the evacuation of survivors found by any one of the search teams.

HMCS *Cayuga* had operated at the saturation point insofar as control and housekeeping arrangements were concerned. If more ground-search personnel had been involved in the rescue, control would have suffered, and some trained members of the ship's crew would have been required for housekeeping duties. Thus the search would have been impaired.

Under the conditions of Operation Brix, a ship like the *Cayuga* provided the most suitable headquarters for the search. A destroyer could provide adequate facilities and, within limits, a reasonable number of men for search parties. With a smaller ship or a larger area to search, ground-search parties would have had to be housed ashore for an efficient and speedy search.

The *Cayuga's* communications officers were kept busy around the clock with the maze of messages. "During the whole operation, our communications staff were kept busy 24 hours a day," Lotzer said. "We estimated that when the mission was over, we had handled over 1,000 messages. Because almost all these messages were classified, they were all encrypted. The same was with incoming traffic, which meant that everything was coded or decoded. It took time and manpower to do all this work. Most was 'priority', which meant that it was to be sent 'now.' All this communication work was done with 10 people."[47]

"The other problem was that our equipment was no damn good," Lotzer noted. "Those radios were absolute junk. Half the time they [the operators] never knew whether they [the radios] worked or not. Half of them was on your back in batteries and half was on your chest."[48]

Recommendations that came out of the rescue reviews included speeding up the availability of aerial photographs. During Operation Brix, the RCAF had not been able to supply the badly needed regional aerial photographs until five days into the search.

A recommendation calling for the establishment of a regional Rescue Coordination Centre was certainly taken seriously. In June 1950, a Rescue Coordination Centre was established for 12 Group at the RCAF Station Sea Island headquarters. From then on, all emergency calls for assistance were passed through this agency, greatly increasing the level of efficiency and decreasing response time.[49]

On March 6, 1950, Major General Roger Ramey, commanding general of the US Air Force's Eighth Air Force, thanked Group Captain J.A. Easton, Headquarters 12 Group RCAF, for the Canadian assistance during the rescue operation. Reports had come to Ramey about the magnitude and the intensity of the Canadian effort in the search and rescue of the B-36 survivors, and the spirit and vigour with which the search was conducted.

On behalf of the officers and men who flew the B-36s, Group

Commander Colonel J.A. Roberts and Wing Commander Brigadier General Irvine, Ramey expressed his heartfelt thanks and appreciation for a job well done. "All these reports indicate that the personnel and units under your control or supervision far exceeded the standards set for search operations set by international agreements. This fine display of spirit and co-operation is most gratifying." [50]

General Hoyt S. Vandenberg, chief of staff of the US Air Force, added his words of appreciation to the personnel of the Royal Canadian Navy for their work in the search for and rescue of survivors of the B-36 crew. Vandenberg said Captain Medland and his men on the destroyer *Cayuga* had been especially helpful in coordinating the ground and aerial searches of Princess Royal Island. [51]

For his part, Captain Medland said that "whilst Operation Brix was essentially peacetime and passive, I have every confidence that in other circumstances, one of [His Majesty's Canadian] destroyers could well act as headquarters ship for landing parties engaged in a more serious business of finding other people who may in [the] future land on the shore of our West Coast." [52]

Soon after the search mission for Bomber 075 was officially terminated, relatives of two of the missing airmen started their own search around Princess Royal Island. The wife of gunner Staff Sergeant Neal Straley and the father of navigator Captain William Phillips looked unsuccessfully for 24 days. After returning to Fort Worth empty-handed, Straley's spouse commented, "What I was searching for was peace and contentment in my own mind. I feel better now." [53]

Straley's widow eventually married Staff Sergeant Trippodi. Fifty years after the crash, their home still displayed pictures of Straley, along with woodwork he had crafted and doilies he had crocheted to calm his nerves after being shot down in the Second World War.

Mrs. Straley's search was the subject of a curious tale, a story not heard elsewhere, that was related by northern BC bush pilot Cedric Mah in 2001. "Ken [Wrathall, who captained a fisheries vessel] told how many months later a widow, unsatisfied with the search report, chartered a floatplane to fly over Princess Royal Island. On a mountain slope she espied the parachute caught up in the limbs of a tree. A search party went in and retrieved the remains of her husband." [54]

The Department of the Air Force kept the five crew members in missing status from February 13 to May 8, 1950. At that date, the department considered the evidence sufficient to establish the fact of their deaths. Shortly after May 8, nearly three months after the accident occurred, relatives were informed that the five missing men were declared to have died officially on February 14, 1950, the date beyond which they could not have survived. The Air Force concluded that the crewmen had parachuted into the waters adjacent to Princess Royal Island.[55]

A few weeks after the end of the search, a US freighter reported sighting what appeared to be the wing tip of an aircraft some 30 miles north of Cape Scott, but an extensive search between March 19 and 23 did not turn up anything.[56]

On July 24, 1950, Mack S. Phillips, a resident of Surf Inlet on Princess Royal Island, reported finding a Mae West between the southeast side of Brooks Point and Red Fern Point. And almost two years later, on May 21, 1952, Lewis Clifton, a Native halibut fisherman from Hartley Bay, made a gruesome discovery off Ashdown Island. His fishing vessel *Collinson* hooked onto a parachute, bearing US markings, entangled with some human bones and tree branches.

Though no positive identification could be made, it was believed the remains might be of an airman from the B-36 bomber. The Prince Rupert detachment of the BC Provincial Police held the parachute and remains until the US authorities picked them up.

On May 27, 1952, six days after the discovery of the human remains, a US Coast Guard Catalina flying boat on an "administrative mission" to Prince Rupert to pick up the parachute and remains crashed into Juan de Fuca Strait near Port Angeles, Washington. The pilot, co-pilot and two others aboard were killed. Eight others were rescued, none of them seriously injured.[57] The Broken Arrow incident of Bomber 075 had indirectly claimed four more lives.

The bones were declared BNR (body not recovered).[58] No identification could be made and they were interred in the Jefferson Barracks National Cemetery in St. Louis, Missouri. The Quartermaster General furnished a monument for the grave on which the names of all five missing men—Lieutenant Ascol, Captain Phillips, Staff Sergeant Pollard, Captain Schreier and Staff Sergeant Straley—were inscribed.

The buried remains included a human foot and a draughtsman's compass, which was also snagged in the net. Since Straley was known to carry a compass in one of his boots at all times, it was assumed the remains were his. One of his relatives still has a photograph of Straley's mother receiving a flag on board the US Coast Guard cutter that brought the remains back from Canada.

After the remains were found in 1952, the next of kin of the five missing airmen received a form letter telling them that the remains had been interred in Grave 135, Section 85, at Jefferson Barracks National Cemetery. They were assured that "the grave will always be cared for in

Staff Sergeant Dick Thrasher—Some Recollections

Dick Thrasher had a run of bad luck with aircraft. In a little over a year, he had experienced two B-36 crashes and a C-54 losing an engine. This apparently made some crew members reluctant to fly on the same aircraft with him. As to being "jinxed," Thrasher shrugged it off, but he was happy to share his experiences.

A year after their harrowing experience aboard Bomber 075, Captain Barry and Thrasher were reunited on another training mission. Barry said, "Is Thrasher going with us?"

Thrasher answered, "Yes, Thrasher is going; this is his crew. When they fly, he flies."

Barry said, "We're bound to have trouble."

"That's the last words I heard out of Barry," Thrasher recalled.[59] Hours later, Barry was killed when a fighter plane crashed into the cockpit of his B-36. As the bomber disintegrated in mid-air, Thrasher managed to jump clear before it smashed into the Oklahoma countryside.

It would seem that Thrasher, nicknamed "Old Lucky" (or Unlucky, depending on your point of view, Thrasher observed) should not be allowed to fly. Old Lucky's flying misfortunes with Captain Barry actually dated back to 1949. The aircraft was another B-36, Serial 034, with Captain Barry as pilot and Captain R.V. Green as co-pilot. The flight engineer was Dudley Gardner and the scanners were Bill Wieter, Clyde Rose and Thrasher.

"It was a test hop," Thrasher recalled. Just before levelling off, Dudley asked the left scanner, Thrasher, to check the No. 3 engine, as he had a fire warning light. "No. 3 looked normal to me and I had just told him so a manner fully commensurate with the sacrifice" the deceased had made for their country.[60] Relatives were invited to attend services at Jefferson Barracks National Cemetery on July 17, 1952.

In another sad aftermath, three of the Bomber 075 survivors were involved in another B-36 accident 14 months later. On April 27, 1951, Bomber 075 survivors Captain Barry and Lieutenant Cox, along with 11 other airmen, were killed in a mid-air collision. Staff Sergeant Dick Thrasher, who was in the rear of the aircraft, survived the accident.

The collision occurred over Edmond, Oklahoma, between their B-36 and an Oklahoma National Guard P-51 Mustang fighter aircraft

when things started to happen, fast!" The cowling turned dark on top and "started to blossom open like a paper burning from the underside." There was no smoke or flame visible. Then No. 3, still turning, departed from the aircraft!

"All this time I'm trying to tell Dudley what I am seeing, but the intercom went dead and I'm not sure how much of it he got. With no contact with the A/C [aircraft] we decided to bail out. We turned the dump valve to 'dump' but didn't know how to stop the pressure from coming in with the cut-off valve. So we couldn't open the hatch... Bill Wieter solved this problem with the crash axe through the right blister."

When they opened the hatch, Rose, who was wearing a summer flying suit with no jacket, said, "I'll freeze to death." So Thrasher tried again to contact the front. "Captain Barry was on intercom No. 2 and informed us everything was under control and to stow all equipment for landing. It was a very smooth landing." The investigation later determined it had been a wing crawlway fire that had crystallized the engine mounts; 034 never flew again.

In May 2000, Thrasher and his family came to Vancouver. "It looked like every time he was on this coast something happened," said geologist Dr. Jim Roddick. "We took him around Vancouver and had him for dinner and then took him to the cruise ship for [an] Alaska cruise." Going up the coast near Glacier Bay, Alaska, the vessel had a fire aboard. "They lost a couple of the crew's bedrooms down near the engine room. The Coast Guard came in to take him off, but the vessel was considered still seaworthy and they continued on to Seward, Alaska.[61]

during a simulated fighter attack. B-36 Serial 49-2658 from 436th Bomb Squadron, Carswell AFB, was flying at 20,000 feet on a training flight in which it assumed the role of an enemy bomber that would be intercepted by four P-51 fighter planes from 185th Technical Reconnaissance Squadron, Will Rogers Field, Oklahoma City. The fighter planes were practising nose passes, diving from high above the B-36. Two swooped by very close. The third collided with the B-36.[62]

According to Thrasher, the B-36 immediately went into a steep dive after the wing tip of the P-51 sliced directly through Captain Barry's cockpit. There was fierce shaking and the B-36 began breaking up. The nose section broke away first. Then a strong fishtail motion began throwing the crew around in the rear compartment.

Of the five crewmen in the rear, only Thrasher went out the hatch. The other survivors remarked how "Slicky Dick" Thrasher dumped the pressure, opened the hatch and cleanly exited. He had done it all before, and it showed.[63] But before the others could follow, the tail section broke off and they were simply thrown out.

CHAPTER 6

Survival Stories of the Crew

"The jump," said one of the crew, "was the easiest part."

Lieutenant Whitfield clearly remembers his bailout: "As I jumped, I rolled over so that I could see the plane pass over me before my chute opened. I saw a brilliant blue-white streamer of fire trailing one engine for as far back as the tail of the plane. I thought that the fire had to be from the magnesium heat exchanger on that engine."[1]

The B-36 manual of bailout procedures called for the crew to drop the nose wheel and then put the aircraft into a slow turn. This would give the crew a better chance of landing close to each other. According to official reports, all personnel accomplished bailout at about 4,500 feet, starting with the men in the nose compartment.[2]

The actual jumping technique used by airmen is very important in an emergency exit from aircraft such as Bomber 075. Staff Sergeant Neal Straley, the first to jump from the rear hatch, followed the official procedures and rolled out in a tight crouch. However, his pack, which included his parachute and a one-man life raft, got hooked on the rim of the small exit hatch. Staff Sergeant Martin Stephens kicked him loose.

Staff Sergeant Elbert Pollard, who went next, had experience bailing out of aircraft, as during the Second World War, he had jumped over Germany and become a prisoner of war. Ignoring the rules, he simply dove out headfirst. Pollard's feet hit the door and the door banged shut.

The door was "kind of tricky" and sometimes shut for no reason, and Stephens had to open it again.

Staff Sergeant Dick Thrasher went next. "I knew we had heavy ice conditions. I was in the aft compartment sweating it out. First thing I knew the pilot said we couldn't hold our altitude any longer. He said we were over Princess Royal Island, and to go ahead and bail out." Thrasher believed that just prior to bailing out, Barry was trying to level the aircraft off. "At one time I believe that the airplane almost stalled because it quivered."

Thrasher got hung up when he tried to bail through the aircraft's small rear hatch. "I have always been told that you are to get your foot at the near edge of the opening and try to roll out in a ball." For Thrasher the size of the opening made this impractical. Stephens, who jumped next, unceremoniously kicked him out and in the process saved his life.

Captain Barry, who left the aircraft through the forward escape hatch, had to crawl out of the aircraft. "I didn't jump hard enough, I just kind of stuck my head out and expected to fall out and the wind pressure held me to the escape hatch but I cleared the propellers by a good many feet." The opening of his B-10 backpack parachute was "pretty good but not terrific."

Stephens later blamed himself for the deaths of Straley and Pollard. "But it wasn't his fault. It really bothered him. [He felt] if he hadn't been in such a hurry to get them out, they might have survived," Barry said.

Lieutenant Cox, who was the third man out of the forward hatch, was one of the first to be picked up by the 72-foot fish packer *Cape Perry*. He landed about 200 yards inland from the western shoreline, a position that supports the possibility that the two who had jumped before him were still over water when they landed. "When I jumped, I cleared the airplane and pulled my rip cord," said Cox. "I landed in a tree and had been there when I heard the airplane coming back; I saw it. It was in a slight left turn. It swung around and turned right over where I landed." It took Cox two hours to get out of his parachute. He dropped his rubber life raft to see how far it was to the ground. Fighting the dark, he sensed a branch from a nearby tree, tossed his parachute to it, swung across and slid to the ground.

Lieutenant Roy R. Darrah, the last man out of the rear compartment, set down within shouting distance of Cox. After landing in a tree that stood about 75 feet from the Queen Charlotte Sound beach, he spent the entire moonless night 16 feet off the ground. "It was raining and snowing and blowing a gale," Darrah said. "In the morning I started to shout and got an answer." Darrah and Cox yelled back and forth, but they did not get together until daylight. The two men walked five miles along the coast, where they were able to start a signal fire. "We were the first two spotted from the boat Wednesday," Darrah said.[3]

Corporal Richard J. Schuler, the aircraft's radar mechanic and the fifth man to leave the front exit of the aircraft, was the "lone wolf" among the 12 survivors in that he was the only one of them who never saw another of his mates between the time he "hit the silk" and the time the *Cape Perry* answered his frantic waving of a piece of white parachute from the beach. When the vessel blew its horn in recognition, Schuler said, "I just dropped to my knees and said a prayer." He had landed in a tree that collapsed his parachute and then had fallen some 20 feet to the ground. "I landed flat on my chin," he recalled. "It knocked me cold. I don't know how long I was out but it was still dark when I awoke. I just lay on the snow and curled up." He then passed an uneasy, wakeful night alone, listening to some animal prowling about his improvised parachute tent. "He was just on the other side of a tree," Schuler said. "I only had a screwdriver but I sure was going to pounce on him if he came after me." In the morning he discovered bear tracks. Disoriented and alone, Schuler first thought he was on the mainland and headed east in search of a road during the first day. The demanding terrain forced him back toward the coast, where he spent a second harrowing night.

Captain Barry and the six men clustered with him at the shoreline all had their stories to tell. Ford had also been hung up in a tree. After he managed to get to the ground, Ford attempted to fall asleep in the snow, but he too was worried about the wildlife. "I heard an animal," he said. "I think it was a wolf, prowling around in the darkness just out of sight. I shouted, and he left but he came back and prowled around all night."

Thrasher, worried about whether he would make land or not, had unfastened his chute in front, thrown it back, got a Mae West and put it on. Finding the chute was tight in front, he fastened it under the Mae West. After Thrasher's chute popped open, he made just one swing to the left and another to the right; then he was in the trees. "I landed in a big tree in the dark. I could not get loose from my parachute, so I cut myself free with a knife." He could feel a big branch with his foot and when his eyes got used to the dark, he discovered that the branch was actually a root. He was only a few feet above the ground.[4]

Right after he landed, Thrasher said, he saw the aircraft he had just exited. "I was still in the tree trying to cut my shroud lines with my pocket knife when the plane came back over. I saw it after it came back over. It was travelling southwest, mostly south, about 190 degrees." Thrasher estimated he landed about 2.5 miles in from the west shore of Princess Royal Island. "I spent the rest of the night in my one-man life raft," Thrasher continued. "I was all by myself. The raft kept me dry. Next morning I was cold, so I climbed the tree to try to get my chute. I wanted to wrap myself in it. When I got to the top of the tree, I began yelling for all I was worth. The navigator and radar operator answered.

"I recognized Jim Ford's, the radio operator, voice when he replied. They couldn't have been more than a quarter mile away." Thrasher made his way toward them. "I headed for small clearings that looked like easier going, but they were actually slush ponds. At a larger slush pond, I inflated my life raft that I was packing with me. Then I sat in it but couldn't make it move." He abandoned the life raft there and went back, going over and under deadfall logs. He finally joined Ford and Lieutenant Gerhart, the radar operator.

"We found another gunner," stated Thrasher, referring to Sergeant Stephens, who had booted him through 075's tiny rear escape hatch. "Then we found another officer [Lieutenant Colonel Daniel MacDonald]. We were weak and decided to build a tent out of our parachutes and a life raft. After a lot of trouble, we finally got a little fire going. We were lucky. We had our lighters and some lighter fluid, but everything on the ground was wet. We had a hard time keeping the fire going through the second night."

Ford picked up the story. "We made a teepee out of a parachute and I remember that we emptied our pockets and wallets of any paper we had to make a fire, except money," Ford explained. "Once we got a fire going, we tried to dry our socks and get warm, but it was a pretty miserable night, although I didn't even come down with a cold after all that exposure."[5]

When morning came, they decided to try to walk out to the coast. On the way, the men followed two sets of tracks and found the aircraft commander, Captain Barry, and co-pilot Raymond Whitfield. They tramped an SOS in the snow and had just started to build a fire when they heard a motor.

"At first it sounded like a plane, then we decided it was a boat. Barry and I walked down to the shore and began shooting flares," Thrasher said. "It was a Canadian fishing boat. I think it was about 2:30 PM, Wednesday. The Canadians really treated us fine. Aboard the boat were three others of our crew members. I was really happy to see the boat, for I fully expected to spend another night in the snow."

In a radio-telephone interview with the Canadian Press from the *Cape Perry*, Captain Barry reportedly stated that he ditched the plane. "I came down in the middle of a lake on Princess Royal Island but made shore safely where I spent the rest of the miserable night. I tried to build a fire but the wood was too wet. My parachute was so wet it didn't do me much good for warmth during the rest of the night."[6] When morning came, Barry was pretty hungry, and when he saw a ground squirrel, he fired at it twice with his .45 and missed both times. "But my shots attracted Lieutenant Whitfield, my navigator [co-pilot]. He blew his whistle and we walked toward one another. We got together and started plodding through the snow and underbrush. It was rough."

Barry and Whitfield had to make one of their toughest decisions shortly after they found each other. Heading toward the coast, they heard the cries of 23-year-old radio operator Vitale Trippodi. The two officers found him hanging upside down from his ankle, weak and almost delirious. They cut him free, wrapped him in his parachute and put him in a recess in the rocks on a bed of spruce boughs. They made a fire to warm him up, gave him their rations and then left him behind to strike out for the beach together; their survival training had taught them that a lone person might not survive the journey.

In a 1997 telephone conversation from his home in Brigham City, Utah, Trippodi, then 69 years old, described how he had hung upside down in a tree with an injured shoulder until he was found.

> I was hanging there in that tree, head down with a foot caught
> in a chute strap. I had lost my right strap on the jump. When

I first landed in the tree, I tried to shake myself loose. I then fell head first. That's when my foot caught. If I hadn't lost that right strap, I would have had something to grab and never would have got hung up. After a few hours, I didn't care anymore. I felt like I was dying. I would hang head down as long as I could, then I would reach out and grab a branch and pull myself sideways. But my arms would get tired and I'd let go. I tried to knock myself out but I couldn't do it. I could not sleep. All the time I hung there my Mae West was choking me. I was sort of dazed.

When my pilot and my co-pilot pulled me down Tuesday and left me lying there, I felt I was dead. They managed to get me out of the tree but I couldn't walk because of frostbitten feet. So they made me comfortable at the foot of the tree and told me that they couldn't stay with me, they had to go find help for the others but that they would be back for me. When they left me, I wanted to go too. I was afraid they would get lost and nobody ever would find me.[7]

That night Barry and Whitfield built a parachute tent and slept in the snow. "We spent all that night trying to keep warm and looking for something to eat. The going was tough. The trip was a mess. The island is hilly and nothing but brush, trees and more brush. Snow, too. We didn't make much progress," Barry remembered.

Next morning, when they reached the coast, they stamped SOS in the snow on the beach and filled the impressions with tree boughs to make the letters more visible from the air. "Whitfield built a fire," Barry said, "and we threw a lot of wood on it. That was the smoke the fishing boat saw."

It was a good thing they set the fire when they did. Captain King would later explain that he was ready to leave the area with the three men he had rescued when they noticed a wisp of smoke that called them back. After the *Cape Perry*'s crew radioed their position, the Canadian destroyer *Cayuga* also arrived to assist in the rescue. They sent a ground party inland who found and treated Trippodi.

According to rescuer Percy Lotzer, the location where Trippodi was found was not three miles inland as reported, but rather less than a mile.

It was certainly tough going, though. Lotzer was following three other men who could walk on top of the snow. But Lotzer, who was carrying his 35-pound radio, broke through at almost every step.[8]

The search continued into Thursday, when the 12th and final survivor, Lieutenant Charles Pooler, was discovered and taken aboard *Cayuga*. In 1997, in a telephone conversation from his home in New Braunfels, Texas, the then 82-year-old Pooler recalled, "Getting out of a tree, I fell 40 feet and broke my right ankle." He limped a mile down the mountain to a frozen lake and settled in to await rescue. "I had one of those search and rescue signalling mirrors and began signalling a rescue plane that flew right over me. It flew over me twice and I could see the reflection from my mirror dancing on its fuselage, but the crew never saw me and the plane flew on off."

Pooler lay there for three nights, assuaging his hunger with a candy bar he had bought on his way to Carswell AFB to begin the flight. "I remember dragging out that candy bar and counting the squares and figuring out that if I ate one square of chocolate a day, I could eat for nine days."

On the morning of February 16, having lost track of time and suffering from exposure, he heard voices calling in the distance. He cried out. "I lay there in that ice and snow for a day or two until I was found by a Canadian rescue team who got me to a ship."

By then the original group of 10 crewmen, brought together and nourished aboard the *Cape Perry,* had been evacuated to Port Hardy, on northern Vancouver Island. Captain King said in a later interview, "I felt pretty good about getting those guys out. We had a bottle of rum and a bottle of scotch aboard and gave them some drinks. Then we gave them some ham and eggs and put them to bed aboard our boat. I never saw a braver bunch of men."

Vitale Trippodi and Charles Pooler waited aboard the *Cayuga* for the arrival of a US Air Force Canso amphibious aircraft, which flew them directly to McChord AFB.

CHAPTER 7

The Official Story

Major General Roger Ramey, commander of the Eighth Air Force and commanding general, Seventh Bomb Wing, Carswell AFB, termed the loss of Bomber 075 a "very regrettable accident" and declared that "no guesses, but a very careful and thorough investigation" was required to find out why it had happened.[1]

By direction of the US Air Force Chief of Staff General Vandenberg, a special Board of Inquiry was formed to investigate the loss of Bomber 075. The board's mandate did not include investigating the search and rescue or the "classified equipment aspects" of the incident. If considered necessary, these additional investigations would be conducted by Ramey. There is no evidence that any follow-up investigation ever took place.

The Board of Inquiry looked first at the qualifications of the bomber's crew. The task force commander of Bomber 075's mission, Lieutenant Colonel Chadwell noted, "Captain Barry is a good B-36 pilot and he has one of the best crews in the group." Captain George N. Payne, from Seventh Bomb Wing Standardization, agreed and said he thought Captain Barry to be "one of our better ACs [aircraft commanders]."[2] Lieutenant Colonel Calvin Fite, Deputy Commander, Seventh Bomb Group, considered Captain Barry a very stable and capable pilot.

Colonel John Bartlett, who commanded Bomber 075's ferry flight to Alaska, considered Captain William Phillips a superior navigator.

Phillips had been Bartlett's navigator on a round-trip flight to Hawaii staged from Fort Worth. Bomber 075's co-pilot, Lieutenant Whitfield, was also a B-36 airplane commander in the 436th Bomb Squadron. At the time of the accident, he had a total flying time of 1,538 hours, 327 of these on the B-36.[3]

Technical Sergeant Jesse L. Fox, Seventh Bomb Wing Standardization, told the board that he had checked out the first flight engineer, Lieutenant Ernest Cox. "He proved very capable at the time I checked him. He was up on all his emergency procedures, engine feathering, engine restarts, altitude restarts…he was a little slow on the panel work, which all of us were when we first got the B-36. Outside of that, he was very efficient."[4]

First Lieutenant Ray Darrah, the second flight engineer on Bomber 075, belonged to the Eighth Air Force Operational Engineering Section and was assigned to the Seventh Bomb Wing at the time. He was considered a superior flight engineer, even though he had not yet had an opportunity to become completely familiar with the B-36. The third flight engineer, First Lieutenant Charles Pooler, had not been checked out before Bomber 075's last flight, but his attitude, knowledge and progress were graded as superior.[5]

As for the aircraft and its equipment, Bartlett stated that the radar was excellent all the way up from Carswell AFB to Eielson AFB. "In fact we were able to see the deviation of high waves off the west coast to Eielson. The waves were so high, you could actually see them on the scope."

He did, however, note a few minor problems with the aircraft. "When we opened the bomb bay doors, the door cables broke on No. 2 bomb. The No. 5 water tank was not repaired; that would have been impossible to do and get the airplane out before it was cold soaked."[6]

Captain Barry himself stated that he did not get a chance to check over the aircraft ferried up to Alaska by Bartlett as thoroughly as he would have liked. This was because some radar work was being done in the nose of Bomber 075. "The radar was not in commission when we took off, and the crew members had to repair the radar after we were airborne. They worked for approximately two hours after [being] airborne before they got the radar set in commission and it was pretty cold work and they did it while we were climbing, and it was strenuous exercise at that altitude to make any adjustments in the aircraft."

Captain Harold L. Barry

Enlisting in October 1941, Barry served as an aircraft mechanic until he got his wings and officer's commission on July 28, 1943. He was assigned to the 25th Bomb Squadron, 40th Bomb Group. Though rated as a pilot, Barry was assigned as co-pilot to a B-17 and later to the first B-29 in the Pacific Theatre. He co-piloted Robert Gaughan's *Gone With the Wind* B-29 for 38 combat missions before returning to the United States as an instructor at Hendricks Field in Sebring, Florida. Less than a month after his return to the US, *Gone With the Wind* was shot down mistakenly by a British aircraft. For his service with the 40th Bomb Group, Barry received the Distinguished Flying Cross, an Air Medal with three Oak Leaf Clusters, and a Presidential Unit Citation with Oak Leaf Cluster.

Following Japan's surrender, Barry joined the 346th and then the 22nd Bomb Groups. From February 1946 to January 1948, he piloted a B-29 out of Okinawa, Japan. Subsequently, he was assigned to Operation Vittles, the massive, round-the-clock airlift to supply Berlin's 2.2 million people with food and fuel in 1948 and 1949. With the 530th Transport Group, 1268th Aircraft Transport Squadron and the 11th Troop Carrier Squadron, Barry flew Douglas C-54s out of Fassberg, West Germany. For his service during the Berlin Airlift he received a fourth Oak Leaf Cluster.

Next Barry was assigned as a pilot for the new B-36. On July 19, 1949, he was piloting B-36 2035 when a fire broke out, which caused the loss of three engines and eventually a portion of a wing. Maintaining control of the aircraft, he was able to put it down on the tarmac at Carswell AFB without any injuries. He received his sixth Air Medal for this achievement. Barry finished his career having earned the Distinguished Flying Cross, an Air Medal with nine Oak Leaf Clusters and numerous campaign medals.

On the actual day of the flight, Bomber 075 had taken off ahead of sister aircraft 083, but was behind it at the time of the accident. Captain Cooper, pilot/commander of 083, said that both aircraft were following the same course but flew in different air lanes down from Eielson. Bomber 083 caught up with 075 on its flight pattern heading south because 075 had trouble getting its inboard flaps up. Bomber 083 then moved ahead of 075 after Barry made a 360-degree turn while 075's Schuler and Gerhart were trying to fix their radar set, and the engineers Cox and Pooler were out in the wing trying to get gas valves in the right position.

Lieutenant Cox told the board, "We started losing airspeed, actually we hit this little bit of turbulence, and we figured we were in. In fact we could hear the ice hitting the airplane. It sounded like hail, so I advised the engineer that I thought we were getting into ice conditions." He also noticed some ice on the instrument landing system antenna. "I believe it got on there during this period that we went through this strip of icing," he said. "You could hear it coming on the airplane; it sounded like sleet... it was not heavy ice, it was just frosty. There was quite a bit of static flying off the antenna. It definitely was not clear ice."[7]

Staff Sergeant Thrasher, who acted as left scanner, observed that the ice on the antenna was clear and estimated it to be about a quarter of an inch thick. He first noticed it about three to four minutes before the aircraft started its climb and saw it build up continuously during the climb.

The scanners, however, could not see whether the aircraft had ice on its wings because the wings were set back from the men's line of sight. Normally, the bombers were equipped with Aldis signal lamps (a visual signalling device for optical communication using Morse code) that could double as spotlights if need be. Cox explained, "We understood our plane had Aldis lamps; we had three outlets for them, two in front, and one in the rear. These airplanes were supposed to have Aldis lamps in them when they got to Eielson, but they could not be found. Colonel Bartlett said they were on there. Possibly they were taken off. I believe he said they used them when they were going up.

"When the propellers first began surging, that is when we figured we had propeller ice." Cox went on to testify that

> the propellers were surging at all powers after the trouble began. The prop was losing its efficiency. We had a very slight rate of climb, but the rate of climb decreased. I wanted climbing power and we started to climb right away and try to get on top of it. We started to climb good and went to 14,000 feet. About 14,500 feet, I noticed it was dropping off a little fast, and from there on it dropped off very fast, until we reached 15,000 feet and then we just couldn't get any higher.

Barry levelled off at 15,000 feet, the highest he could go. Then his air speed fell off. Cox explained:

That was maximum and just about that time we had a fire in [engine] No. 1. About the time we levelled off to 15,000 feet…the scanner called in, 'Fire in No. 1 coming out around the airplug.' The engineer feathered it and turned the manual switch to stop it. The scanner called fire in No. 2; so he feathered that one, and between the fire in Nos. 1 and 2 the engineers changed seats.

So he was about getting things settled down when the right scanner called fire in No. 5, so he feathered that one, and by that time we were losing altitude quite rapidly in excess of 500 feet a minute and I asked the radar operator to give me a heading to take me out over the water. We kept our rapid rate of descent and we got out over the water just about 9,000 feet. The co-pilot ran to the bomb bay doors and hit the salvo switch and at first nothing happened, so he hit it again and this time it opened. The radar operator gave me a heading to take me back over land; the engineer gave me emergency power to try to hold our altitude.[8]

When questioned by the board about how icing might affect the B-36, Mr. R. Fitzgerald, chief test pilot for Convair, testified, "The airplane is an anti-icing [prevention through the application of heat] airplane, and not a de-icing airplane. Where you anticipate icing, the heat should be on."

Barry was uncertain how long he had the anti-icing system on prior to the accident. "I am not sure when we turned it off, partway down the coast or not. I know we had it on right after takeoff to try to lose some of the ice we had on the airplane when we got off the ground. We took off with a thin skin of ice on the outboard panels. And I don't remember whether we had turned that off at any time or not."

Lieutenant Stacker, flight engineer on Bomber 081, which had been part of the 10-bomber exercise, explained to investigators why B-36 crews seemed to be reluctant to turn on the anti-icing heat and often turned it off. "You get a terrific flexing of the metal on the leading edge of the wings when the heat is turned on. If you could see 081, you could see the permanent marks resulting from the use of anti-icing on the wings this flight. We even burned the paint off the leading edge of the wings and tail.

After a long period of time, you would undoubtedly cause fatigue of the metal."[9]

Carburetor icing is a phenomenon associated with ice buildup in the carburetor throat that may lead to restriction of inlet airflow and subsequent loss of power. The icing causes the carburetors to run too rich, leading to a buildup of raw fuel in the exhaust system and possibly to fire. In most aircraft, the carburetors are located in the rear of the engines. This arrangement permits the warmed air from the engines to flow around the carburetors and prevents all icing except throat icing. In the B-36, with its rear-facing engines, the carburetors were in front of the engines and thus constantly subjected to cold air from outside the engine. In addition, the relatively warm ocean currents that flow along the British Columbia coast cause heavy fog, even on the coldest days of winter. This results in an abundance of moisture in the air above the coastline, from which ice forms.

The B-36's carburetor consisted of two separate chambers for air intake, which fed two different sections of the carburetor with an opening in the baffle plate to separate the two sections and permit a pressure balance to be maintained. It was suggested that this opening became covered with ice and caused both halves to run rich. The constant rich mixtures resulted in a buildup of raw fuel in the exhaust systems that eventually ignited and caused the engine fires.[10]

In its summary, the board concluded that the loss of the aircraft was not caused by crew error but by heavy icing of the underside of the wings, which disrupted lift; heavy icing of the propellers, which caused surging; and ice within the carburetor, which closed the impact tubes and caused the carburetor to meter raw fuel into the engine. The raw fuel was then pumped into the exhaust system, where it caught fire and burned through. Furthermore, the forward-mounted carburetors meant they received no heat from the engines.[11] Upon further investigation, the board learned that there had been numerous instances of emergency situations similar to 075's in other B-36 bombers. Prior to the Alaskan manoeuvre and just a month before Bomber 075's fatal run, a case of suspected carburetor icing had occurred on Bomber 074.

Also of interest is the fact that Bomber 075 was actually the third B-36 to develop mechanical trouble over the Pacific Northwest in a 48-hour period. The other two made emergency landings at McChord AFB on

"Accidents Will Happen"

Although Major General Roger Ramey, the Commander of the Eighth Air Force, declared that the Bomber 075 mishap was the first in two years of Eighth Air Force operations with the B-36, and that "accidents will happen as long as we operate machinery, whether it be roller skates or aircraft," the loss of Bomber 075 was actually the second major mishap involving a B-36 of the Eighth Air Force. [12] On the night of September 15, 1949, B-36B, Serial 44-92079, crashed into Lake Worth, Texas. Of the five crew members killed, one died from impact injuries and four others from drowning. The pilot claimed that the propellers switched to reverse thrust on takeoff, but no one believed him. Later, as another B-36 was on approach to landing at Carswell AFB, a propeller on each wing switched to reverse thrust. The subsequent inquiry into the crash revealed that two propellers had indeed inexplicably reversed, serving as a brake on the aircraft's takeoff speed. This corroborated the pilot's story from the Lake Worth crash.

To prevent such accidents from recurring, a procedure was drawn up for checking out each propeller prior to takeoff. The procedure called for all props to be checked from outboard to inboard, and was referred to as the "LeMay Shuffle." On the end of the runway, before a B-36 took off, one of the crew members in the forward compartment would jump out to see if all engines were blowing in the same direction, toward the tail. In later models, propeller reverse lights were installed to give pilots an indication of the problem.

February 12. One had been southbound from Alaska, the other on a routine training flight from Fort Worth.[13]

To avoid future exhaust-system failures, the Board of Inquiry recommended the installation, in production and on a retrofit basis, of a mechanical linkage system to the carburetor mixture controls on all B-36 aircraft. Starting February 15, 1950, each B-36 flight at Carswell AFB had to be cleared personally by the Commanding General of the Seventh Bomb Wing. Flights were carried out under detailed, carefully briefed and controlled flight-test procedures.

Bomber 075 carried a large complement of safety and survival gear, exposure suits, one-man dinghies, five E-18 Arctic survival kits and one "Gibson Girl" survival radio set, type T47/GRT-3, with parachute. However, not all the required emergency equipment was on board the aircraft, and articles like food were missing. "Though all they had to do was salvo their E-18 [Arctic survival kit], which was stored in the rear bomb bay, the crew did not drop it," Captain Barry testified. "The only personal kits we had were the E-18; five of those…they were probably salvoed when we salvoed the load because both doors were open and I don't know whether the bombardier salvoed them with the salvo lever or not."

When asked whether he had at any time considered abandoning the aircraft, Barry answered, "No, sir. Well, there had been some talk a while back about ditching airplanes, but the last four or five months they had said it would be better to bail out over the water than try to ditch the aircraft. Consequently, they had taken out all seven-man life rafts."

Barry stated that not all the crew members were wearing their proper bailout equipment. "Some men had on Mae Wests and some had on dinghies. However, they didn't all have dinghies…The men that took the dinghies with them were in better shape; at least they had a dry place to sleep the first night."

The crewmen on Bomber 075's final flight were still wearing their "dry" suits. Though the plan called for them to change to "wet" suits during the flight, they had not done so. The dry suits were made of a porous material that could breathe, allowing air circulation and drying of perspiration. This proved to be a major problem for the airmen after they bailed out, because their clothes soon filled with water and they remained cold and wet until they were rescued.

The crew members were dressed identically in regular Arctic-type winter flying clothes—most unsuitable, as they became wet and extremely heavy in a very short time. They did not all carry exposure suits and would not have had time to put them on before bailing out. The incident revealed a definite need for clothing suitable for the conditions the crew had encountered. It was recommended that nylon-pile aircrew suits be tested to see how wearable they would be under similar circumstances.

To improve the level of technical training in the Seventh Bomb Wing, the investigation determined that arrangements should be made with Convair to begin special training classes at their factory immediately. Classes of approximately 250 officers and men would attend eight hours a day, six days a week. Almost 8,700 airmen went through this process.

Inside the US government, the more serious questions pertained to

The "Gibson Girl" Radio

The "Gibson Girl" radio was an early emergency radio transmitter and part of the aircraft survival kit. The radio had a distinctive hourglass shape and was named after a series of cartoons drawn by Charles Dana Gibson at the turn of the twentieth century. The cartoons featured statuesque young women possessing an hourglass figure, who became known as the Gibson Girls. Designed originally for the US Army Air Force, the device was used to transmit a distress signal in case of a crash or forced landing. Large in size, it incorporated a generator operated manually by a hand crank, a transmitter-receiver and a long wire antenna held aloft by a box kite that was included in the kit. The whole rig, including the kite and a helium balloon to fly the antenna, was packed in a padded case. To make it air-droppable, it had a small parachute attached to it. The Gibson Girl radio was housed in a large box that had indentations on either side where the operator could place his knees for stability. A wide, webbed strap secured it around his legs. The operator then cranked away on the generator while a distress signal was automatically transmitted. There was even a Morse key on top to tap out messages. As a backup for more state-of-the-art emergency signalling devices, the Gibson Girl remained part of the survival gear on Canadian Aurora patrol aircraft until 1994.

the loss of one of America's most advanced nuclear weapons. The Atomic Energy Commission (AEC), which officially owned the bomb and its core, demanded details about the crash from the US Air Force. The USAF tried to hide losing this valuable and secret nuclear bomb as long as possible. When Bill Sheehy, an AEC official and member of the Joint Committee on Atomic Energy, first asked whether a bomb had been on the B-36 lost off the British Columbia coast, Colonel Richard T. Coiner told him that the US Air Force was not yet certain. Sheehy demanded answers. In one memo, he asked if Bomber 075's crew had dropped the bomb in the ocean or left it on the aircraft. His question was met with silence.

It would be 11 days after the accident before the senators of the AEC were advised that the weapon indeed had been jettisoned *but not detonated to destruction* (italics are mine). Still, Air Force officials were reluctant to give any details. On February 28, two weeks after the event, General William Evans "Bill" Hall, Deputy Director of the Legislative and Liaison Section, said he refused to tell the AEC the status of its bomb without a written request.

Faced with this lack of co-operation, Sheehy contacted his boss, William Borden, executive director of the Joint Committee on Atomic Energy, to try to get a response. In frustration, Sheehy wrote, "I am not willing to sit back and wait until the Air Force gets damn good and ready to tell us what the hell they did with one of our atomic weapons."[14]

On March 9, 1950, Borden wrote the US Air Force demanding to know what had happened to the bomb. Major General Thomas White's answer was short and blunt: "The bomb was jettisoned, *presumably* [italics are mine] over the sea, and it exploded while in the air." Unfortunately, no further follow-up correspondence could be obtained under the Freedom of Information Act. Even 60 years later, the American and Canadian publics have been denied full disclosure of what remained on board after the crash.

The Air Force Special Weapons Project requested that Strategic Air Command provide answers to several questions: "Which items were left aboard when the aircraft was abandoned? How long would the aircraft fly after it was abandoned? How far might the aircraft reasonably be expected to go before crashing? Did the aircraft send radio signals after abandonment? If so, were the signals used to locate the position of the aircraft at any given time? Have any reports been received by the Air Force indicating the possible location of the crash site of the B-36?"[15]

The USAF obviously had some explaining to do. It was bad enough that they had just had their first loss of a nuclear weapon, on loan for the first time ever from the AEC. They were also just at the beginning of an important testing program with a new and deadly weapon. They had not even finished their very first test with it, and now it was gone! How could they admit that it was out there somewhere like a sitting duck, ready to be checked out by the Russians? The easiest thing to do was tell the AEC that the bomb had been destroyed. Otherwise they risked never again being trusted with a nuclear bomb. Although the US Navy was dispatched to drop depth charges in the general area where the bomb was supposed to have exploded, the Air Force was left with a big dark secret.

In a 1998 interview with Don Pyeatt, a historian with the Seventh Bomb Wing B-36 Association, co-pilot Whitfield stated, "We as a crew believed that we were carrying the real thing." According to Whitfield, the aircraft was carrying a real, fully functional atomic bomb that used a lead rather than a plutonium core. "Without a real bomb, the support systems could not be tested," Whitfield observed. "There were some dummy bombs made of concrete that were used for load testing, but we weren't carrying one of those. This mission was to be as real as it gets, short of war." [16]

It was common practice on training flights for bombers to carry dummy cores for practice. These dummies or "shapes" looked exactly like the real thing, having the same shape, size and weight. They were filled with concrete to simulate the weight of a real plutonium core. To make them more realistic, dummy cores were made out of low-quality uranium.

"Even if they were carrying a dummy, these were still kept secret from outside bystanders. When we loaded these practice nukes, they enclosed the bomb bays with black covers and brought the device in under the covers on covered trailers," B-36 veteran Bob Preising recalled.[17]

During his research, Don Pyeatt found an inconsistency in one of Whitfield's earlier statements. Originally Whitfield had stated that Captain Schreier had placed the core into the bomb to make it operational: "Schreier entered the bomb bay, armed the bomb, placed the core [in its box] on the bomb bay doors, and returned with his Mae West on over his chute. The bomb and the box containing the core were dropped together. The core was jettisoned to keep the Russians from finding it. No mention was made of any salvage of the core."

Whitfield returned Pyeatt's first draft of his article based on their interview with a note that it had not happened that way, that the core was *not* in the bomb. "He [Whitfield] decided that he didn't want to go public with any statement about the bomb," Pyeatt said. "I edited the draft, sent it back to him, got a few minor changes, and that is the version on the website now." [18]

The unarmed bomb, fused to explode at a pre-set altitude of 3,800 feet, was dropped from 8,000 feet, just before the men jumped. According to Radar Operator Paul Gerhart, "it was about midnight when I salvoed the bomb. It detonated about 4,000 feet above the Pacific." [19]

Minutes before, Gerhart had carefully placed a detonator in each of the 32 high-explosive (HE) charges, or "lenses," surrounding the spherical core. When triggered by the detonators, these charges would compress the core, initiating a nuclear explosion. If an active plutonium core was removed for safety reasons, a casing of uranium would remain inside the bomb.

Declassified information released in the early 1980s by the US defense department states that B-36 075 was carrying an 11,000-pound Mark IV "Fat Man" nuclear bomb. The Mark IV was considered a relatively large bomb. Staff Sergeant Trippodi described it as being bigger than his Volkswagen. At the time, Air Force personnel were used to the 24-foot "grand slam" high-explosive bombs. Although the Mark IV A-bomb was not as large in size, it had much greater power.

American military officials have consistently denied that a plutonium core, an object weighing 13.4 pounds and about the size of a softball, was ever aboard the bomber. But with all the paranoia over the Cold War, and with communist hordes at their doorstep, one has to ask how likely it was that the Americans would have admitted that Bomber 075 was carrying a real capsule.

US Air Force documents state that the Mark IV bomb aboard Bomber 075 was armed with a dummy capsule instead of a live one. If the capsule did not have a plutonium core, it would have contained natural, rather than enriched, uranium, which would emit a very low level of radioactivity. Thus when a bomb such as the one carried on Bomber 075 was detonated using only its high-explosive content, the blast would have caused neither a nuclear explosion nor significant contamination.

A Pentagon information officer also stated that such a bomb, stripped of enriched uranium, could not cause a nuclear blast. The core is necessary to cause an atomic chain reaction in the bomb. Without the core installed, the blast would not trigger a nuclear reaction; it would only destroy the bomb. Lieutenant Colonel Rick Born, the US defense department's public affairs officer in Washington, DC, said standard procedure called for tests to determine whether there had been radioactive fallout from nuclear accidents. Department documents indicated there was no fissionable material aboard 075 and that it was not the practice to carry nuclear warheads on training missions. "It was not a bomb that could have been a nuclear bomb."[20]

In the event of an accident with a real bomb equipped with a real plutonium-uranium core on board, procedure called for jettisoning the core so that it could be recovered. Recovery was very important so that none of this equipment would ever fall into enemy hands. Also, the core was very expensive, costing millions of dollars, and at that time very few were in existence. On these harshly realistic training flights, only the weaponeer knew for sure whether the core was real or a dummy. Bomber 075's weaponeer was among the five men who were never found.

It was US policy that if a nuclear bomb was lost, no record of its exact location was to be kept, so that no one could go and look for it. One reason for exploding the bomb was to prevent enemies from trying to find it later. Since the location of a nuclear weapon is classified information, it is also US Department of Defense policy to neither confirm nor deny the presence of nuclear weapons at any specific place. In the case of

A Second Broken Arrow Incident over Canadian Soil

Although the US Air Force released an account in 1977 of the loss of Bomber 075, it did not get much publicity at the time. In later years, however, this nuclear accident did occasionally receive attention in the news. Early in 1997, it came up again in a report released by Canadian military historian Dr. John Clearwater. The study was based on just-declassified US and Canadian records showing that the US Air Force dropped two nuclear bombs over Canadian territory in 1950. Besides the bomb lost from Bomber 075 in February 1950, a somewhat similar loss happened near Rivière-du-Loup, Quebec, only 10 months later. This accident, later described as nuclear accident No. 5, was on November 10, 1950, and involved a Boeing B-50 Superfortress. The aircraft, one of a group of 11 that had been deployed at Goose Bay, Labrador, since August 1950, was returning to Tucson, Arizona.[21]

During the flight, three of the aircraft developed engine problems. The lead aircraft dropped its Mark IV nuclear bomb, which did not contain its core, over water from an altitude of 10,500 feet. Just before 4:00 PM, an explosion rocked the small town of Sainte Alexandre-de-Kamouraska on the south shore of the St. Lawrence River near Quebec City. The 4,840-pound charge used to detonate the Mark IV bomb caused a thick cloud of yellow smoke to spiral up 3,300 feet above the middle of the river, which is an accident involving nuclear weapons, its location may or may not be divulged at the time, depending upon the possibility of public hazard or alarm. Also, the US does not specify the location of accidents that occur on foreign soil, due to diplomatic considerations.

Pentagon information officer Captain Virginia Pribyla stated that Bomber 075 crew's action of dropping the weapon was in accordance with a standing order to go out over open water and jettison such a bomb. "We simply do not have an accounting of where it was dropped and at this stage have no means of knowing how far out into the Pacific the plane went," Pribyla said. "In those days the crews had orders to jettison the bomb in such a configuration that the H.E. would go off and destroy the bomb without causing contamination. When it did, we did not have to go out and try to recover the weapon."[22]

It turned out that the 075 crew did not go out very far over the Pacific

12 miles wide at that point. Then came a low rumble that shook houses for 25 miles around.[23]

A high-explosive detonation at an altitude of about 2,500 feet was observed. The blast scattered 100 pounds of uranium. According to the Center for Defense Information in Washington, DC, there is no record of recovery of this nuclear weapon.[24]

The US Air Force immediately covered up this incident by saying a load of 500-pound conventional practice bombs had been jettisoned. It was not until the early 1980s that the Air Force confirmed it as a nuclear accident, saying only that the bomb was dropped "over water, outside the United States." The B-50 bomber landed safely at a USAF base in Maine.

Clearwater said that the nuclear core had been removed from the bomb. Such blasts are non-nuclear, instead relying on the powerful chemical explosives used in every atomic bomb.[25] When the crew dropped its bomb, only some extremely low, virtually undetectable levels of radiation might have been released.

Clearwater's study indicates that it was US policy to deny that nuclear weapons were involved in any accidents.[26] According to the surviving crew members of Bomber 075, the order to detonate bombs whenever aircraft developed problems was intended to safeguard nuclear-bomb-design secrets.

Ocean to drop the bomb. During the debriefing, the crewmen confirmed that shortly before bailing out, they had jettisoned their nuclear bomb load somewhere along the north coast of British Columbia, possibly in Estevan Sound or Squally Channel. A declassified document gives the location of where the bomb was jettisoned as 53°0'N, 129°29'W.[27] This puts it in the Inside Passage between the Estevan Group and Campania Islands.

Sound and shock waves reportedly followed the observed bright flash. In the February 14 issue of the *Fort Worth Star-Telegram*, there was an account of a Seattle radio operator reporting an RCAF message that an unidentified light had been observed in Queen Charlotte Sound and that they were sending planes to investigate.[28]

Frank Rickey was in the US Coast Guard at the time of the accident. Rickey was serving on the cutter *Winona*, which was dispatched to aid in the search for survivors. One of its missions was to find the crash site and guard it so that the Soviet Union could not salvage the bomb.

Painting of Bomber 075 by Kamloops artist John Rutherford. About 162 feet long, almost 47 feet high and with a wingspan of 230 feet, the B-36 was the largest bomber ever built.

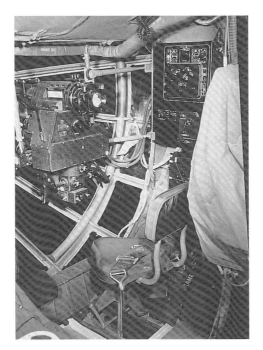

A typical gunner's station in a B-36. The sight functioned like a periscope for the gunner.

The crew of Bomber 075 lined up for inspection prior to takeoff; Captain Barry is at the far right. US AIR FORCE

Captain Barry inspects crew members (left to right) Staff Sergeant Elbert Pollard, Staff Sergeant Dick Thrasher, Captain Harold Barry, Lieutenant Paul Gerhart, unidentified. US AIR FORCE

The official US Air Force portrait of weaponeer Captain Ted Schreier, the one person who could have shed light on what really happened on Bomber 075's last flight. US AIR FORCE

The Sikorsky 51 helicopter 92011, seen here at Butedale (now a ghost town) on Princess Royal Island, was one of two US Air Force helicopters involved in the early part of the search for the missing crewmen. CEDRIC MAH

The search for the missing airmen became known as Operation Brix. USCG *Winona* (WPG65) was one of four US Coast Guard cutters involved in the operation. FRANK RICKEY/US COAST GUARD

A search and rescue team leaving at first light in a desperate bid to find the remaining missing airmen. Left to right: Royal Canadian Air Force Para-Rescue Sergeant George Lecki, and Royal Canadian Navy personnel Petty Officer Stan James, Petty Officer J.M. Pitts and Chief Petty Officer C.J. Padget.

DEPARTMENT OF NATIONAL DEFENCE E-010858702

The destroyer HMCS *Cayuga* (DDE 218), based in Esquimalt, BC, was dispatched to the search area to assume on-the-scene coordination of the air and ground searches.

DEPARTMENT OF NATIONAL DEFENCE DNS-30115A

At a briefing in *Cayuga*'s operations room, Lieutenant Commander C.R. Parker assigns search areas to ground crew. Clockwise from bottom left: Petty Officers James Brahan, James Ridout, Jack Strachan and Vincent Mielin.

Sergeant Trippodi in a Neil-Robertson stretcher as *Cayuga*'s motorboat is lowered to take him to a US Catalina flying boat to be flown to McChord AFB for treatment.

This old newspaper clipping shows some of the survivors warming up with a mug of coffee at Port Hardy, BC, after being rescued. Seated (left to right): Sergeant James R. Ford, Corporal Richard J. Schuler, Lieutenant Paul E. Gerhart, Lieutenant Colonel Daniel V. MacDonald, Sergeant Martin B. Stephens. Standing (left to right): Lieutenant Ernest O. Cox Jr., Lieutenant Raymond P. Whitfield, Captain Harold L. Barry, Sergeant Dick Thrasher, Lieutenant Roy Darrah. THE VANCOUVER SUN

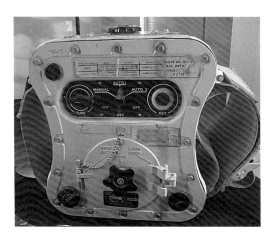

The Gibson Girl emergency radio, widely used during the Second World War, was still in service with the RCAF in the early 1990s. At 1:42 AM on February 14, 1950, a series of SOSs was received on a frequency of 495 kilocycles per second, almost identical to 075's frequency. Could the SOSs have originated on Bomber 075? DIRK SEPTER

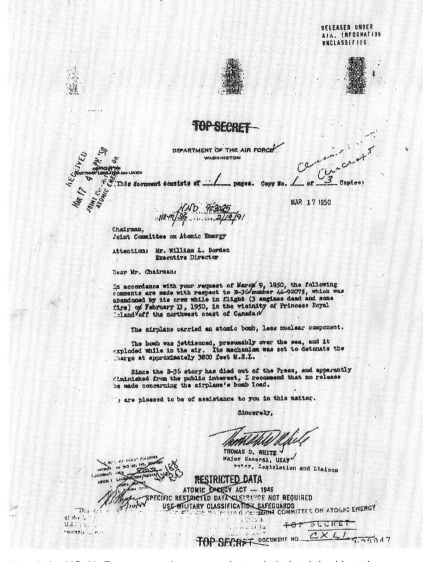

~~TOP SECRET~~

DEPARTMENT OF THE AIR FORCE
WASHINGTON

This document consists of ___1___ pages. Copy No. ___1___ of ___3___ Copies)

MAR 17 1950

Chairman,
Joint Committee on Atomic Energy

Attention: Mr. William L. Borden
Executive Director

Dear Mr. Chairman:

In accordance with your request of March 9, 1950, the following comments are made with respect to B-36 number 44-92075, which was abandoned by its crew while in flight (3 engines dead and some fire) on February 13, 1950, in the vicinity of Princess Royal Island off the northwest coast of Canada.

The airplane carried an atomic bomb, less nuclear component.

The bomb was jettisoned, presumably over the sea, and it exploded while in the air. Its mechanism was set to detonate the charge at approximately 3800 feet M.S.L.

Since the B-36 story has died out of the Press, and apparently diminished from the public interest, I recommend that no release be made concerning the airplane's bomb load.

We are pleased to be of assistance to you in this matter.

Sincerely,

THOMAS D. WHITE
Major General, USAF
Deputy, Legislation and Liaison

RESTRICTED DATA
ATOMIC ENERGY ACT — 1946
SPECIFIC RESTRICTED DATA CLEARANCE NOT REQUIRED
USE MILITARY CLASSIFICATION SAFEGUARDS
JOINT COMMITTEE ON ATOMIC ENERGY

~~TOP SECRET~~

~~TOP SECRET~~ DOCUMENT NO. _CXLI_

It took the US Air Force more than a month to admit that it had lost the bomb that was on loan from the Atomic Energy Commission, and even then it recommended that the Peacemaker's bomb load not be mentioned to the media. US AIR FORCE (OBTAINED UNDER THE FREEDOM OF INFORMATION ACT)

The Smithers airport, photographed here in August 1953, was used by the USAF in its 1954 mission to the wreckage of Bomber 075.

The September 1953 US Air Force salvage team, under the command of Captain Paul Gardella, included helicopter pilot Captain Horace Skelton, weapons officer Captain James Bailey and Sergeants Charles Toulbert, Harold Harvey and Jerre White.

An SA-16 Albatross rescue flying boat parked at the Smithers airport, September 1953. The 1953 Air Force salvage team used two of these aircraft in the first attempt to reach the crash site. LOUIS SCHIBLI

In 1956 the Geological Survey of Canada's Operation Stikine mapping crew accidentally stumbled upon the wreckage of Bomber 075 while on a routine geological traverse. Left to right: Doug McCartney, Mildon Porteous, Bob Hutt, Fred Rayer, Doug Craig, Bob Baragar, Mike McMullen, Eddie Schiller, Evan Bullock and Gordie Peters. COURTESY OF DR. JIM RODDICK

The Canadian Armed Forces–Environment Canada team used such high-tech equipment as this BTI Microspec-2, which detects, identifies and measures ionizing radiation. DOUG DAVIDGE

In 1992, Scott Deaver and the author tried to locate Bomber 075's crash site. Deaver had some special sweatshirts made to celebrate the expedition. DIRK SEPTER

The inside of the explosives case found at the wreck site shows the 36 receptacles that housed the bomb detonators. Only 32 detonators were needed to arm the bomb, but 4 spares were also included in the case. The close-up shows one of these spares. DOUG DAVIDGE

Doug Craig crawls into the fuselage of the wreck in August 1997.

Scott Deaver and Dick Thrasher pose with the birdcage (the lead-lined container used to carry an atomic bomb's nuclear core) at the crash site on August 1, 1998.

In September 2003, Myth Merchant Films spent seven days at the crash site filming footage for the documentary film *Lost Nuke*. Left to right: John Clearwater, Jim Laird and the author.

A "Mae West" life preserver that inflated automatically and an unused parachute were found inside the fuselage. Were these Captain Schreier's? DIRK SEPTER

The three most important items located inside the wreck were the explosives (detonator) case, the bird-cage and the kit used for arming an atomic bomb with its nuclear core. DOUG DAVIDGE

This is one of several containers of TNT that was dropped to the crash site by helicopter in 1954 as part of a US military mission to destroy what was left of the crashed bomber. DOUG DAVIDGE

This dramatic photograph shows the resting place of Bomber 075 and the beginning of the stripping of the wreck, starting with its most distinctive feature, the Stars and Stripes emblem.

DOUG DAVIDGE

Jim Laird inspects parts of the wreckage with a Geiger counter (used to measure radioactivity) in September 2003. The only radiation detected was from the radium dials on the aircraft's gauges and instrument panels. MICHAEL CARROLL/MYTH MERCHANT FILMS

In early February 2004, Michael Jorgensen (filming) and the author returned to the crash site to get some winter footage for the *Lost Nuke* documentary. The site was covered with at least 20 feet of snow.

DIRK SEPTER

The cover assembly for the upper turret ammunition box shows Bomber 075's serial number. DIRK SEPTER

The aircraft's flight and landing directions just before impact could be determined from engine No. 1's upslope location. DIRK SEPTER

An emergency exit sign from one of Bomber 075's escape hatches.

DIRK SEPTER

Jim Laird and John Clearwater examine an escape hatch cover.

This shot gives an overview of the crash site.

1 This is where the nose (radome) of the aircraft hit the top of the ridge.
2 These are the remains of the port wing.
3 This is a massive crater, which is the result of an explosion in the bomb bay behind the cockpit.
4 Here are the two escape hatches through which the crew jumped.
5 This is where engine No. 1 was found.
6 The rock here was coloured by burning fuel when the bomber crashed.

PART 3 : The Mystery of Bomber 075

CHAPTER 8

Surprise Discovery

More than three years after the loss of Bomber 075, American and Canadian searchers were deployed to look for a New Mexico millionaire, oilman Ellis Hall, whose aircraft had gone missing on a flight from Annette Island, Alaska, to Bellingham, Washington.

On September 3, 1953, three days before the official search for Hall ended, one of the Annette-based search aircraft spotted wreckage on Mount Kologet, on the west side of the Kispiox Valley, northwest of Smithers, BC.[1] Later that day, the US Air Force headquarters in Washington, DC, received an unclassified message that read, "B-36 aircraft located at 56 degrees 03 minutes north 128 degrees 23 minutes west at 6,000-feet level. Plane has Eighth Air Force insignia. Number on nose wheel door is 511. Believed to be aircraft missing since yr. 1950 en route Eielson–McChord."

It came as a complete surprise that the wreckage of Bomber 075 would be found in this spot, some 200 miles in the opposite direction of where it was last seen heading and almost 6,000 feet above sea level in the Coast Mountains of BC.

The discovery caused a flurry of activity as the US Air Force prepared to immediately send an investigation team to Smithers. One of the team members was First Lieutenant Paul Gerhart, the radar operator of Bomber 075 and a survivor of the accident. He was recalled from the South Pacific, where he was involved in nuclear weapons testing.

During the reconnaissance mission, Gerhart's team flew over the wreckage in a helicopter, taking aerial photographs. Due to icing problems, they could not land at the crash site and had to abort efforts to recover any sensitive materials. As fate would have it, this helicopter never did make it back to its US base. While returning south it encountered mechanical difficulties and went down in the Fraser Canyon, luckily without any loss of life.

A ground crew of six American service personnel was dispatched to Smithers for a second attempt to reach the crash site. Arriving on September 21, 1953, the team, commanded by Captain Paul Gardella, included helicopter pilot Captain Horace Skelton, weapons officer Captain James O. Bailey, sergeants Charles Toulbert and Harold Harvey, and weapons technician Jerre White.

Officially, their mission was to salvage certain parts of the plane and personal effects of crew members. The wreckage was also supposed to be marked from the air so that it would not be reported again. It is not known whether the US government requested permission from the Canadian government to conduct this operation.

On September 22, Gardella's team left Smithers, bound for Hazelton, about 43 miles distant. There, Kispiox resident Jack Lee, reputed to be the most experienced guide in the region, joined the six Americans. Lee was a former bronc rider, described as "slight and wiry with quick slogging strides, like a woodsman's goose step, for covering the ground."[2] Eighteen years earlier, Lee had trekked more than 200 miles from Caribou Hide, an outpost in the Stikine region due north of Smithers, into the Skeena-Kispiox country.

Gardella had engaged Smithers resident Jack Chapman to take their supplies by truck from Smithers to Marty Allen's ranch in the Kispiox Valley, the starting point for the intended overland expedition on horseback. Here they planned to access the old Dominion Telegraph Trail. Allen had come to the valley in the late 1940s and had trapped along the old telegraph line and worked for Dominion Telegraph. In 1948, he married Dorothy Love and settled on the ranch site that had always been a welcome stopover for anyone trekking the Telegraph Trail.

Once Jack Lee had his party on the trail, the team's S-51 Sikorsky support chopper dropped supplies along the route. The trail could get the men within eight air miles of the crash site.

Photographs taken on the reconnaissance flight had shown some of the engines, the remainder of the fuselage and the tail section visible above the snow. Sergeant Harvey, one of the crew members who flew over the wreck the next summer and airdropped supplies nearby, confirmed this. "As I recall, most of the fuselage was intact," Harvey said later.

The supplies included metal barrels containing bricks of Compound "B," a form of the high explosive TNT. "The crash site was about 75 to 100 feet from the top of the ravine heading north...I drop[p]ed the explosives above the crash site in the trees, maybe 100 feet above the site, using red cargo parachutes."[3] At least one Geiger counter was dropped at this time.

Aerial shots taken by Gardella clearly show Bomber 075's tail section. Gardella had managed to secure prints of two of his photos by gaining access to the USAF photo lab through a friend who worked there. While his photos were being processed, Gardella secretly pocketed two rejects that had ended up on the floor, both of poor quality and printed in reverse from the original black and white slides. The US Air Force has never released any of these photographs.[4]

The snow conditions and the extremely rugged terrain in the Mount Kologet area made the team's progress very slow. Additional food supplies were airdropped on September 26 and 29, for both men and horses. Protective clothing was also dropped to shield them from the harsh conditions. Originally, the expedition was expected to take no more than eight or nine days, round trip. An amphibious aircraft based in Tacoma, Washington, and flying out of Smithers kept in contact with them from the air. On the evening of October 10, the team returned to Smithers, completely exhausted. They had endured 19 days of extremely arduous travel and had failed to reach the wreckage.

A third attempt to reach the wreckage before the end of October 1953 also failed: the crew of American servicemen encountered snow six feet deep. This time a helicopter was used to lift a ground party from its base at a small lake north of Hazelton. Dennis Garon, an assistant forest ranger in Hazelton, clearly remembers that one morning while he was preparing breakfast a large US military helicopter landed near his cabin. An officer introduced himself and asked whether he could leave one of the crew members behind to make room for the Love brothers, two local guides who were to take the crew north into the upper Kispiox Valley. Later that fall, Garon was asked if he wanted to accompany another Air Force crew travelling by pack train to the crash site. Knowing winter was near, Garon politely declined. "I had second thoughts about the trip. I decided against it, as there was a scent of snow in the air and I did not relish going into the high mountains and accumulating saddle sores."[5]

Storms assured the team that the bomber would be covered with snow until spring, so the men returned to the US on October 31, their mission also not accomplished.

Smithers resident Marcella Love, Jack Lee's sister-in-law, remembers that expedition well. Marcella moved to the Kispiox Valley two years before the crash was discovered. She is quite sure that poor weather forced USAF personnel to turn back without reaching the crash site.

Pierre Cote, master corporal in the Canadian Rangers, knows the mountainous terrain. He too believes that the group never reached the site that autumn. He can't see how they could have gotten in and out in the allotted time. "They were running into quite a bit of snow and it's not the easiest of hikes. It's quite ugly at the north face and the east face, the only routes that you would have in and out. The other two are not passable because of the amount of drop-off on either side. You've got a glacier on one side and a huge drop-off on the other."

Cote also noted that while the S-51 helicopter had enough power to fly over the site and drop supplies, it would not have been able to land. Given the thin air at that altitude, he noted that they would have to "kick it off the mountain to get it in the air."[6]

Still, there has been much speculation as to why the first helicopter did not land. One reason might have been fear of radioactivity, if the crew believed a plutonium core was aboard 075.

Some researchers have theorized that the USAF helicopter actually did land at the crash site and that the Air Force did recover the deadly plutonium core of the Mark IV bomb.

Kim Lee, Jack Lee's granddaughter, claims that her grandfather did get the Americans to the wreck in 1953. According to Kim, the Americans made Lee hold back just before reaching the site. They went ahead by themselves and blew something up. Those who remained behind heard some explosions.[7]

It has also been suggested, because of Strategic Air Command's declaration in July 1950 that B-36s should carry a second nuclear bomb, that 075 may possibly have been testing its performance with this additional cargo.

It was early August 1954, when the snow had melted enough to expose the remains of Bomber 075, that a fourth and final attempt was made to reach the wreckage. It is fair to say that the magnitude of this recovery exercise raised a few eyebrows around Smithers. To land at the site and deliver supplies, a Sikorsky H-19 helicopter (Serial 13866) was brought up from McChord AFB, along with two SA-16 Albatross amphibian aircraft (Serials 0174 and 0177). Once the salvage crew was on Mount Kologet, the SA-16s airdropped supplies to the crash site, using the Smithers airstrip as their operations base.

Coincidentally, there was one man in the area at the time who was quite familiar with Bomber 075's fateful story—Percy Lotzer, a radio operator on HMCS *Cayuga* during Operation Brix in 1950. Lotzer, who in 1954 was assistant general manager of Skyway Air Services, a water-bomber enterprise retained by the British Columbia Forest Service, was on a base-inspection trip. "Smithers was invaded by a large contingent of US Air Force aircraft and helicopters," he recalled. "A shroud of secrecy was wrapped around this event."

Lotzer had good reason to be both angry with the US Air Force invasion of Smithers and suspicious of what was going on. In spite of vigorous objections by both the BC Forest Service and Skyway Air Services, the Canadian military ordered them to vacate their hangar and hand it over to the US Air Force.[8] "They were overruled by the Canadian military. In these matters, the militaries on both sides of the border considered secrecy paramount and diplomacy secondary," Dr. Jim Roddick, from the Geological Survey of Canada (GSC), observed.[9] When asked how much notice they were given to vacate the hangar, Lotzer said, "None! We had an expensive engine inside that had just been overhauled. The last thing you want to do is to haul it outside in the open. That's no place to put an engine. Outside it was dusty as hell!" Lotzer asked the US military to sign a document saying they would pay for any damage. "No problem," was their answer.[10]

Bush pilot Cedric Mah, who was temporarily stationed at the MacLure Lake floatplane base in nearby Telkwa at the time, recalled the excitement. Upon landing at MacLure (Tyhee) Lake he reported to the BC Forest Service in Smithers. At the airfield Mah discovered furious activity around the forestry hangar and that the premises were off limits. The US Air Force had taken over and the US Coast Guard and army helicopters were flying back and forth. "At the airport I was told that the BC Forest Service and Airspray [Skyway] were kicked out of the hangar," Mah said. "The US Air Force had priority and had requisitioned it for some kind of program. No one knew what the exercise was about. Everything was supposed to be secret, so no one questioned it."[11]

In a 1997 CBC interview, historian John Clearwater downplayed the shroud of secrecy. He believed that the secrecy about the site itself was not due to the presence of an atomic bomb, but to the fact that the aircraft contained many secrets of the early nuclear age. He suggested that various pieces of equipment and records were considered far too sensitive to leave for anyone to find. One such device was the Norden bombsight, even though it had been around since the Second World War. In fact, some critics claimed that the military often seemed as eager to retrieve the bombsight as they were to rescue downed crews. At the time they were very concerned about the security of this technology.

Secrecy at the time of the 1953 and 1954 missions was accompanied by a lack of disclosure, either intentional or unintentional, in ensuing years. For example, secrecy surrounded the location of the remains of Bomber 075. It was the summer of 1956 when Dr. Jim Roddick became intrigued with the Bomber 075 story. That July, almost two years after the 1954 salvage and destroy mission by the US Air Force, two of Roddick's field assistants, Bob Baragar and Doug Craig, stumbled onto the wreckage of the B-36 while on a routine geological mapping traverse in the Mount Kologet area. Though he reported the wreck and its location to the Canadian authorities, they did not show much interest. The scene of the wreck site stayed clearly in Roddick's mind and finally, upon retirement in 1996, he dug out his notebooks and confirmed a disturbing fact. The coordinates of the crash site in the official American documentation that had been released for public access were wrong.

Officially, the objective of the 1954 military mission was two-fold: to recover certain aircraft parts and to destroy the remainder of the wreckage. A four-man team was taken to the high-altitude site by the S-19 helicopter. Captain Guy Hayden and Staff Sergeant J. Stephens were accompanied by Captain Bailey, the only team member who had been part of the earlier attempts to reach the bomber in 1953. Hunter Simpson of Smithers, who did a lot of prospecting in the area with his brother, accompanied the three USAF men. Simpson was a lineman for the BC Telephone Company and was reportedly a childhood friend of one of the US servicemen. Simpson would be the only civilian who knew first-hand what actually happened during the 1954 recovery and demolition operation.

Between August 7 and 16, the team stayed near the 5,800-foot level on Mount Kologet. The bomber was still largely covered with snow. Contact was maintained on a regular basis by a USAF SA-16 Albatross. Toward the end of their 9-day mission, when poor visibility and weather conditions prevented the team from being brought out, supplies were airdropped.

Finally, on August 19, bold headlines in the *Interior News* read, "Wrecked Bomber Mission Fulfilled." Some sensitive materials, such as radar and the tail gunner's electronics, were recovered. Several cases of explosives were used to blow up the wreckage. Simpson, who witnessed the operation, said that no pieces "bigger than a football" remained of the wreckage. In the end, the aircraft's huge tail section, with its vertical and horizontal stabilizers, was completely destroyed. Using dynamite and incendiary grenades, the crew destroyed whatever they did not want to fall into the wrong hands.

The dynamiting may have triggered rockslides that buried part of the wreckage. However, Jack Lee's son Wilf thinks that large parts of the aircraft were never blown up. According to information from his father, the aircraft wasn't demolished because the location of the bomb was not known. Instead, they blew up the side of the mountain above the wreck in order to bury it. Marty Allen's version of events is slightly different. "First they dynamited the plane. Then they triggered explosive landslides to bury what was left of it."[12]

USAF servicemen had told Smithers resident Marcella Love that they were looking for "an object about the size of an 8-inch ball, contained in a lead box... it was of the utmost importance to recover it and if the thing exploded, it would take the whole [Kispiox] valley with it," according to local resident Harry Kruisselbrink. He also noted that Marcella's sister-in-law Ruth Love independently confirmed the description of what the Americans sought.[13]

Later, Marcella Love changed her story. "It was a secret mission and little was said about it. Rumours were that something had to be removed from the plane." Contradicting her detailed earlier statement, she said, "Personally I didn't see or meet any of the US Air Force personnel. I never heard what or if anything was brought out in 1954."[14]

When Kruisselbrink subsequently questioned Love about her earlier statement about the "ball in a lead box able to blow up the Kispiox Valley," she told him that was "the word going around the valley" when the US Air Force team was there. "It's a little different from what Marcella told Joe [L'Orsa] and I at the [Bulkley Valley] Museum's annual general meeting in 1998. Perhaps she was a bit carried away in the excitement of the moment," Kruisselbrink said. "However, it still has some validity, because how would the public know about a ball in a lead box, etc.? So one of the men must have blabbed."[15]

The Americans' vigour in destroying the aircraft fuelled speculation that either the nuclear bomb or the plutonium core had still been aboard. These are indications that the core carried on the bomber may have been real and not a dummy or practice nuke, as claimed. The fact that at least one Geiger counter was airdropped near the crash site may also point in this direction.

B-36 researcher Scott Deaver believes the Geiger counter was dropped as standard equipment when the supply people knew only that the accident somehow involved an atomic bomb.[16] There certainly was not a lot of concern about the aircraft's only other source of radiation, its instrument gauges, which were coated with radium to glow in the dark.

Within an hour of their return to Smithers, and without a word about their mission, the Air Force party was on its way back to the US.[17] "There was something on it [the B-36], but they kept that quiet," Marty Allen told reporter Jeff Nagel in 1992. "Whatever it was, they took it back with them. They were very secretive about it."[18]

At the time, it was generally believed that one of the missing crew members, likely Ted Schreier, might have stayed with the aircraft after the others had bailed out. Official reports state that no bodies were found at the crash site. But Allen was always adamant that skeletal remains were brought out in 1954. Operation Brix search master D.G. Bell-Irving stated later that one of the crew members did not bail out and that his body was later found in the wreck of the aircraft.[19]

If the remains of a body had been removed in 1954, would this have been reported to the Canadian authorities? "I doubt it," said Dave Coverdale, regional coroner at Prince George, BC. "You know how the [US] military acted in those days!"[20]

Even five decades after the crash, one enticing morsel of new information came to Smithers unexpectedly in October 2002. A US security agent walked into a local convenience store while screening the area in preparation for a planned fishing trip to the "Babine Hilton" by then US vice president Dick Cheney.[21] The agent was drawn to a cluster of photographs lying on the counter. They had been taken by a Canadian Ranger who had just returned from the most recent Ranger exercise to rid the crash site of unexploded ordnance. The Ranger's wife, who worked there, recalled a "very important military-looking man" walking into the store, looking at the pictures and then questioning her in a "very authoritative manner." The American later told her that during the many years at his job he had seen classified files of the B-36 crash and the files indicated that a body had definitely been removed from the crash site in 1954.[22]

A declassified government document does indeed mention the finding of human remains. "The widely scattered wreckage was later found...on September 2, 1953, with the body of one crewman in the wreckage."[23]

CHAPTER 9

What Was Known About the Incident?

When the wreckage of Bomber 075 was found in a mountainous area hundreds of miles from where its crew had bailed out, many questions were raised about the previously accepted story of its fate. How could the aircraft, last seen flying at an altitude of about 1,200 to 1,500 feet, end up high on a mountainside some 200 miles northeast of where it was last seen? After all, before the crew had jumped, Captain Barry had put the aircraft on autopilot to fly southwest. At the rate the aircraft was losing altitude, it should have crashed in less than 10 minutes. How did the bomber manage to keep aloft for nearly three hours?

The questions began with what the crew members saw after they bailed out late on February 13, 1950. That night, as the crew of Bomber 075 drifted down on their parachutes, their aircraft circled over Princess Royal Island more than once. Lieutenant Cox watched the B-36 veering around after the crew bailed out. "It suddenly appeared in the distance coming towards me. It was making a gradual left turn. I thought it was coming right at me. Then it turned and went right by. It went inland, then to sea." He did not see where the gigantic bomber finally went down.[1]

In an interview with the International News Service shortly after he was rescued, Captain Barry said: "The ship was on automatic pilot and somehow it turned in the air and came back over us. There were three engines burning and I could follow the ship's progress as I went down in my chute. But I don't know where it crashed."

Although the automatic pilot had been set to accomplish a gentle turn toward the sea, flight engineer Cox stated that after he hit the ground, he saw the bomber in a gentle bank to the left. He told the USAF's Board of Inquiry that he saw the aircraft come over about five minutes after he had landed in a tree on Princess Royal Island. "After I landed, when I first heard the airplane it was to the northwest of me, passed over me in a slight shallow turn to the left, and when I last saw it, it was heading east. I could hear it turning around to the north. The last time I saw it, it was still in a slight left turn, a shallow turn. Last time I heard it, well, the airplane was probably 15 degrees off of north, what I thought was north."

Estimating that the B-36 was flying at an altitude of about 1,500 feet, Cox believed it would hit the water. "It was still in a left turn. I was a little excited at the time, when I saw it coming in. It looked like it was losing altitude, but it looked like it was coming toward me. The bomber was headed in a northeasterly direction when I last saw it, I believe. It was still in this turn which would have brought it out to the west." The aircraft's remaining three engines were all operating at the time.[2]

Staff Sergeant Thrasher stated that he'd expected the aircraft to crash on water, "because the last I saw of it, it was coming over at about 1,200 feet, turning to the left. It was headed inland [NE to E], but was turning to the left, back towards the ocean. I kept listening to hear it crash, but it droned on out to where I could not hear it." He also explained about the power settings at the time: "They had emergency power, but it was making plenty of noise for three engines."

The Board of Inquiry recorded that Captain Barry had set the automatic pilot for a clockwise curve, which he thought would lead it to crash in Queen Charlotte Sound. "It is clear, however, that his setting caused it to fly in circles. The circle size was not large, as he had seen the plane pass back over him before he landed."[3]

At the time of the initial search, the radar operator at Port Hardy confirmed that the B-36 had gone back to sea. But then, he said, it made a 180-degree turn and flew back to Princess Royal Island, where he lost the blip in the ground clutter.[4]

The B-36 actually circled over Princess Royal Island more than once. The caretaker of the Surf Inlet mine and his wife heard it come over "a couple of times" after it woke them from a sound sleep.[5]

Before jumping, Bomber 075 radio operator Staff Sergeant Ford secured the HF radio's push-to-talk transmitter key to transmit continuously on the frequency of 8,280 kilocycles per second. For about three hours after the crew jumped out of the crippled bomber, Eielson AFB in Alaska kept receiving steady, continuous carrier-wave transmissions from the aircraft and also heard an SOS at 8,280 kilocycles per second around this time. Signals were also received on the bomber's other frequencies of 3,105 and 6,240 kilocycles per second.

At 12:22 AM on February 14, Civil Aeronautics Administration (CAA) officials reported that a steady carrier wave was heard by various stations at a radio frequency of 3,105 kilocycles per second. Around 2:30 AM, a weather reconnaissance B-29 aircraft in the vicinity of Vancouver Island was reported to be monitoring the 3,105-kilocycles-per-second and emergency frequencies.

At 2:46 AM on February 14, a station identified as Bedford Radio informed Air Rescue Station "C" Flight at McChord AFB that the RCAF had reported receiving a steady carrier wave on 4,495 kilocycles per second and that they were hearing the same transmission. Bedford believed it to be a Canadian Radio Telephone circuit, but they were unable to make bearings on it, as their direction-finding (DF) equipment was undergoing an inspection. Instead, the US Federal Communications Commission at Portland, Oregon, was requested to take bearings on this transmission. About an hour later, they reported that the signal heard near 4,495 kilocycles per second was calibrated as 4,501 kilocycles per second and was a Canadian Radio Telephone circuit using scramble speech.

The continuous carrier-wave transmission ended abruptly at 2:55 AM on February 14. This would fix the exact time the B-36 went down at Mount Kologet. This also closely matches the last time of transmission reported in the Prince Rupert *Daily News* one day after the B-36 crashed. In large print, following the headlines on the front page, it read, "The six-engined plane was last heard from at 2:54 AM when it radioed that one engine was afire and the pilot contemplated 'ditching' in the water."

But could it be that the first part of the sentence was correct, namely that "when it radioed" referred to an actual voice transmission by the pilot just one minute before impact? The first media reports are usually the most accurate. Could this transmission at 2:54 AM on 3,105 kilocycles per second have been made by the pilot, and the transmission with the screwed-down key have been made one minute later on 4,495 kilocycles per second when the aircraft crashed?

Another newspaper reported that at about 3 AM, the aircraft was forced to ditch in the waters approximately 460 miles northwest of Seattle. The *Nanaimo Free Press* reported: "Mackay Radio said it picked up a message at 2:54 AM PST, in which the plane…said, 'One engine on fire, contemplating to ditch in Queen Charlotte Sound between Queen Charlotte Island and Vancouver Island. Keep a careful lookout for flares or wreckage.'"[6]

Long after the bomber actually crashed, steady carrier-wave signals and SOS reports kept coming in. At 3:05 PM, CAA officials relayed a report that the Vancouver airport tower was hearing a signal at 4,495 kilocycles per second. They said that it sounded like an SOS being transmitted three times, followed by N-O, then a figure 52 or 53, which blocked out, and the rest of the transmission was unreadable. This was received by intermittent carrier wave, or ICW. Thirty-five minutes later, CAA reported that the SOS heard at 4,495 kilocycles per second was just below the foreign broadcast band, which was always heard at night on that frequency. This message could indeed have come from Bomber 075, indicating the location where it came down. The latitude and longitude of the crash site did contain those numbers and an N.

At 3:25 PM, Walla Walla Airways and Seattle Overseas CAA Station reported a constant carrier wave at 8,230 kilocycles per second transmitting a series of short and long dashes. Did they actually mean 8,280 kilocycles per second? The Federal Communications Commission was informed and asked to try to get bearings. Just before 4:00 PM, Seattle Overseas Station reported picking up a strong carrier wave, again on 8,280 kilocycles per second.

Earlier, Carl Miller, a ham radio operator in Bremerton, Washington, reported receiving a series of SOSs on 495 kilocycles per second. The series of six SOSs had apparently been followed by a series of letters and some numbers (AAA AAA DC CN SS F32L). The frequencies recorded may have been scribbled down in haste and possibly should have been 8,280 and 4,495 kilocycles per second, respectively. The latter series could certainly have been 495 kilocycles per second, which was extremely close to the 500-kilocycles-per-second frequency used by the Gibson Girl emergency radio.

Search headquarters received Carl Miller's message at 1:25 AM on February 14. The US Coast Guard later reported that it had investigated the report, but added that several false alerts had been received from him in the past. "He is regarded as a very unreliable source and we recommend that this report be disregarded."

Was Miller actually an unreliable source, or was he made out to be because the military authorities did not want it known that the B-36 was sending messages, thereby indicating someone was actually at the controls at the time?

Radio transmissions received at 3:25 PM and just before 4:00 PM were well after the one received at 2:54 AM, when the aircraft had presumably crashed. Had somebody tried to send an SOS message with a latitude and longitude to pinpoint the location of the crash site?

A former radio operator on the B-36 explained that the aircraft's radio system was still rather primitive. Part of the radio operator's job was to pick up a list of various frequencies that were to be used on that mission. Every time the pilot wanted to talk on a specific VHF frequency, the radio operator would go to a tray of crystals issued for that particular mission. When the pilot wanted a different frequency, the radio operator would change the crystals again. Clearly, somebody had to be on board to physically change the crystals.

"This would explain why after everyone bailed out, the communication from the flight deck was on the HF radio. The pilot could select VHF or HF from a selector panel by his seat, just like we have in airplanes today," B-36 historian Barry Borutski explained in 2002. "The pilot could tune into any frequency he wanted. As some of the HF frequencies were encoded, only certain military bases could hear and understand this radio traffic. And since civilian authorities, such as the Vancouver Control Tower, would not be able to understand these, messages would have to be un-encoded... Based on the above information, whoever remained aboard the aircraft was talking to military bases and to civilians," said Borutski.[7]

"These multiple radio frequencies put the pilot on board," geologist Doug Craig pointed out in 2000. "You have an aircraft that flew hundreds of kilometres, maybe or maybe not on its own. There's just enough here that's tantalizing to keep the questions coming."[8]

The *Vancouver Province* reported at the time of the accident, "Planes...will circle a spot in Queen Charlotte Sound where a position-fix was made on a continuous carrier wave heard overnight on the distress frequency. [US] Air Force officials say this may have come from the emergency transmitting equipment which is carried on the aircraft's life rafts." The article continued, "Sharp-sighted lookouts reported a second column of smoke in mountains east of Price Island. RCAF officials believe the smoke may be significant because its location checks with the position of a large oil slick sighted this morning, and with a wireless signal heard overnight. An RCAF spokesman said the wireless signal could have been made by the emergency equipment of the missing B-36."[9]

The RCAF later relayed ground observers' reports of a large aircraft seen near Nimpkish Lake and Alert Bay on the north end of Vancouver Island at about 2,000 feet, heading west at 12 minutes after midnight. A second report stated that a large aircraft was seen near Passes Lake, also near Alert Bay, at about 1,000 feet, heading south and apparently in trouble at 12:15 AM. The RCAF transmitted a list of ground observers' reports, mostly from persons on Vancouver Island, either seeing or hearing a large aircraft "apparently in trouble."[10]

Twelve minutes after midnight on February 14, the bomber was reported over Nimpkish Lake at the northern end of the island, flying at 2,000 feet on a true west heading. Three minutes later, it was seen over Tahsis Inlet. The aircraft, now at 1,000 feet, appeared to be in trouble and flying true south. Later, several persons in the village of Tofino on the west coast of Vancouver Island saw a B-36 circle three times and then proceed in a true south direction. The exact time of these last sightings is unknown.[11]

A later message identified this aircraft as Bomber 083, even though it was flying at 17,000 feet. At 12:28 AM, Bomber 083 relayed 075's last known position, estimated to be over Port Hardy and given as 53°N and 129°29'W, heading in a roughly northeasterly direction.

The US Air Force's version of what the observers had seen and heard was that it was not the missing bomber. After leaving the area where Bomber 075 encountered trouble, Bomber 083's track extended over Alert Bay, down across Vancouver Island to Tofino and thence to Neah Bay, Washington. This aircraft's flight might have accounted for the many observers' reports from this area that night.

The wreckage of Bomber 075 was found at an elevation of approximately 5,800 feet, but to get there, it would have had to climb several thousand feet higher than the bailout altitude. "The automatic pilot, like a human pilot, could not control the elevation of the plane while the engines were behaving erratically," researcher Jim Roddick explained. "Lessening of the fuel load, possibly de-icing [due to probably drier conditions inland], and the fact that Barry had left the engines at full throttle, possibly caused the plane to climb. In fact, it must have climbed in order to clear the intervening terrain, much of which is considerably higher than 5,500 feet. At the end, the automatic pilot may have regained some control over the wildly enthusiastic engines, and may have been in the process of bringing the aircraft down at whatever rate setting Barry had made when it crashed."[12]

In a 1998 interview, Bomber 075 co-pilot Lieutenant Whitfield said he found it incredibly hard to believe that the abandoned B-36 flew more than 200 miles in a northeasterly direction, finally crash-landing at an elevation of nearly 6,000 feet on the side of a mountain in the Kispiox Valley. Asked whether this could be explained by the engine fires having melted the carburetor ice, thereby restoring some power to continue on the course set by the autopilot at the time of bailout, Whitfield answered, "I doubt it, but the functioning engines might have regained enough power to allow the plane to climb two or three thousand feet. I am very surprised that it could go so far and climb at all."[13]

US rescue-helicopter pilot Lieutenant Richard Kirkland speculated that the de-icing process may have contributed to the erratic flight path of Bomber 075. Kirkland described what he thought could have happened after Barry set a course out to sea and then jumped:

The aircraft then entered a layer of lower, warmer air. I verified that this existed from old weather reports for that day. The ice melted off one wing first, and the big bird went into a bank. Then, as it completed its 180 [degrees], the ice slid off the other wing and it leveled.

Now, with tons of ice gone, the nose came up on that big monster and it climbed up over the mountain range behind Princess Royal Island and flew, crewless, for hundreds of miles into the interior. It flew into an area we'd never dreamed of searching, because how could a faltering aircraft that was about to crash climb over 12,000-foot mountains?[14]

Farther north, eyewitnesses saw Bomber 075 hours after the crew had bailed out. One claimed to have seen it flying up the Skeena River, while another described a starry night and the mystery plane making a slow bank up the Kispiox Valley with all lights on and no flames.

Before 1:00 AM, "the US military contacted the Terrace airport about the possibility of Bomber 075 making an attempt to land there. The commissioner who was on duty at the Terrace airport was informed that the bomber was going to try and do an emergency landing in Terrace," researcher Pierre Cote stated.[15]

The later moments of the flight and subsequent crash of Bomber 075 were actually witnessed by some local residents who did not realize what they were seeing. A man who lived just outside Hazelton at the time heard the aircraft. His sister in Hazelton also heard it. "He said that his sister had seen it fly over Hazelton, making a hell of a lot of noise, which they did. She looked outside and saw the aircraft on fire," said Barry Borutski.[16]

In the upper Kispiox Valley, Elsie Wookey was sitting up late that night, sipping a cup of hot chocolate. She heard a heavy aircraft fly over and wondered what it was doing there that late. She went outside and shortly after witnessed a flash. She saw a glow that lit up the sky for a considerable period of time.[17]

The Terrace *Omineca Herald* reported that forestry officers and police in Terrace had been alerted of planes being heard over Aiyansh in the Nass Valley; Reverend S. Kinsley, missionary and local postmaster,

Even before the remains of Bomber 075 were spotted north of Smithers, there was a documented case of a B-36 flying some distance without a crew. On February 7, 1953, US Air Force B-36H, Serial 51-5719, of 492nd Bomb Squadron, Seventh Bombardment Wing, flew crewless about 30 miles before it crashed on farmland near Lacock, Wiltshire, England. This aircraft had run short of fuel after two missed approaches to the Royal Air Force Fairford base, forcing the crew to bail out. The 15 crewmen parachuted to safety and were found scattered across three counties, Oxfordshire, Berkshire and Wiltshire.[18]

reported that he had heard an aircraft circling at two o'clock that morning and then moving on.[19]

Despite reports of a blazing aircraft overhead that night, no official air search was organized because no aircraft had been reported missing in the area. In fact, a search was started on February 14 by the residents of Kispiox to look for the cause of the flash, but was unsuccessful.[20] The sky may have been lit up for some time by the burning of the aircraft's magnesium skin.

In the 1970s, surgeon Dave Kuntz talked to many people who were living in the area at the time of the crash. During his time working at the Kitimat General Hospital, he lived with his family at their ranch in the Kispiox Valley, not far below where the B-36 had come down some 25 years earlier.

What puzzled Kuntz was that nobody ever told him about the existence of the B-36 wreck. Why not, and why this secrecy?[21] The more Kuntz thought about this mystery, the more questions he had. One thing that neighbour Marty Allen told Kuntz was that he had seen "UFOs" or some suspicious lights on the mountainside. Kuntz wondered, "Were those the lights of landing helicopters at the crash site, or just scare tactics to get me to leave the valley?"

Regardless of its route, the fact is that Bomber 075 ended up on Mount Kologet at about 5,800 feet in elevation. And there Bomber 075 was first identified from the air by the number on the front wheel cover of the landing-gear door. "And not by the fin or anything else, which would mean that the aircraft's landing gear was down," B-36 historian

Borutski later observed. "The only way they could have identified that was if the aircraft's wheels had been down, otherwise the flaps would have been hidden."

It appears that the B-36 crashed in stall position with its landing gear extended. "The aircraft had its gear dropped and then the pilot just smacked her in. It worked like a toboggan cutting through butter," Borutski explained. The fact that the aircraft's propellers were bent and not curled meant that the engines were feathered during the crash.

"The site is the only place you could crash-land an aircraft in the mountains. I think we can prove someone on board landed it there in the deep snow."[22]

Pierre Cote believed that the location of the crash, in a broad alpine bowl surrounded by high ridges, indicated that the aircraft was deliberately landed at the crash site. "There's no way the plane got to where it got without someone piloting it there," he asserted.

"If an engine is running on impact, the associated propeller will have all three blades bent in a spiral pattern around the propeller shaft," Goleta Air and Space Museum curator Brian Lockett said. "If the engine is not running, one or two propellers will be bent towards the tail of the airplane."[23]

"I think the gearing of the B-36 propellers may have caused a slighter damage profile than I would expect," B-36 historian Don Pyeatt suggested. "Looking at a picture of engine No. 1, the [Bomber] 075 blade tip on the ground appears pristine." This engine seems to have been feathered. The missing blade likely sheared off on impact without touching the ground. Pyeatt added, "Because the propellers rotate counter-clockwise, as viewed from the rear, for it to break by ground impact, the blade following would have dug through the ground and damaged the tip. If an engine is not running when it hit the ground, [the wing would have to] hit the ground at a high angle and speed to shear the blade and collapse the engine cowling into the accordion [bellows] shape. Also, there is no indication of [engine] fire."[24]

To conclusively establish the aircraft's running state at impact requires good pictures of the landing gear and props, according to Borutski. "If you show that every prop blade had been feathered, then that is pretty well conclusive that that thing was flown in and basically with the wheels down, bomb bay doors open. The pilot kind of stalled it right into that particular area and she [the aircraft] came in intact."[25]

"Another key point is the landing gear, to see what kind of pressure was put on those struts," Borutski continued, "because he was coming down with the wheels down. But in 15 to 20 feet of snow, they probably would just act as a big plough. They were strong and powerful and were designed to carry the whole load of the aircraft, which never would hit any surface rocks. She would just cut a trail."[26]

While at the crash site in the late summer of 2003, researcher Jim Laird and I tried to determine whether the aircraft crashed or came down in a controlled flight into terrain. We were able to positively identify engine No. 1. Located near the top of the ridge, it obviously had not moved very far, at least not upslope. With this engine located on the far left of the port wing, the aircraft's actual heading before it came down could be determined as approximately 75 degrees.

The aircraft would have just cleared a ridge below Mount Kologet, then passed through a little saddle in that ridge and hit another one across a narrow valley. The aircraft was roughly on an easterly course when it struck the edge of the final ridge top. The fragments visible today are lower down the slope, probably thrown back by the explosion or carried downhill by subsequent snow slides and clean-up missions.

"Looking at the map, the pilot would be setting a course using a LORAN [long-range navigation device]," Borutski said. "Were they aiming for Watson Lake, or were they trying to go back to Anchorage? I believe he was heading toward Watson Lake because that was a well-known base and a staging point during World War II."[27]

One can only speculate how much the US Air Force knew immediately following the incident. Why, for example, did it send at least one of its aircraft up the Nass River and Nass Bay inland as far as Aiyansh on the very first day of the air search, even though the aircraft was supposed to have crashed somewhere in the Pacific Ocean?[28]

Whatever the circumstances, the US military authorities must have been aware that after its crew bailed out, the bomber kept on flying for a little over three hours. Did they actually instruct the pilot to turn around and fly the aircraft in a northerly direction, either to take the aircraft and its sensitive payload back to Eielson AFB or to just try to land it at a remote location easily accessible from the Annette Island air facility in Alaska?

Doug Craig wondered why the aircraft might have tried to return to Anchorage instead of just flying on to Seattle. The pilot could have tried to land at either McChord AFB near Tacoma or returned to Eielson AFB in Alaska. But landing the huge, stricken aircraft with a live bomb single-handedly was likely just too risky. The pilot's priorities would have been to avoid a nuclear explosion, save his precious cargo and, last but not least, save his own life—altogether no simple task. First he would have to find an out-of-the-way place where he could put the aircraft down more or less in one piece. It would have to be somewhere in the middle of nowhere, yet close to a US military or Coast Guard base.

The big snow-covered glacier in the Kispiox Mountains would fit the bill. This northwest corner of British Columbia was in the 1950s a very isolated spot with hardly any settlements or road access. The US Air Force could not have picked a better location for a secret salvage operation. It would be fairly easy to access the downed aircraft and its sensitive cargo without anybody knowing about it. Moreover, at this high elevation, everything would be safely covered in snow for most of the year. The bomber would also be conveniently close, as the crow flies, to the US Air Force Annette Island air facility. Assuming that the US military was fully aware that Captain Schreier had remained on board and flown the aircraft back north to an isolated location near the Alaska Panhandle, this would have to be kept secret at any cost. Also, knowing that it would be next to impossible to immediately salvage anything from the crashed bomber in the middle of the winter in the mountains on foreign soil, it was of the utmost importance that none of this information be leaked.

Sooner or later, the US Air Force would have a helicopter strong enough to lift whatever needed to be removed from the crash site. After they secured what they needed from the site, the US Air Force would just have to sit back and wait until someone else eventually spotted the wreckage from the air. Subsequently, the US military would only have to go through the motions of acting surprised and do a casual investigation of the wreckage.

Lieutenant Cox is skeptical that the aircraft could have flown for another three hours in the condition it was in when he left it. "When it came down to warmer temperatures and got rid of some ice, it could have, or maybe the carburetors cleared up, but it seems doubtful to me the way we were losing altitude. It was in a bank when I last saw it."[29]

The B-36 is not difficult to manoeuvre with some inoperative engines. The ease of manoeuvrability results from the free-floating characteristic of the servo-operated control surfaces and positive means of trimming the airplane.

Others disagree. Flying a B-36 single-handedly on only three engines on a black, stormy night would indeed have been a demanding job, to say the least. A situation with "three turning, three burning" would have been very difficult to keep flying in.[30] And a B-36 flying on the power of just three engines would barely be able to stay in the air, as it would not be able to fly much faster than the stall speed of about 120 miles per hour.[31]

CHAPTER 10

What Did the Government Know?

The ultimate question is whether the US Air Force was aware that Bomber 075 had gone down in northwestern British Columbia and not somewhere in the Pacific Ocean. Though the aircraft was supposed to have crashed somewhere in the Pacific, why had the US Air Force, on the first day of the search, sent an aircraft inland up the Nass River? This isolated secondary search, far from the media and the Canadian search commander, must have taken place for a reason.[1]

A day after the crash the *New York Times* reported, "A general air of secrecy surrounded the plane after last reports were received that it was in distress."

General John Montgomery, Operations Officer of the US Air Force Strategic Air Command, issued orders forbidding survivors to talk to the press until they were "thoroughly briefed" by the US Air Force. The fact that Montgomery was personally and directly involved in the incident was itself quite significant.

Lieutenant Richard Kirkland, and possibly everybody else assembled in that briefing room at McChord AFB for the rescue operation, immediately realized that having a general and a squadron of B-29s involved in a search and rescue operation for downed airmen was highly unusual. It certainly suggested that there was more to this mission than a missing aircraft and its crew.

Kirkland recalled that the general came right to the point. "Gentlemen, I am General Montgomery from Strategic Air Command headquarters. We have lost a B-36 on the Alkan [Alaska–Canada] route." Montgomery could not over-emphasize the importance of locating the aircraft and its crew at the earliest possible moment. "Critical... urgent... international repercussions... top, top priority" were phrases that stressed the urgency of the matter.

"I'm here because your rescue unit will have primary responsibility for conducting the search and rescue mission and I want to emphasize the importance of locating this aircraft and its crew at the earliest possible moment." Montgomery continued, "Gentlemen, there is classified equipment aboard the aircraft, and therefore this mission has the highest priority, right from the top."[2] Then he paused for a moment to let this information sink in.

The general did not actually say the B-36 had an atomic bomb aboard, "and I realized that, of course, he couldn't," Kirkland said. "That was top-secret stuff. But he didn't have to say it. We all knew, and we all realized there was a lot at stake here.

"Wow, I said, it was something big, alright! I had only seen the B-36 flying over, because it was too heavy to land at our base. We all knew they flew daily secret missions from their SAC bases to wherever. When one came our way, it was generally headed for Alaska, which was one stone's throw from the USSR.

"Their route up there was called the Alkan Route, and it was our responsibility to provide search and rescue coverage. They had never required our service before now, but that bird flew so high and it had so many engines that we never expected to get a call."[3]

Kirkland wondered what effect an incident like this would have on the whole nuclear retaliatory program. "What were the consequences of a lost atomic bomb? Was it armed? Could it go off? It all seemed too big and too frightening to comprehend."

Immediately after the accident, a deliberate effort was made to cover it up. Besides hiding some pertinent facts, the US Air Force promptly began their calculated efforts to change the facts. Soon after Major Bush Smith assumed duties as mission commander, it was reported that "all information, repeat, all information relative to the incident will be released through Commanding General Eighth Air Force [Major General Ramey]."[4]

Although a B-36 pilot was available at McChord AFB for liaison duty, no public information officer was available there. Because of the "international status and classified nature of the incident," no attempt was made during Operation Brix to solicit observer reports through commercial radio and press.

On February 15, the first message received about survivors from the missing bomber read: "Handle this with care. Just talked to Vancouver RCAF. Two survivors in good condition picked up near Ashdown Island by two fishing boats. That is about all I have now but expect more shortly. Will pass on without interrogation. Again, handle this with care. No leaks."[5]

As soon as the survivors were rescued, US authorities firmly informed Canada that from that time on, debriefings would be a totally American show. Canadians would be left in the dark about the fact that the Americans' first accident involving nuclear weapons had occurred over Canadian soil. The truth was not revealed until nearly 30 years later when the government documents were declassified.

The USAF sent advisories out to Port Hardy regarding press interviews. A naval message clearly stated, "it is decreed that survivors should not give interviews to members of press or other unauthorized persons." Interviews were restricted to Lieutenant William Kidd, RCN, or other service personnel. CBC reporter Ross Munroe was later one of the few to interview Kidd about the rescue for *CBC News Roundup*.

On February 16, USAF search commander C.L. Brady recorded a short speech in the 12 Group commander's office. The recording was made by Vancouver radio station CKWX engineers and was later broadcast over that station. The speech was mainly designed to "inform the public of the excellent co-operation, which existed between the services of the two countries during Operation Brix and to combat idle rumours of the number of survivors found."[6] In an unprecedented move, the request from US Air Force headquarters asked the Canadian Department of Transport to have an area within a 100-mile radius of a point, 53°05'N, 129°10'W, made into a prohibited zone for civilian aircraft until further notice. Though this was officially to ensure that civilian aircraft would not interfere with the search, the US Air Force may not have wanted anybody in this huge chunk of British Columbia's coast for other reasons. Since the 12 survivors had been located in a small area on Princess Royal Island, why was such a big area declared out of bounds?

The proceedings of the US Air Force Board of Inquiry were obviously kept secret. Due to the "highly classified nature of the accident," all witnesses appearing before the board were read regulation AFR62-14A, essentially an oath of silence, and clearly advised "not to touch on anything that might involve highly classified material." Nothing could be mentioned about the bomber's cargo.

Around the middle of March 1950, Major General Thomas D. White, US Air Force director of legislation and liaison, wrote to the executive chairman of the US Congress Joint Committee on Atomic Energy, William L. Borden: "The airplane carried an atomic bomb, less nuclear component. The bomb was jettisoned, presumably over the sea, and it exploded while in the air. Its mechanism was set to detonate the charge at approximately 3,800 ft. . . . Since the B-36 story has died out of the press, and apparently diminished from the public interest, I recommend that no release be made concerning the airplane's bomb load."[7]

A Canadian naval message states, "Eielson reported hearing signals between 0705 Zulu [11:05 PM on February 13] til [sic] 1055 Zulu [2:55 AM PST on February 14] on 6,240 Kcs. The radio operator at Eielson believed the transmissions came from mission B-36 with key screwed down."[8] If the key was tied down at 8,280 kilocycles per second, how could the aircraft also transmit at 6,240 kilocycles per second?

General Montgomery immediately contacted Eielson AFB by phone to correct the frequency to 8,280 kilocycles per second. The message added: "General Montgomery will explain fully upon arrival."[9] Was this an attempt by Montgomery to suppress information? What was it that he explained "fully"?

On February 19, Colonel John Bartlett, commanding officer of the Fort Worth squadron to which the missing B-36 belonged and also the pilot of Bomber 075's ferry flight from Texas to Alaska, thoroughly interrogated three of the rescued crew members: Captain Barry, Lieutenant Gerhart and Staff Sergeant Stephens. Bartlett reportedly gained much useful information concerning the bailout and ultimate crash.[10]

Was this reference to the "ultimate crash" just a slip of the pen, or had the crash actually already been discussed in detail by the US Air Force? Either way, since signals were received from the aircraft on three different frequencies until just before 3:00 AM, it is safe to assume that the authorities were aware that the B-36 had been in the air for another three hours beyond the official time of the crash.

Geologist Doug Craig, who'd accidentally stumbled onto the wreck during a routine ridge traverse in 1956, believed that the reference to "the ultimate crash" was not a mistake but rather an intentional effort to steer attention away from the wreck. Was the reported sighting of an aircraft's wing tip some 30 miles north of Cape Scott on Vancouver Island, allegedly part of the missing B-36, also an intentional false trail to divert attention from the real location of the wreck? "Since the aircraft was missing for three and one half years during a time when the US Air Force would not like it to be found, there could well have been various deceptions, which are now in the records, such that it would be difficult to separate fact from fiction," Craig speculated.[11]

Jim Roddick was back at the survey team's base camp when the wreck was discovered. He also suspected efforts were being made to keep the wreck out of the news, even by the Canadian authorities. Roddick recalled, "Later, from our base camp, we made radio contact with the RCAF in Whitehorse, Yukon Territory. The officer who answered was polite but distinctly restrained about what we considered to be our great find... In fact, he clearly did not enjoy the conversation, but heard us out with minimal comment. At the end, he conceded that they already knew [of the wreck]. He would say nothing more and concluded with a terse, 'Thank you. Bye.' This was our first encounter with the military secrecy that shrouded this wreckage for decades."[12]

Crew members later testifying during the closed-door Board of Inquiry hearings were warned not to mention any of the classified aspects of their mission, despite the fact that the reviewing committee was made up of senior members of the US Air Force, including a general. For the USAF, it was a closed case.

No mention was ever made of there having been a nuclear weapon on the lost aircraft. The bomber's real mission wasn't even mentioned at the time of the crash. The Commander of the Eighth Air Force, Major

General Roger Ramey, told journalists only that Bomber 075 had been on a routine training flight. In light of this, it is doubtful that Canadian officials were told about the aircraft's potentially deadly cargo.

Copies of US Air Force reports on the August 1954 salvage operation remain unavailable. Though the Air Force Historical Research Agency at Maxwell AFB searched the unit histories of organizations that might have mounted the operation, including the 824th Operations Squadron, the 824th Air Base Group, the 43rd Air Rescue Squadron (ARS) and the Fourth Air Rescue Group, no mention was found about the operation. The Fourth Air Rescue Group's unit histories for August 1954 indicate that the ARS's geographic zone of responsibility included British Columbia. As the expedition in question was mounted by helicopter, there is a good possibility that the 43rd ARS conducted it. However, the agency apparently has no means of validating this or of determining what units or personnel may have participated. Neither did they have the means of locating information on Captain Hayden, Captain Bailey and Staff Sergeant Stephens, the three US Air Force servicemen who took part.

Considering the scope of the operation on foreign soil and the urgent attempts to get into the crash site to recover whatever they were looking for, one might expect the US Air Force to have detailed reports of the mission, but none have ever been acknowledged or released.

In 1953, after the wreckage of Bomber 075 was accidentally discovered, Staff Sergeant Denzel Clark and the others who had been on sister ship Bomber 083 that night in February 1950 were called in for a briefing. They were told that Bomber 075 had been located. "They were told certain things were found and that certain things were done," said Jim Laird. "But he [Clark] wasn't too specific about that." B-36 crew members all had to take an oath of secrecy and Clark was a member of a crew covered by that order.[13]

Many of the local residents in the area where Bomber 075 crashed may also have been sworn to secrecy.

In 1951, bush pilot Cedric Mah was flying up and down the coast for Central BC Airways on the Kitimat Alcan aluminum smelter project. He first heard about the lost bomber in the spring of 1950. "I had just returned to Vancouver after a stint of six years, first flying the 'Burma Hump' from 1944 to 1946," he said. For the next four years, his trips into the British Columbia Interior and elsewhere brought him into frequent contact with friends and schoolmates from his hometown of Prince Rupert. He learned from them that many had been on the search for the B-36 along the BC coastline. He also kept hearing rumours that the nuclear bomber had actually crashed in the Kitwanga Valley.

"Nearly always the case of the missing nuclear bomb arose," he recalled. One of his friends told him, "They were searching in the wrong area. It didn't go down in the Queen Charlotte Sound but up near Kitwanga Lake... No one could pinpoint its location, but the scuttle-butt was that the Americans had gone in and retrieved what was salvageable and had burned or buried the rest."[14]

Mah's friends in Prince Rupert and the BC Interior could supply no answers: "It was hush-hush and it was said that the guides were sworn to maintain complete secrecy."[15]

While Kispiox Valley resident Marcella Love disagrees, "Local residents were not aware of the event until Jack Lee was contacted for hiring with his pack horses to reach the [crash] site in September 1953," others concur with Mah.[16]

In September 1968, a writer from North Vancouver who was in the final stages of completing a book on flying in Canada contacted the Smithers *Interior News* for photographs of the wreck. The writer added, "I know prospectors who finally spotted it and took photographs. I believe the name of one was Mr. Roddick." The newspaper managed to contact one person who had photographs of the wreck in his possession. However, that person refused to release them to the *Interior News*, apparently due to instructions of secrecy.[17] That person was likely Hunter Simpson who had witnessed the 1954 salvage and destroy mission.

Harry Kruisselbrink, a former colleague of Simpson's, confirmed that during the time they worked together, Simpson never spoke about this event. It was well known that he was "sworn to secrecy."[18]

Obviously Simpson's statement to the *Interior News* in August 1954 that no pieces "bigger than a football" remained of the wreckage was gross misinformation.[19] Was he told to make this statement to discourage future visits to the crash site because there would be nothing left of interest there anyway? Until his death in 1972, Simpson never changed his story, even though Smithers resident Joe L'Orsa recalled Simpson indicating with his hands how big the pieces were after the aircraft was blown up.

Misinformation or not, small pieces of the destroyed wreck were found much later, after they had washed down into the main stem of the Kispiox River. In the mid-1970s, an elderly Native man showed L'Orsa a small piece of aluminum from the B-36, which he had found in the river.[20]

One of Simpson's relatives agreed to an interview with Pierre Cote but said, "You ask the questions and I'll only say yes or no." However, Cote recalls him relating how intact the aircraft was. Other Kispiox residents also remain tight-lipped about what went on around the wreck of the B-36.[21]

Marty Allen is another witness who rarely spoke about the event to strangers, not even to close friend Dave Kuntz, who moved to the Kispiox Valley years after the crash and lived there for 10 years without a clue about the B-36 wreck on nearby Mount Kologet. "I'm sure the B-36 event was being discussed by the immediate Love and Allen families, both long-time residents in the valley and who had intermarried. If they did, they only talked amongst themselves about it. But not one person said a word about it, and it wasn't that we were strangers," Kuntz said.

During his time off from work, Kuntz loved flying his private Bell 47G helicopter throughout northwestern British Columbia, including the Kispiox Mountains. In the decade that Kuntz lived in the Kispiox Valley, nobody ever mentioned the B-36. Several years later, in 1999, Kuntz read some of the articles I had written about this Broken Arrow incident. Suddenly, a lot of things made sense to Kuntz.

"Dorothy and Marty Allen came over and cooked the food for our wedding. Marty was best man at the wedding," he said. Billy, Marcella Love's son, worked on Kuntz's ranch skidding and falling, and Kuntz had operated on members of the Love and Lee families. The Kuntzes were good friends with the Love family, but people just didn't want to talk.

"Especially when I started to fly my helicopter in these mountains, this must have made some people worried. I'm sure the immediate Love and Allen families may have discussed the B-36 event. But most likely they were all sworn to secrecy."[22]

Other long-time Kispiox Valley residents never mentioned anything to Kuntz about the B-36 crash site either. Considering the fact that Kuntz had easy access with his helicopter to the site, and as pilots are often interested in aviation history, this seems odd.

Kim Lee confirmed that over the years this topic was indeed often discussed over the dinner table between her father and grandfather. She also wondered why the air in the Kispiox had always been tested when she lived there. "Was it for possible radiation?" [23]

A report jointly published by the US Departments of Defense and Energy, *The Histories of Nuclear Weapon Accidents 1950–1980*, stated that the aircraft wreckage was found on Vancouver Island. Another official US report pinpoints the B-36 accident as happening in Puget Sound, Washington.[24] Yet another official US report, dated January 14, 1992, repeats the statement that the aircraft wreckage was found on Vancouver Island.[25] Were these efforts to divert attention away from the crash area?

Even military historian John Clearwater, when interviewed on the CBC radio program *As It Happens* on January 27, 1997, repeated the claim that the B-36 wreckage had been found on Vancouver Island.

A few weeks after the CBC broadcast, the *Fort Worth Star-Telegram* erroneously reported that after the five missing men had jumped and apparently landed in the Pacific, "the flaming bomber had reached British Columbia's Vancouver Island, and the 12 survivors landed in the heavy growths of pine trees that covered the island."[26]

The official 1950 search report on Operation Brix has a handwritten note added later giving incorrect coordinates for the B-36 crash site. Both the latitude and longitude were given two minutes short, thus throwing the location off by two miles in each direction—just enough to mislead people trying to find the site. "The coordinates of the wreckage site in both the RCAF and USAF files were in agreement, but wrong," Jim Roddick observed. "Close, but not sufficiently accurate that one could fly directly there. The only accurate location-data were in my old 1956 [Geological Survey of Canada] notebook."[27]

In August 1992, in an effort to locate the crash site, Scott Deaver and I chartered a small fixed-wing aircraft in Smithers. Harold Harvey, who had dropped the explosives above the crash site, warned us that it would not be easy to find the site and wished us luck. Having the wrong coordinates, and further limited by a fixed-wing aircraft with a low-horsepower engine, we were unable to locate the wreck.

It was not until early in 1997, after Jim Roddick and Doug Craig provided the right coordinates, that the wreck could be identified on aerial photographs taken in the summer of 1950 as part of an ongoing program of aerial-photo coverage of the whole country.

Studying air photos of the position originally reported had not shown anything simply because the crash site was actually on the next flight-survey line. The site is already hard enough to spot from the air in the rough mountainous terrain, let alone using the wrong coordinates.

The location of 56°05'N, 128°34'W provided by Roddick made more sense. It showed a pond that corresponds with the pond Captain Paul Gardella mentioned in his report. The 1:30,000 scale photos, which have very low resolution and deep shadows, show enough detail to identify the crash site. At the bottom of a glacier, between patches of permanent ice, a 1/16th-inch dot can be seen with little dots around it. The top of the rise on the north side shows the shadow of the aircraft's tail, and the terrain contour exactly matches the description of the site provided by Gardella, leader of the October 1953 search and destroy mission.

A 1965 photo of the site shows a series of depressions where the wreck had been before it was blown apart. These depressions are visible as blotches on the ground. The scar of a fresh landslide is visible near a sharp peak south of the site, possibly caused by the explosions.[28]

In 1997, just prior to joining the Canadian Armed Forces survey team going to the crash site, Doug Craig and Doug Davidge were driving up to Stewart, BC. "While stopping for a break, we watched a honking great olive-drab helicopter churn over us," Craig recalled. "We idly wondered whether it was to be the one that we would use on the succeeding days. We were smarter than we knew. We [soon] met the four-man flying crew and two nuclear engineers from Ottawa. The flight crew had been flying around, looking for 075 remains."[29]

The helicopter crew did not have the correct coordinates of the crash site, but instead were using the ones originally indicated on the crash-position map of the RCAF. "And they presumably persisted with these right up until the day before the eight of us flew up there." Craig could not refrain from speculating, "Were the RCAF coordinates a simple mistake? Some of those maps were not precise. Or was this a modest error by design?"[30]

Dave Kuntz concurred with the theory of an intentional cover-up by the US Air Force. He also strongly suspected that the site was, and likely still is, being protected and monitored by a number of people. Appointing some local residents like members of the Allen and Lee families would be the most obvious choice. This would not cause any suspicion.[31]

Scott Deaver, who lives in Green Farms, Connecticut, has been chasing the story of Bomber 075 for many years. He describes himself as a "semi-employed carpenter with a love of airplanes I inherited from my late pilot father."[32] In the early 1990s, he bought a technical manual on the aircraft. He was visiting a friend, whose father was an author and had many old newspaper clippings. Deaver put the manual down on a stack of newspapers. When he picked up the book, he noticed it was sitting on a *New York Herald* with a front-page headline about a B-36 lost in British Columbia, Canada. "It's a true story. When I saw that, I had to find out more."[33]

Deaver has done extensive research on this Broken Arrow incident but still hits brick walls in Washington because some materials are even now classified and top secret.

"There is still something they are hiding and not letting out to this day," said Barry Borutski, a B-36 researcher who has been to the crash site at least twice. "They basically say, 'We have the information but it's classified,' and that's the end of it. Deaver has done some fantastic research; he knows the system in and out. And when he hits a brick wall, you can be guaranteed it's a brick wall."[34]

Few of the surviving crew members are willing to talk about the incident. "You don't want to make it possible for somebody that wanted to do damage to the country to maybe have some information that they could...use," Raymond Whitfield said. "It's just better not to talk about things like that." Dick Thrasher agreed, "Yeah, there's still things that I can't talk about, that I won't talk about."[35]

Not only were US military personnel required to take an oath of secrecy, appeals were also made to their patriotism. Not maintaining their oath by breaking their silence meant breaking rank. Moreover, Americans generally have great trust in their government.

"I know there is a lot of interest in what happened," said Vitale Trippodi, "but I think the incident is kind of like an Indian burial ground and should be left alone."[36]

CHAPTER 11

What Did the Crash Site Reveal?

On July 23, 1956, almost two years after the 1954 salvage and destroy mission by the US Air Force, Geological Survey of Canada (GSC) geologist W.R.A. "Bob" Baragar and his assistant Doug Craig stumbled onto the wreckage of Bomber 075. They were members of a surveying crew on a routine geological mapping traverse in the Mount Kologet area. It was part of Operation Stikine, a GSC field program. Their helicopter-established base camp was within four miles of the wreck site.

Just below a ridge, the two young geologists found four small fragments of the aircraft. Strewn about the mountainside were one of the big engines and some smaller pieces of aluminum. On the northeast side of a ridge, they found an orange flare parachute with an attached five-gallon US military steel drum with a nice thick pad on the bottom. The well-protected keg contained a fairly standard Geiger counter. The packing date on the parachute was 1951, and the place of origin was McChord AFB.

This was a Geiger counter the US team had airdropped at the crash site in 1953. Some people speculate that several Geiger counters were airdropped. However, one of the crew members involved in the airdrop said they only dropped one Geiger counter and that the wind blew its chute to the other side of the ridge, where it was lost. It may have blown off course somewhat, but in any case, the US Air Force demolition team never found it. The two surveyors did not look any farther over the ridge, but reported their find to their crew chief, Dr. Jim Roddick.

Roddick would spend half a century working for the Geological Survey of Canada. His career as a reconnaissance geologist was devoted mainly to the geological mapping of large regions of Yukon and British Columbia that were previously blank spots on the map. In 1953, he pioneered the use of helicopters for geological mapping in mountainous terrain.

After he completed his Ph.D. in 1955, Roddick spent the next field season participating in Operation Stikine in northern British Columbia, which would result in the first of 29 new geological maps (mostly at a scale of 1:250,000) that covered a total area of 177,600 square miles, about the size of California and Maryland combined. The fieldwork involved many 400-hour helicopter seasons with many assistants and a lot of luck in having no fatalities in spite of the rugged terrain.

On July 25, two days after Baragar and Craig found the Geiger counter, Roddick visited the crash site with Evan Bullock, a helicopter pilot, and Gordon Peters, an aircraft maintenance engineer with Okanagan Helicopters. Going over the ridge, they found the main wreckage of the B-36, including the wings, more engines and a 45-foot chunk of fuselage. Even though it was late July, glacial ice and snow covered most of it.

Not knowing what the wreckage was, Roddick started checking for possibly significant serial numbers. Soon he came across a fragment of aluminum cowling jutting out of the snow. "The words on it were wholly unexpected: Engine No. Six!" This was definitely not the remains of a bush plane as he had expected; this was a big aircraft! Being a pilot himself, Roddick had some knowledge of aircraft. "I was pretty sure I knew what this was," he recalled. Confirmation soon came from some lettering on a blister cover: "Spec. No. 98-26751-H; Model B36B; Consolid. Vultee Aircraft Corp.; Date of manufacture—5/28/49; Airforce—US Army." There was no doubt in Roddick's mind now: "I was looking at the remains of a B-36 Peacemaker!" He made the following entries in his GSC field notebook:

> The wreck is located at El. 5500, Long. 128°3', Lat. 56°05'. The aircraft was apparently on an easterly course when it struck within 100 ft. or so of the ridge top. The fragments now

visible are lower down the slope, probably thrown back by the explosion or carried downhill by subsequent snow slides.

The wreckage is concentrated in about a quarter mile circular area. The upper part of it was covered by deep snow. The exposed wreckage shows very little linearity except for a slight elongation downslope. Most of the pieces are very small, the largest being the propeller blades (3), several panel fragments from wing or fuselage and a tail fragment.

There is considerable emergency gear such as canned goods and clothing, etc., also armaments (incendiary grenades and 20-mm cannon shells). Although clothing is quite common there is no indication of bodies. One fragment of a duffel bag has the name attached to it, H.L. Barry Capt. AO-808341.[1]

Tucked under a rock ledge was a canister containing a large number of phosphorous incendiary grenades. The grenades must have been flown in at a later date, probably to destroy the remnants of the wreck, although the crew with Roddick did not notice much evidence of fire. The crew's cook amused himself throwing the grenades around camp, and into the water; they still worked.

Craig, who kept one of the grenades, described it as "smaller than a can of Campbell's soup, say 1.2 inches in diameter and 5 inches long." Some of the grenades were also used to heat the lake water near the shore at base camp. While the young man was joyfully tossing the grenades around, Craig had apparently been assigned to another camp. At least, he was not in camp when Roddick returned from the crash site. Craig remembered being "a bit cheesed off at such fun without being involved!"[2]

Despite this, Craig did end up with several items from the crash site, including a canvas duffel bag, the Geiger counter, some of its desiccant bags and a 20-mm aircraft cannon projectile, which rattled around in his possession until he realized that it still contained its explosive charge. "I heaved it into the Liard River off the [Liard River Suspension Bridge on the Alaska Highway] in 1971. The grenades/canisters and the Geiger counter parachute were so disposed that there was no reasonable doubt that they had been brought in at a later date when a demolition crew of the US Air Force went over the wreckage. For many years, the dining-tent storytelling would get around to the B-36."[3]

Finding a Geiger counter near the crash site by no means proves the presence of radioactive material, but it does indicate that the crash site investigators were aware of this possibility. "That four years earlier, the aircraft were flying with apparently fully operational, shaped charges, 11,000-pound packages in the No. 2 bomb bay," Craig explained, "and lead warheads elsewhere in the aircraft and the possibility at least that the weaponeer was the only one who knew that the warhead was a dummy, is simply not relevant."[4]

Many aircraft of Second World War and postwar vintage used glowing radioactive materials as a way of providing orientation inside a darkened aircraft. Also, many of the instruments on the instrument panels would have slightly radioactive parts. A Geiger counter would have been useful in the search for missing pieces. "We...attached much weight to the Geiger counter as indicative of the cargo on the aircraft," Craig explained.[5]

Though the GSC team did have at least one Geiger counter in their camp as part of their scientific-instruments set, it did not occur to Roddick at the time to check the crash site for radiation. A few days later, Roddick wrote a two-page report of the wreckage to the RCAF in Whitehorse, Yukon. He also reported the serial numbers, dates and manufacturers' names of the automatic pilot and other components.

Roddick was told the RCAF knew about the wreckage and would get back to him later. The RCAF never contacted him again.[6] The RCAF was obviously reluctant to have the matter publicized.

By coincidence, the GSC team found another link with the B-36 crash later that same summer. The last days of Operation Stikine were spent in a cabin at the old Big Missouri mine, north of Stewart, BC. In the shack they were occupying at this shut-down mine, they came across a 1951 edition of an adventure magazine that featured a cover story about the harrowing experience of a B-36 crew off the coast of British Columbia in February 1950. Roddick kept the magazine, called *True Adventure*, for many years, but then lost it. "The story was heavy on anecdotes and skimpy on details, but the name of the pilot was Harold Barry. Clearly it was our plane!"

Roddick recalled the magazine story explaining that the aircraft was on a flight from Alaska to Seattle when fire developed in three of the six engines. When the pilot realized that altitude could not be maintained, he decided the crew should bail out over the nearest land. The article concluded that 12 were rescued, 5 disappeared "and the plane crashed into Queen Charlotte Sound. We knew it had not."[7] There was no mention of an atomic bomb. Unfortunately, the magazine has not been located.

Armed with the date of the incident, Roddick checked the Vancouver newspapers of the time. "I found that it had been headline material during the Valentine week of 1950. In fact, the articles were much more informative than the magazine story. Yet, the plane was still supposed to have crashed in the sea. Interviews with the survivors left no doubt that they believed it had. How and when the crash site was first discovered still remained a mystery to us."[8]

There are two more curious coincidences between members of the GSC crew and the B-36 wreck. Sixteen years later, Roddick happened to charter HSRV *Montagnais*, one of the RCAF crash boats involved in Operation Brix, for his 1972 field season. Also, Craig had met the prospector Hunter Simpson before either was involved with the B-36 crash site. Craig was hitchhiking between Smithers and Terrace in the late spring of 1954 when he got a ride from Simpson, who would lead the first successful recovery attempt that summer.[9]

In November 1981, the Vancouver *Province* published a short article with the lurid headline, "That's an A-Bomb There." On that day, the Bomber 075 incident was revealed in a list of nuclear weapon accidents released by the Pentagon. The article stated that there were 17 men aboard the B-36 and all were rescued. It also reported that the aircraft crashed on Vancouver Island.[10]

A similar article in the *Vancouver Sun* the next day stated that only 12 were rescued, and that the wreckage had been found north of Smithers "three years later," which would be 1953. The *Sun* quoted the Pentagon's story that the bomber jettisoned an unarmed nuclear bomb off the coast and that the crew saw the flash. Headlined, "Pentagon doesn't know where A-bomb was lost," the article said, "The Pentagon said today it has nothing on file to indicate where in the Pacific off the B.C. coast a crippled B-36 bomber jettisoned an unarmed nuclear bomb in 1950."[11]

The newspaper's version conflicts with what Roddick read in the magazine. "The crew obviously had no interest in heading out to sea to unload any cargo. They were desperately hunting for land, and wanted only to be safely out. I am extremely skeptical that any crew member could see anything happening at sea level that night except a full scale nuclear explosion," he said. "The plane seems to have flown in a big circle and was going east when it hit the ridge," Roddick speculated. "But then again, the story that the pilot dutifully pointed the aircraft out to sea before jumping may be fiction, as he would have risked jumping into the water."[12]

Forty years after Doug Craig stumbled upon the crash site in 1956, he still wondered about how the crash had happened. During all those years, the wreck of the enormous B-36 haunted him. "You're out in the complete wilderness, standing on this ridge crest that's littered with mechanical debris. It felt kind of strange; you never get away from it. It's as pristine as you can imagine and it's cluttered with old military stuff." Retired as the head of the GSC's Yukon office and interested in environmental issues, Craig was still bothered about the presence of that Geiger counter found at the crash site. "It was the first and most important thing we found," said Craig. "It led us to believe there was probably atomic ordnance on board."

He knew B-36s sometimes carried nuclear bombs during the Cold War, when air-raid towers and fallout shelters were being built everywhere. Why otherwise would the demolition crew need a device to measure radioactivity levels? he wondered. If the nuclear bomb had been dropped over the ocean, could it be that the bomb's plutonium core remained on the aircraft when it crashed on the mountainside?" By this time an environmental consultant, Craig had grown more concerned over the years about possible contaminants, especially radioactive ones. There has been plenty of evidence of pollution by the US military in the Canadian Northwest, including abandoned Distant Early Warning Line sites, tar pits in downtown Whitehorse, and barrels of DDT unearthed at Rainy Hollow, BC.

In 1996, Craig felt compelled to disclose his personal knowledge of the crash site and raise his concerns that the site might be contaminated with radioactive material. "The possibility of radioactive material on the site was what attracted me to stir the pot when I did." He began an extensive correspondence with Yukon Member of Parliament Audrey McLaughlin, and with personnel at Environment Canada, the Department of National Defence (DND) and the US Department of the Air Force.

First, Craig approached the Environmental Protection Branch of Environment Canada for the Pacific and Yukon Region. Despite all the information Craig had gathered, there was no clear evidence or paper trail on whether or not the bomber was carrying a nuclear payload or device when it crashed. Unfortunately, neither Environment Canada nor DND seemed to be able to locate any official records about the crash. The official response from the US Air Force in 1954 and again in 1996 was that the B-36 had not been carrying a nuclear bomb or warhead.

Craig teamed up with Environmental Assessment Officer Doug Davidge from Environment Canada's Whitehorse office, and the two men started their own probe in the mid-1990s. They decided to see if they could establish that there was a nuclear warhead on board. "Surprisingly, a few people knew a lot about it," Davidge said. "We made general inquiries through newsgroups on the Internet and got positive feedback from people."

In August 1996, Craig contacted DND officials in Ottawa to address his concerns and to seek their opinion of the wreck and the possibility that there was a nuclear warhead on board. Their discussions continued through the winter of 1996–97 while more information was gathered. DND believed it was "reasonably certain that the bomb was dropped over the Pacific and exploded." Inquiries through a US liaison office determined the information was still classified. Efforts to obtain the official 1954 US Air Force crash-site-investigation report through government channels were not successful. "There were no good answers when we could get any [answers at all]," Davidge explained. "In May, we decided to investigate the site."

The possibility that the plutonium core had remained with the bomber was a real concern. A Canadian military report dated May 21, 1997, raised the question of what had happened to the bomb's core. It would make sense, the report reasoned, that the core would have travelled with the bomb, in case the weapon was needed in short order.[13]

To put all speculation and fears of contamination to rest, DND and

Environment Canada reached an agreement that month to conduct a field assessment of the crash site for radioactive contamination and other dangerous goods. More than 47 years after Bomber 075 crashed, and stimulated only by environmental concerns about radioactive contamination, the crash site would finally be checked for radiation using modern methods.

A joint ground survey of the site was coordinated between Lieutenant-Commander David Knight of DND and Doug Davidge of Environment Canada. DND agreed to provide the air transportation, ground support, technical expertise and equipment for radiation detection. In addition to Craig and Davidge, the team consisted of David Knight and Chris Thorp of Nuclear Safety Compliance, DND Ottawa. The helicopter crew from the Canadian Forces Base at Cold Lake, Alberta, included Captain Wayne Tidbury, Lieutenant Jeff Wedman and Master Corporals Greg Sawchuck and Jim Cudmore.

Between August 11 and 14, 1997, the DND–Environment Canada team did an extensive survey of the site. Using a military Bell 412/CH-146 Griffon helicopter, they took daily flights from Stewart, BC. The area of the crash site was still partially covered with snow, up to six feet deep in some areas.

Although the site may have seen the occasional visitor over the years, members of the DND–Environment Canada team were the first people to officially visit the site since the Geological Survey of Canada crew had been there in 1956. Although melting snow and ice hampered the team, they found the site still contained most of its artifacts.

The geographic setting of the crash site is in a land formation called an alpine cirque. The team found the site pretty much as Doug Craig and his crew had seen it in 1956.

However, Craig noticed that the snow cover was greatly diminished. Earlier, a small glacier had occupied most of the cirque. Though the crash site was basically untouched, a great deal more ground, and thus also more of the wreck, was exposed than when the site was visited in 1954 and 1956. "It was quite dramatic," said Craig. "I stood on the ridge exactly where I had been 41 years before. This is what I'd thought about as a dream for some years and now it was a reality. It was dramatic and hard to explain in simple terms. I found the pillow [casing] of the Geiger counter. That's how I knew I was standing at the exact same spot I had 41 years earlier."[14]

Before allowing other personnel into the crash zone, Knight and Thorp conducted a preliminary survey of the wreckage for radioactive sources. When no elevated radiation levels were detected, each member of the team was furnished with accumulative-radiation detectors for the duration of the survey, to measure total dosage received while on the site. Following a cursory survey of the crash site by team members, Knight and Thorp established a survey plan to sample for radiation sources.

First, a random but fairly thorough visual examination of the crash site was conducted on both sides of the saddle formation at the top of the mountain. Aircraft wreckage was distributed over a large area along a steep westerly facing boulder-and-scree slope in a geologically unstable area, prone to movement and slides.[15] Part of the aircraft's tail section, the port wing and three engines were scattered along a small ridge above the main fuselage wreckage.

The site was sampled at regular intervals using equipment that included a general purpose survey meter to detect X-ray and gamma radiation, an advanced survey meter to measure alpha/beta radiation particles, and a multi-channel analyzer with E-probe for isotope gamma energy discrimination. The team took measurements inside the wreck itself, particularly of the aft fuselage section, and of the dials and instruments where possible. The aircraft electronics and gauges were the only radiation sources detected at the site. The radiation sources were identified as radium, a material once widely used to illuminate dials and gauges on instrument panels.

The team took soil and biological samples, largely of mosses and lichens. At the time of the survey, the ridge was almost completely free of snow. The extensive series of measurements indicated there was no high-level radiation contamination on the crash site, nothing significantly above background levels.

The surrounding area outside the main crash site was searched for ordnance and other debris. Although no high-level radiation material was detected, some hazards associated with conventional explosives were found. A considerable quantity of unexploded ordinance littered the site, both from the aircraft itself and from the demolition team. Many hundreds of unexploded 20-mm rounds of ammunition were also still scattered about the site. The B-36 carried 16 20-mm machine guns with 600 pounds of explosive-tipped ammo for each gun.

As well, canisters containing about 100 pounds of weathered TNT explosive, left behind by the 1954 demolition crew, were found. The yellow metal canisters, with a capacity of about 15 to 22 US gallons each, were still attached to a parachute that was frozen into a snow-and-ice field, and therefore assumed to have been airdropped by the demolition team. One canister appeared to have remained unopened until this visit.

The individual explosive TNT charges were each slightly larger than a chocolate bar, approximately 20 per layer, with perhaps six layers present, or some 100 charges in all. Depending on the way charges responded to the weather, they could represent a safety hazard. (During a subsequent visit to the wreck site on September 20, 1998, Pierre Cote found another canister of TNT.)

Apart from scattered small-arms ammunition and a small number of unexploded 20-mm cannon shells, the greatest potential problem encountered at the site was a metal-shielded suitcase containing four electronic-type detonators for the nuclear bomb. The case and enclosed documentation identified the detonator components as being intended for use in a Mark IV nuclear bomb. The case, marked serial #103 Mark IV and prominently labelled "Explosives," was found inside the aft fuselage section. It was approximately 8 inches thick, 18 inches wide and 20 inches long. An inner lid warned, "Do not break this seal unless authorization has been given."

Beneath the inner lid in the foam-rubber-lined suitcase were 36 depressions, or receptacles, like those in an egg carton. Thirty-two of the depressions were empty; the remaining four contained small machined assemblies, each about the size of a small salt shaker. They were apparently made out of brass, about an inch long and an inch and a half in diameter. The assemblies had two brass horns, possibly electric terminals, projecting from the side of the larger brass cylinder. Inside the larger cylinder was what appeared to be a smaller steel cylinder about an inch long and three-quarters of an inch in diameter.

The detonators were small, hand-grenade-like explosive units that are initiated by fuses to cause the massive high-explosive lenses to explode.

Each detonator has to start the explosion of about 65 pounds of high explosives. The detonators were used to cause an implosion of the mass; properly used, they would all detonate at the same time. Thirty-two detonators plus four spares were carried for each bomb.

In the Mark IV Mod. 1 and Mod. 2 bombs, these detonators are pre-installed. In fact, it is not possible to reach all the detonator installation points from the bomb's nose and tail openings without partially dismantling the bomb. The first version, the Mark IV Mod. 0, did not have all detonators pre-installed, but access was restricted by design and construction. The weaponeer was assigned to install them. This explains the detonator case found at the crash site. Installing the detonators was a ground-based job, and, once installed, they were not disturbed during the flight. It would be the weaponeer's job to install the 32 detonators before the aircraft left Texas. He would then take the case with the four remaining spares and leave it in the aircraft. When the B-36 returned to its home base, the detonators would be removed and put back into that special case.

The case found at the crash site had 32 detonators missing, leading Davidge and Craig to suspect the Fat Man's warhead was armed with its detonators. "We did find four spare detonators and the 'suitcase' for a Mark IV device in the wreckage, suggesting there may have been an actual nuclear device on board, minus the plutonium warhead," Davidge explained.

"The IFI tool was designed to replace red with green plugs to 'make it go.' Apparently there were four lenses, four 'go' plugs and four 'no-go' plugs, that had to be switched. What colour were the ones in the case?" Jim Laird asked. "Red or sort of rusty orange-red colour! These were not spares and not detonators: they're the ones they took out of the bomb. Put the green ones in; you've got somewhere to put those things. They had to have four of the things to change over to make it live." [16]

The question remains, was there an active core on board? The case of detonators found at the crash site may point in that direction. To arm such a nuclear bomb, 32 detonators would have been placed inside the bomb. They would all implode within, perhaps, one-hundredth of a second of each other. Their implosion would set off an eight-inch-diameter core the crew would have placed, by hand, in the centre of the bomb.

The bomber was carrying more than 300,000 pounds of gear, fuel and weapons. The manifest of the bomber's load list mentions an 11,000-

pound item, the "Fat Man" bomb, and also a 67-pound item, locked away in its own compartment. The manifest does not specifically identify what this item was, but its weight "is in the exact right range [for a plutonium core]," said Craig. "They wouldn't mention it unless it was important." This is actually the first item on the list under "cargo and miscellaneous."[17]

This evidence does not convince Scott Deaver that the plutonium core was on board. "It would have been historically impossible. The Atomic Energy Commission, a civilian body, had exclusive control of the plutonium balls; the military didn't have access," he said. "They always used fake or dummy ones [made of lead] for practice. They'd never risk putting a real capsule into this thing in case it crashed. They practised with dummy ones until the late '50s. Then they phased them out and they all became self-arming."[18]

Faced with the manifest and the four plugs Craig assembled, Craig and Davidge came to believe there indeed *was* a nuclear bomb on board. "I was skeptical there would actually be a bomb on board," Davidge admitted. "But with the information we've found out [in the manifest], and the evidence we found at the site [the four plugs], I've started to sway the other way."[19]

With regard to the plutonium core, which when inserted into the bomb would trigger a nuclear explosion, there are three possible scenarios. It was either not carried on the aircraft; it was jettisoned prior to the bailout of the crew; or the US Air Force recovery-and-demolition team recovered it intact in 1954.

The DND–Environment Canada team on Mount Kologet left the detonator case with its four remaining detonators inside the fuselage of Bomber 075, where it had been found. Because of the detonators' unknown characteristics, the team was not sure how unstable they might be and decided not to remove them by helicopter. The TNT and some other ammunition were also left on site to be disposed of by the DND Explosives and Ordnance Demolition (EOD) group. The team was only checking the site for radiation; explosives experts would have to revisit the area at a future date. Souvenir hunters later removed this case and at least one of the detonators from the site.

Strewn among ice and jagged rocks, the remains of Bomber 075 were a garden of twisted steel. The widely scattered debris was strongly concentrated in an area of about 165 feet downslope by 100 feet across the slope. Major components such as a wing panel, engines, burnt cockpit, main fuselage, landing gear and an unburned section of tail fuselage were within this zone, with a sparse scattering of smaller debris spread over a much larger area.

This wide scattering of artifacts was the result of the demolition work done in 1954. Engine components, consisting of cylinder and piston fragments, were blown over the saddle up to 500 feet from the main wreckage zone. The remains of the starboard wing and engines were located immediately adjacent to the main fuselage. Portions of the aircraft forward of the wing, including the main landing gear, forward bomb bays and cockpit, appeared to have been completely destroyed by a fire.

Evidence of demolition by high explosives was found, with pieces of the engines, wing and turret scattered a considerable distance from the wreck site, in some cases up to 1,600 feet away. A section of the aircraft aft of the wings, including portions of the rear bomb bay, several engines and three 20-mm twin-gun turrets, was found to be relatively intact. The bomber's aft portion appeared to be inverted and almost collapsed upon itself, but there was no evidence of fire or demolition by high explosives.

"I would say about 20 percent of the aircraft is still visible, all of which is pretty much collapsed or in relatively poor shape," said Davidge in 1997. "The remainder either burned on impact or was destroyed by demolition and is strewn about in tiny little pieces, some 1,640 feet away from the crash site."[20]

Scattered around the crash site were many of the crew's personal effects: a cologne bottle, hairbrush, a small souvenir totem pole purchased in Alaska and an insignia pin from the Seventh Bomb Wing with a motto that translates as "Death from Above." There were also leather flight caps with goggles, propeller blades and a ball turret with 20-mm guns.

Partly covered in the snow was a metal barrel still attached to a parachute. The barrel, which would have been airdropped to the demolition crew, contained weathered bricks of TNT. The 1954 demolition team apparently had missed a 36-foot-long section of fuselage and several engines. This aft section, just forward of the tail, was probably covered with snow and ice at the time.

Late in the summer of 1997, after more snow had melted, more artifacts came to light: survival kits, suitcases, things that had just been freed from the ice that summer. The remainder of the aircraft's wreckage consisted of waste metal and other miscellaneous debris. Survival equipment, oxygen cylinders, instrumentation and engine covers were scattered around.

The nose section of the B-36 was still easily recognizable. It was bashed in, and a large area of rock in front of the aircraft's nose was discoloured, probably due to fire. Though the windshield wipers were still there, all instruments had been removed. All but one: Bomber 075's compass was still recognizable from the flight deck.

Parts of the shattered housing of the aircraft's radome, however, were found quite a bit farther upslope, at the edge of the ridge.[21] As the radome was the part of the aircraft to hit first, the nose of the aircraft probably originally ended up near the top of this little ridge. Over time, it worked its way down as the result of gravity, downslope movement of snow and ice, and possibly the demolition operation.

An aerial photograph of the wreck taken in 1954 clearly showed bomb bays No. 1 and No. 2 right behind the wings. Farther back, in the largest part of the fuselage that was pretty well left intact, were bomb bays No. 3 and No. 4. Even farther down was the location where the tail section was blown up.

Immediately behind where the cockpit used to be, a crater was clearly visible. The hole indicated that a big explosion took place in this spot— an explosion that destroyed the part where bomb bays No. 1 and No. 2 would have been, where they would have carried the Mark IV nuclear bomb. That a big explosion took place in this spot was obvious. But what kind of an explosion?

The B-36 contained a lot of magnesium in its airframe. Once that caught fire, the magnesium burned so hot that water, and thus snow and ice, were broken down into oxygen and hydrogen, which in turn fed the fire. The heat caused incredible destruction and melted the aluminum and magnesium into slag. The main parts of the aircraft that were affected by the burn included the first, second and third bomb bays, the forward turret area, the forward crew area and the cockpit. There was nothing recognizable in bomb bays No. 2 and No. 3 as a result of the fire.

Only the bomb shackles in bomb bay No. 1 survived and were found well ahead of the area where the bomb bay should have been. Perhaps they were blown clear by the explosions.

Bomb bay No. 1 contained two shackles used to hold a Grand Slam/ Blockbuster conventional bomb or a Mark IV atomic bomb. Each of the two shackles had two release clips. All four shackle-release clips still grasped the lug from a massive object like a Mark IV bomb. Bomb bays No. 1 and No. 3 also carried giant fuel tanks to extend the range of the aircraft. These empty tanks were hung from the major bomb racks, just like the Grand Slam bomb.

The main instruments were just slightly uphill from the cockpit, and pieces of the bomb bay were found far up the hill toward the aircraft's wing showing the giant "USAF" marking. This USAF wing sign was probably the underside of the port wing. Perhaps during an explosion the wing broke away and flipped over while the main body of the aircraft slid downhill.

The rear No. 4 bomb bay survived fairly intact. The rear crew compartment was torn apart and lay almost totally upside down. The bomb-bay doors were missing, but the opening faced up the side of the hill. The rear-turret area was also mostly on its side or upside down.

It is not clear how much of the wreck actually burned on impact. At the time of the crash, the aircraft should still have been carrying an estimated 18 hours' worth of fuel. Although there was evidence of fire at the crash site, the thousands of gallons of fuel certainly did not cause much of the aircraft to burn. The aerial shot taken in 1997 from the helicopter right over the wreck showed that the ground directly below the wreckage, but not much else, had burned.

Barry Borutski is an avid B-36 researcher whose obsession with solving the mystery of Bomber 075 has taken him to the crash site on at least two occasions. He was an avionics technician with Smithers-based Central Mountain Air when he first visited the crash site on August 2, 1998. Borutski speculated in 2002:

> Our idea is that because there was so much snow there when she [Bomber 075] landed, I don't think she burned. I think she was sitting there intact with fuel in the tanks and when

they blew it up, the fuel caught fire and burned the ground.

And if you take a close look at the picture, you can see where there had been only a little bit of fuel left. Because when they did detonate the aircraft, she caught fire and burned the ground a little bit. You wouldn't have seen that if there was 15 or 20 feet of snow, like she had come in on. If she would have broken up [on landing], the fuel would have exploded and then it would have burned. But there would be no surface residue left on the ground. She wouldn't have burned 15 feet of snow.[22]

Borutski also commented on the airplane's front end. "The nose of the bomber showed no impact damage at all. The front windshield there, which shows a nice big silver piece going around there, that is actually part of the fuselage, was completely intact. And there was no damage on the window lattice. Usually the nose would start to feel the impact. And then you would get all the crush damage as you went further back. But it's completely intact."[23]

In an article in *Flight Journal*, Borutski described the crash scene as it appeared in August 1998, possibly the most snow-free of any year the site had been inspected.

To our right, down a small slope, was a container labelled "Geiger counter." Its original packing lay to one side, undisturbed for 44 years. A bit farther on was the site of the recovery team's base camp. Old, intact military rations lay exactly where they had been placed. They were still quite tasty despite their exposure to the elements. Mess kits, old bayonets, and flashlights were left as though the team would be right back. As we climbed on the ridge, I could identify the top of the vertical stabilizer, which was a short distance away from what remained of the tail. Because the tail was 46 feet high and contained no electronics, no explosives had been placed in it. It was mangled, but the pieces were substantial.

Close to the vertical stabilizer lay the remains of a fire-damaged 20-mm M-24 cannon. A number of 20-mm shells lay scattered in the same area; all showed evidence of extreme heat or explosion…As we stood halfway up the ridge, we could see the biggest piece of intact debris: the tail section, which was inverted with its huge bomb bay doors facing the sky. It was about 50 feet long, and the Stars and Stripes were still visible, their colours bright and solid. Huge landing gear struts formerly concealed in the large wings lay on their sides, ravaged by the fire.

From our vantage point, we could see one of the B-36B's six Pratt & Whitney R-4360 power plants [engines]. As we walked up to the engine to examine it, my first impression was that it had just been removed for service. There was no corrosion at all; its fittings and attachments were still shiny. This particular locale is uniquely suited to preserving crash debris because it is snow-covered much of the time. There is, however, only a six- to eight-week window of opportunity to visit the site before the snows commence.

Climbing onto the tail section, I was presented with a view of the bomb bay area where the Mark IV once lay secure in its bomb rack. A small control panel, still clearly marked, "Aft Bomb Bay Door Emergency Switches," gave silent testament to the past.

Alongside the fuselage lay huge black electronic boxes that had once been used for the upper and lower 20-mm gun turrets. Though these arming and aiming systems for the 20-mm cannon are large by today's standards, they were state of the art back in 1950. It was a surprise for me to discover so many black boxes, as they were supposed to have been destroyed in 1950. I could also easily identify the computer, the thyraton controller and gun synchronizer. I did not observe any material or parts from the AN/APG-3 [General Electric tail-gun-aiming] radar system. It would appear that the recovery team had been very efficient in their demolition of this system.

At the midsection of the tail, I discovered a spectacular example of the defensive firepower of this huge aircraft.

Peering into the tail cavity, I quickly identified two complete General Electric 20-mm gun turrets. Upside-down, protected from the elements, both turrets were in excellent condition. The 20-mm cannon barrels on the inside turret still showed the protective paper wrappings from the factory. These guns were installed but never fired; the tied-back electrical connectors confirmed this. Although each gun magazine held 600 rounds of 20-mm cannon shells, evidence points to the fact that this particular flight was not a live-fire exercise.

The defensive components of this aircraft were only for weight considerations. At the very end of the tail section, where the vertical and horizontal stabilizers should have been, was the only evidence of personal effects and survival gear. Military flight bags and personal luggage revealed an assortment of items, all abandoned on that fateful night in 1950. A plastic soap container, once used by some crew member 50 years ago, revealed an intact, still-fragrant bar of soap and yellow B.F. Goodrich survival suits with unused rafts and Mae Wests.[24]

When I visited the crash site during the shooting of the Discovery Channel production *Lost Nuke* in late August 2003, the conditions were ideal. A mild winter followed by a warm summer had left very little snow around the wreck. In the valley below the crash site was the campsite that was used in 1954 by the US Air Force Special Operations team that destroyed the B-36 bomber. Littered across the site were dozens of objects, ranging from empty food tins and cargo boxes to grenade pins. As a longtime Smithers area resident, I immediately recognized a porcelain cup bearing the name Heggies. At the time, this was the restaurant/coffee shop in Smithers, only a block away from where Hunter Simpson used to work.

Among the artifacts in the main debris field was a plethora of objects. For example, some 330 feet from the impact site lay the rubber sole of a Bristolite boot.

Closer to the fuselage was the luggage of a crew member: many clothes, including dress shirts, toiletries, toothbrush, comb, brush, some purple slippers, woollen socks and still neatly folded army-issue handkerchiefs and underwear. Everything was lumped together near the remains of a suitcase. In a crack between rocks were two epaulets, sporting a metal leaf rank insignia, identifying them as belonging to Lieutenant Colonel MacDonald, one of the survivors.

In the snow near the receding ice was a notebook or diary. It was wet and could not be opened, so it was freeze-dried to later reveal its contents. Scattered in the remains of the rear crew compartment were seats, coffee machines, gunsights and a lot of survival equipment. All of the tools found near the wreck were common toolbox items. There were still at least three one-man life rafts and one immersion suit. Nearby was a large white silk parachute in almost perfect, new condition. Why was this crew parachute not used?

Probably the only important nuclear weapon artifacts left at the site were the H-frame supporting the bomb shackles and four sway braces, as well as one of the giant bicycle chain hoists used to lift the Mark IV bomb into the forward bomb bay. The H-frame was almost totally intact but had some melted metal on it, and one hoist was missing. All the sway braces were still in their final loaded position. The bomb shackles that steadied the bomb while in flight were located as well.

Photographs taken of the wreckage by the Canadian military in August 1997 had revealed the presence of the detonators needed for exploding a nuclear device, the in-flight-insertion toolkit and the "birdcage," the lead-lined container used specifically to carry the bomb's deadly plutonium core. All of these important nuclear weapon artifacts soon went missing from the wreck. During its visit in August 1997, the DND–Environment Canada team did not find any obvious human remains at the crash site. However, four small bone fragments, possibly from a limb bone, were found near a boulder about 30 to 40 feet to the rear of the fuselage. They measured about two to three inches in length. They were photographed and left on site. There was no clothing associated with the bones, and Doug Craig suspected that they were probably caribou rather than human bones. He considered them to be fairly recent and certainly not bones that had weathered for more than 40 years.

After more snow and ice had melted, however, a discovery was made in the receding snow and ice near the wreck. Glenn Miller was up north visiting his friend Corporal Gordon Sims, head of the Stewart detachment of the Royal Canadian Mounted Police (RCMP), when he heard about all the activity surrounding the B-36 crash site. Miller had a special interest in the B-36 crash. Before joining the Seattle Police Department, he had served in the US Navy, flying North American AJ Savage and Douglas A3D Skywarrior jets.

On September 10, 1997, Miller chartered Vancouver Island Helicopters to take him to the crash site. Miller found skeletal remains partially buried in a snowbank within 30 feet of the wing. Close by, the helicopter pilot found US Air Force identification tags belonging to Captain Ted Schreier, one of the lost crew members. Miller described them as standard round tags, consistent with the Navy identification tags in the 1950s. Miller held them in his hand and clearly remembers seeing co-pilot Schreier's first name on it. "The first name on the tag was Theodore," Miller recalled. "I remember that name, which is not the most common one, because one of my relatives is named Theodore."[25]

Unfortunately, the military dog tags Miller found later disappeared. They were last seen in the possession of the pilot who flew Miller into the site. Is it possible that when the RCMP later questioned the pilot about the tags, he was worried about being fined and denied having them in his possession?

Later, Miller suddenly denied any knowledge of the tags. When asked whether the helicopter pilot who flew him into the crash site had the identification tags, Miller answered, "No, that's incorrect; I don't know where that came from. Some miscommunication there."[26]

The Stewart RCMP was initially very concerned about the possibility of human remains at the crash site. Yet no one ever took any action to retrieve them nor was a coroner brought to the site. It is not known whether this was due to budgetary restrictions or because they were discouraged from doing so for other reasons. The heavily censored RCMP file about the crash site, obtained under the Access of Information Act, only mentions the possibility of visiting the crash site.[27]

The coroner's office in Prince George, BC, received pictures of the bone fragments collected in 1997 by the DND–Environment Canada team and, later, two sets of actual samples. One set of fairly recent-looking, small fragments was received from Gordon Sims of the Stewart

RCMP detachment. The other fragment came via one of the Broken Arrow Aircraft Society (BAAS) members who visited the site.

Before being posted to Trail, BC, Corporal Sims had given BAAS member Pierre Cote permission to collect some bone fragments during his next visit to the crash site. In November 1999, Cote handed over one bone fragment to Constable Jeff McArthur of the Stewart RCMP Detachment. McArthur noted that it "appears to have marrow left inside, which does not seem consistent with it being from a 1950 plane crash."[28] In early 2000, the approximately 7-inch piece of bone was sent to Dave Coverdale, the coroner in Prince George.

On September 12, 2000, while at the crash site to explode the dynamite and some of the detonators, Cote collected some bone fragments and sent them out to a pathologist to determine once and for all whether these were animal or human bones. Both sets were later determined to be animal bones.[29]

Asked whether he knew anything about human remains found at the crash site, Coverdale said that anything that had been brought to him so far had been animal bone.[30] A skeptical Doug Craig later said, "I hope he sent them to a Canadian pathologist!"

On August 1, 1998, during his first visit to the crash site since 1956, Jim Roddick did not find any bone fragments. "There was no snow or ice or anything over there. It was completely clear, a beautiful day actually, and we sure as hell didn't see any bones," Roddick recalled.[31]

In early September 2003, I also collected some weathered bone fragments. These were taken to Professor Ryan Parr at Lakehead University in Thunder Bay, Ontario. Parr had made the news in 2002 by solving a 90-year-old mystery through his positive DNA identification of an unidentified 13-month-old drowning victim from the Titanic. However, he determined that the bones were from a mountain goat, not from a missing crew member.

In early 2000, the US Air Force's Mortuary Affairs office at San Antonio, Texas, asked the Stewart RCMP Detachment for information about the B-36 crash. "In 1952, unknown [human] remains were recovered in a lake." They wanted to know whether there was any kind of coroner's report.[32] Coroner Coverdale later said that they actually requested information about the human remains found attached to a parachute near Ashdown Island in 1952. Unidentified at the time, these remains had been buried in a mass grave somewhere in the United States, possibly with one or more of the other missing crew members. A relative of one of the missing crew members had requested that the remains be exhumed for DNA testing to determine their identities.

"If I understand it correctly, this was the opening of a mass grave," Coverdale said. "Unidentified human remains of military personnel are usually buried in a mass grave." Coverdale later stated that the US Air Force "didn't like much publicity about this issue. You know what you are running against here."[33]

It was Ann Roberts-Snitsky, a relative of Lieutenant Holiel Ascol, who united the families of the five missing crew members and succeeded in obtaining permission to exhume and test the unidentified remains. Roberts-Snitsky is a retired lieutenant colonel in the US Air Force who lives in the eastern United States. When still on active duty, she was told that remains had been found by an undisclosed source. But Roberts-Snitsky had no knowledge of a USAF parachute found and considered it just a rumour.

Roberts-Snitsky was told that relatives of the missing crew members had given blood samples. As this is considered confidential and sensitive information, she was not told who supplied them. Offspring cannot give samples, only siblings or family from the maternal side.

Dr. Thomas D. Holland, the scientific director of the central identification laboratory at the Joint POW/MIA Accounting Command at Hickham AFB, Hawaii, oversaw the exhumation of remains related to Bomber 075 at Jefferson Barracks National Cemetery in Missouri. Although the process was supposed to start in July 2001, a year later there were apparently no results. The attempts to obtain DNA from the recovered remains proved unsuccessful.

"That's certainly possible," said Coverdale. "Bone loses DNA material over time. Sometimes you're lucky and you'll find some still there; sometimes you're not. If there's some skin left or something, you're okay."[34]

During the Korean War era, it was standard practice for the US military to dust all human remains before burial with a white powder that acted as a desiccant. With the discovery of and advances in DNA technology, the exhumed remains could probably have been positively identified if DNA was recovered, but the desiccant used some 50 years earlier had the effect of stripping DNA from human remains. Consequently, even well-preserved remains have no genetic markers.

"The current thinking is that the remains were treated with a formalin-based substance prior to burial and that the formaldehyde in the formalin has either destroyed the DNA or has cross-linked it in such a fashion that we are unable to extract it using normal procedures," Dr. Holland explained. "We are continuing to work on this case with the expectation that, at some future date, we will be able to obtain sufficient DNA to allow for an identification."[35]

In September 2000, Land Force Western Area of the Canadian Forces conducted an operation to destroy the unexploded ordnance still littering the crash site. On September 10, a Canadian Armed Forces CH-146 Griffon helicopter arrived in Smithers from Edmonton. With a crew of six, including two Canadian Forces Rangers, they left the next morning for the B-36 crash site but had to return because of bad weather. The helicopter went out again on September 12, dropped off the two Rangers and returned to Smithers. The captain in charge said there was a lot of snow on the site. The wings were still completely covered and only half of the fuselage was exposed. There was too much snow on the ground to see anything else.[36]

The EOD team destroyed a substantial quantity of unexploded material. Master Corporal Pierre Cote of the Terrace Patrol, British Columbia Detachment, Fourth Canadian Ranger Patrol Group (4 CRPG), was one of the Rangers who exploded the dynamite, two detonators and "what not." These two remaining detonators were found sitting by the fuselage. The Rangers were picked up again in the afternoon and the helicopter left Smithers the next day.

Canadian military explosives personnel flew into the crash site once more in late September 2002 in another attempt to detonate unexploded material left behind at the site. Shifting ice and melting snow had exposed more debris and more unexploded ordnance.

The mission was dubbed "Misplaced Arrow," an obvious reference to the crash's designation as a Broken Arrow. With the support of a pair of military Griffon helicopters from 408 Squadron, another EOD team detonated explosives. The military helicopters and explosive-ordnance team came from Wainwright, Alberta. Civilian helicopters assisted in the advance work for the mission.

The team of 40 included 30 members of 4 CRPG out of Victoria, as well as Rangers from communities in northwestern British Columbia, including Terrace, Kitimat, Smithers and Stewart. In addition to cleaning up the site, the Rangers also used the mission to simulate their emergency response to a military plane crash.[37]

At a small, level area about 4,000 feet below the crash site, the EOD team unloaded its explosives and set up a small camp. Weather conditions were difficult, trapping a team on site overnight. In preparation for the main body of Rangers to be flown in from base camp, an advance party inspected the crash site. After the 45-minute hike up to the site, Rangers performed a number of line sweeps. As on previous visits, local Ranger Pierre Cote was one of the crew scanning for explosives.

More explosives abandoned by the US demolition team in 1954 were destroyed. Rounds of 20-mm cannon shells with explosive tips from the bomber's anti-aircraft guns were also found. The explosives experts were able to explode the remaining detonators. In all, the Rangers filled eight sandbags with about 250 pounds of various forms of ordnance. All of this was added to a drum of TNT found by the advance party the previous day. The gathered explosive materials were overlaid with 120 pounds of C-4 plastic explosive and blown up. Al Beattie, Ranger Patrol Leader for Kitimat, said that they heard the boom in their base camp 12 miles away. "What they lit off there was enough to get rid of most of Kitimat," he recalled.

"We destroyed the canister[s] of collected ordnance at the top of the mountain, one beside the fuselage and two canisters to the right of the fuselage. And there's another 1,500 and 2,000 pounds still loose on the site. The canisters that we found last year were probably canisters that hadn't seen the light of day since 1954," Cote said. "They were freshly painted and the parachutes were in mint condition. There was about five feet of snow, plus one and a half to two feet of ice on top of them."[38] The explosives had to be destroyed because they were unstable.

CHAPTER 12

What Was Known About the Bomb?

On June 8, 1989, Lynn Hunter, the New Democrat Member of Parliament for Saanich–Gulf Islands, quizzed External Affairs Minister Joe Clark in the House of Commons about the atomic bomb dropped off the British Columbia coast in 1950.

In response, the Canadian government dismissed the allegation that the US Air Force had dropped a live nuclear bomb. An external affairs department spokesman said the government knew in 1986 of a US Department of Defense report acknowledging that Bomber 075 had dropped the bomb with a dummy nuclear warhead. He said that the bomb drop and subsequent crash (reportedly on Vancouver Island) had been acknowledged in a 1986 letter from then-Associate Defence Minister Paul Dick to Jim Fulton, New Democratic MP for Skeena. Dick wrote that the unarmed bomb had been ditched in international waters and that since there was no nuclear material involved, the incident could not be considered a threat to Canadian health and safety. "There's nothing new here. It's an old story," the spokesman said, after Joe Clark confirmed the incident in the House of Commons. "When there are nuclear weapons, there are going to be accidents."

Clark said later that day outside the House of Commons that he was unaware of the US report and that it was only an allegation by an environmental group, Greenpeace. Josh Handler of Washington, DC, a

Greenpeace research coordinator, said it was just "plain dumb luck" that the bomb did not contain nuclear material because US aircraft carried nuclear bombs at the time. Hunter maintained that the bomb was "an operational weapon" and that people had the right to know of any danger. She expressed skepticism about the US report of there being no danger of a nuclear explosion, adding, "It would not be in their interests to admit that type of accident because it would impair relations with Canada."[1]

Glenn Miller, a former US Navy heavy delivery/nuclear weapons specialist, is sure that Bomber 075 had *two* weapons on board, one being an early version of the Mark V. "Even when I was in [the service], we carried Mark Vs. The only difference with the ones we had and the ones that were in the aircraft [Bomber 075] is that they were an implosion type where they had the detonators that caused the pressure from all sides [as] opposed to the shotgun version."[2]

Chris Thorp, a member of the DND team that checked the crash site for radiation in 1997, said the team did not find any evidence to indicate that the bomber had carried a second nuclear bomb or core. "Our indications say no. We went there to prove whether it was still, in fact, on site and everything we accounted for definitely seems to indicate that there was nothing not explainable on that site."[3]

With some early models of nuclear weapons, the standard procedure during most operations was to keep the nuclear core separate from the actual weapon for safety purposes. It was also standard procedure to store the nuclear cores in lead boxes, commonly known as "birdcages." Since the early cores were extremely valuable as well as dangerous, much effort went into their preservation. The early birdcages had parachutes attached to them. In case of over-water flights, these birdcages also had to have an automatic self-inflating one-man dinghy attached.

"According to the Canadian military historian Dr. John Clearwater, they could have thrown the warhead out of the window," said Doug Craig. "I am wondering a little bit if they in fact did. They almost certainly dropped the 11,000-pound shaped charge without the warhead in it [but armed] with those 32 detonators. But not the warhead. Maybe they did in fact throw the warhead out separately."[4] An anonymous former B-36 and B-52 pilot told Jim Laird "that if I was in that situation with a 'pit' on board, I would have chucked it into the sea."[5]

Less than two months after the crash of Bomber 075, a Boeing B-29 with a nuclear bomb aboard crashed in New Mexico. The detonators were installed in the bomb. Both the weapon and the capsule of nuclear material were on board, but the capsule was not inserted for safety reasons. The bomb case was demolished in the crash and some high-explosive material was burned in the gasoline fire that ensued. Four spare detonators in their carrying case were recovered undamaged.

After the wreckage of Bomber 075 was eventually found, independent research at the crash site suggested that there was not a core on board Bomber 075. Craig thought that the aircraft did not contain a "real" bomb, since no gamma ray contamination was found at the crash site. "There is no radioactive material on site because there never was any in the aircraft. Had there been a bomb there, whether it was still in the crate or carried separately, it would have [contaminated the site] the same way as the nuclear reactor in Pickering, Ontario, which contaminated the structure of the building. And the sensitivity of our scintillometer [a scientific instrument that measures ionizing radiation] was such that it would have been blown off scale by the contamination of the structural members of the aircraft. They [the instruments] went just crazy near the cockpit dials."

The DND–Environment Canada team took a gamma ray spectrometer reading within about three feet of the crate. "So that tells you, and even if it would have been [encased in] lead, those instruments would have responded. Highly penetrated radiation, buried or otherwise, probably would even have made the rocks radioactive," Craig explained. "If somebody would have picked it up and moved it a mile, the structure of the aircraft would still be radioactive. All this can easily be verified."[6]

As Bomber 075 was officially only on a training flight, Chuck Hansen, author of two books on US nuclear weapons, does not believe that the bomb aboard was equipped with a radioactive core.[7] B-36 researcher Scott Deaver also believed that the B-36 did not carry a real core, "because they were not carrying them until several years later. At the time, even though it was during the Cold War, the AEC controlled the real capsules and bombs. In order for the Air Force to arm a bomb, they needed permission from the US president... The first time real capsules were released was in 1951, during the Korean War."[8]

"The first transfer of nuclear material to the [US] Air Force on April 10, 1951, is well documented and considered historically important,"[9] insisted Deaver. "To arbitrarily say that the Air Force was actually training with real material a year earlier would rewrite the history books and demands further explanation. One would have to assume that the 1951 Presidential papers on first transfer, the 1950 complaint letters by SAC General LeMay that he has no [nuclear] weapons, and many others, are fakes and forgeries—all of it a cover-up so a B-36 can carry plutonium in February 1950.

"None of the 'plutonium-site theorists' has ever explained how to get around this point, preferring to ignore it," Deaver continued. "Beyond that, even if the Air Force had real capsules in 1950, real capsules were not used to practise-arm the early bombs and were not carried on training missions. Dummy capsules were used for training, and you would expect one to be on this flight. Again, the conspiracy theorists do not address this."[10]

Dr. John Clearwater also believes that the US Air Force did not have custody of nuclear weapons at the time. "Before 1951, the AEC, and not the US military, had control over nuclear bombs," Clearwater notes. "As a result, the US Air Force borrowed the bomb for the exercise."[11]

"This is an important fact, as it shows that it is almost impossible for there to have been a nuclear capsule on board the aircraft at the time of the crash. The Mark III bomb, identical to [the bomb] dropped on Nagasaki, took many technicians a couple of days to assemble into strike configuration, thus further mitigating against an assembled nuclear bomb being present."

Clearwater believes that Bomber 075 actually did carry a nuclear weapon. "There is indeed a nuclear weapon involved, and it did have at least 40 kilograms of depleted uranium inside, although no plutonium core...I believe there was a nuclear weapon on the aircraft and that this weapon was jettisoned far closer to the Canadian coast than reported by official documents. This has been proven to be true in the case of the Mark-43 lost in the Sea of Japan; it was far closer to Japan than reported."[12]

Pierre Cote disagreed and believed that Bomber 075 did carry a live core. The Soviet Union had detonated its first atomic bomb just half a year before Bomber 075's last flight. The Soviet Union's exploding its own nuclear weapon heightened Cold War tensions. "There was no way they were flying without a live core," said Cote.

Cote observed that no more clues in this regard were expected to come to light until after 2010, when more US military documents were due to be declassified. Unfortunately, the terrorist attack of September 11, 2001, has resulted in permanent closure of all US classified military files.

Whether or not the bomber carried an operational core, the fact is that it had a real atomic weapon on board. After all, Bill Sheehy and William Borden of the AEC were pretty anxious to know "what the hell they [the US Air Force] did with one of our atomic weapons."[13] Although Major General White stated that the bomb did not contain the plutonium core, he did not mention what happened to it.

If there was a nuclear core on board, the crew may have bailed out with the core or jettisoned it. It is more likely, however, that the core stayed on board the aircraft until it crash-landed. US military personnel either then recovered this highly secret device in 1954 or it is still under the debris, snow and rocks on the crash site. In that case, it may not be detectable as the cores were housed in shielded cases, Cote said.

CHAPTER 13

What Happened to the Bomb?

The crash of Bomber 075 happened at a time when the Cold War was heating up. Though several of the official documents dealing with this accident have been declassified and are available under the Freedom of Information Act, an unknown amount of information is still held in top-secret files and cannot be accessed. The very fact that the US Air Force has been evasive and misleading with both official and unofficial representatives from Canada since 1950 perpetuates suspicions regarding their motives, actions and inactions. To enforce the secrecy of the US Air Force Board of Inquiry, witnesses were all read Air Force regulation AFR62-14a, which is essentially an oath of silence. Why were the proceedings of the board kept secret? Why could no reference be made to what the aircraft was carrying?

Given the confusion right after the crash, it is not surprising that there would be conflicting reports. With the US military suppressing information and altering facts, everything became even more muddled.

The day following the accident, several newspapers reported that transmissions, presumably received from the missing bomber, ended shortly before 3:00 AM. At that time, the aircraft's last message would have been from the pilot who was contemplating "ditching" in the water.

Did the US authorities give out this time, or did it originate from the transmissions received by civilian operators? Was the part about "ditching" in the water intentionally added to ensure that the bomber had "disappeared"?

Obviously, Captain Barry and his co-pilot, Lieutenant Whitfield, did not get their stories straight about how the bomb was jettisoned. Barry testified in secret that the bomb-bay doors and salvo mechanism did not work the first time, but that the co-pilot was able to drop the load on a second try. According to Whitfield, however, because the bomb doors had jammed, he had ordered the T-handle to be pulled, allowing the weapon to be dropped through the partially opened bomb doors.

The bomb was reportedly dropped and detonated. Crewmen testified to seeing the bomb explode 3,600 feet above the water. Given their circumstances, hastily preparing to jump into a pitch-dark night, how could they possibly have been able to ascertain the height at which the bomb detonated?

Over the years, the mysteries surrounding the fate of Bomber 075 have continued to fuel suspicion. And suspicion leads to more questions and more discoveries. Was there, for example, a possibility that the bomb reportedly ditched in Queen Charlotte Sound was not destroyed as some surviving crew members had described? Not long after Bomber 075 disappeared, the US military dropped a series of depth charges in the area without ever telling the Canadian government why they were doing it there.[1] After all, a bomb the US Air Force jettisoned over the Savannah River at Wassaw Sound on the Georgia coast in 1958 did not detonate.

Did the crew not drop the bomb? Or did they just drop the "dummy"? The aircraft may have carried a second bomb, another Mark IV, or as Glenn Miller claims, an early version of the Mark V bomb, which stayed on the aircraft.[2]

Although the US military claimed that the bomb did not contain an active core, it did contain 2.5 tonnes of high explosives and 88 pounds of uranium. If the bomb was dropped and exploded, depleted uranium would have been scattered over the Pacific Ocean.

There are also unanswered questions about the wooden box thrust from the aft escape door of Bomber 075 amid the five bailouts that occurred there. Did the box really contain "radio parts"? And why was it so important to drop this box ahead of crew members?

Crew member Dick Thrasher, when questioned decades later about this wooden box, emphatically denied that such a box was thrown from the rear compartment before he bailed out third. Thrasher had some trouble with his own exit, being caught momentarily in the small hatch. Was that enough to cloud his memory? Surely the man who was jumping right after valuable time was spent pushing out the box would have remembered waiting for that!

Bob Baragar considers it odd that Thrasher would have no knowledge of the wooden box. He speculated that since Staff Sergeant Stephens and Lieutenant Darrah bailed out of Bomber 075 after Thrasher, one of them might have kicked out the box after Thrasher jumped.[3]

Scott Deaver did not think there was anything unusual about the box. "The 'radio parts' must have been vacuum tubes or electronics of some kind, based on the description of the finders. The tubes from everything from the radio to the radar to the tail gun set might have been considered secret enough to throw out," he suggested.[4]

Any vacuum tubes or other electronics jettisoned without a parachute, however, would certainly not have survived the landing undamaged. This may have been done on purpose. On the other hand, if it were done to prevent these sensitive materials from falling into enemy hands, would it not have been better to leave them on board the aircraft?

Thrasher's denial, however, did not surprise Doug Craig. When he first started looking into the possibility of a contaminated site in the late 1990s, Craig got in touch with a former US Air Force pilot. "I think he was a B-36 pilot, but certainly a B-52 pilot." This man gave Craig quite a bit of background information and then suddenly said, "This probably has all been in the press. You probably already have heard it, but please don't attach my name to it."

"And that's only six or seven years ago," Craig added. "In other words, he's doing the same thing as Thrasher, basically denying it. They say, 'That's a closed book; forget it.' But when I ask, 'What about letting me have a peek at it,' they say, 'Bugger off.' They were certainly trained to be close-mouthed, weren't they? So whether you can put something else of equal strategic value [on board], it would take some doing because it would be pretty conjectural, wouldn't it?"[5]

If this was just a routine flight, why was a high-ranking officer such as Lieutenant Colonel Daniel MacDonald on board? Referred to as "being of the office of director of plans and operations in Air Force headquarters, Washington, DC" or sometimes just as a "passenger," MacDonald's official position on the aircraft was that of an "ORT Observer." Was MacDonald the bomb commander?

As previously noted, carrying an operational nuclear bomb required a special two-man crew: the bomb commander and a weaponeer. The bomb commander, usually a colonel, was responsible for coordinating the bomb assembly and delivering the bomb at the loading site. He also supervised the weaponeer and certified the bomb as ready. It was the weaponeer—Schreier, in 075's case—who armed the bomb.

Despite rumours that skeletal remains were found on the aircraft at the crash site in 1954, why is it not possible to get any information about Captain Schreier from the US Air Force? There must be records somewhere indicating whether he is still officially missing or if his remains were buried in 1954. Endless queries to the Air Force Historical Research Agency at Maxwell AFB and the US Total Army Personnel Command have gone unanswered.

Perhaps because several crew members were aware that Schreier was not the second-last man to jump, Captain Barry was later told to change his story. Also, in the official accident report Schreier's name is spelled "Scherier." It's the only misspelled name; was this just a typo, or an attempt to hide the real Schreier?

Why did Schreier risk his life by staying on the aircraft? "Schreier was either a fanatic or suicidal," argued Doug Craig, a firm believer that Schreier flew the bomber inland. "Fact is that he almost landed the aircraft because it was largely intact."[6] Did Schreier risk and ultimately lose his life in a single-handed attempt to keep US nuclear weaponry and secrets from falling into enemy hands? Was it a live core that kept him aboard? Could this explain the Geiger counter found at the crash site in 1956? Since the site proved to be uncontaminated, could the capsule have remained undamaged and been recovered in 1954?

"It all points to one thing. Granted, the plane was worth saving, but what the hell was he protecting?" asked Jim Laird, another who believes that Schreier had stayed aboard.[7] Historian Barry Borutski speculated that it was the plutonium core. Former weapons specialist Glenn Miller offers a more expansive theory. "The aircraft carried two nuclear weapons, one actually being an early version of the Mark V."[8] Miller may be wrong about the Mark V, but maybe Bomber 075 was armed with two Mark IV bombs.

According to the research of Dr. John Clearwater, the US Air Force did indeed have two Mark IV atomic bombs on loan from the Atomic Energy Commission in February 1950. After these had been picked up from one of the two storage sites, two Boeing B-50 Superfortress bombers had flown them to Carswell AFB, where they were loaded on B-36s for the ferry flight to Eielson AFB. "44-92075 [Bomber 075] was not alone on the mission. It was joined by 44-92083 [Bomber 083] of the same squadron, and also armed with a real Mk-4 atomic bomb."[9] But as a crew member of Bomber 083, Staff Sergeant Denzel Clark would certainly have been aware of having a Mark IV aboard his aircraft. Since no other references were found about Bomber 083 carrying a nuke, Bomber 075 may have carried both of the bombs on loan.

There is some reference that during the atomic bomb tests in the Pacific, a B-36 was modified to carry two nukes, a small one ("Little Boy") and a large one ("Fat Man"). In the context of space and weight, a former B-36 crew chief observed that the aircraft's two bomb bays could either hold one H-bomb each or two A-bombs per bomb bay. For A-bombs of the "Fat Man" class like the Mark IV, this would be possible with regard to capacity, though the 11,000-pound weight of these units would have been a serious gross weight consideration. "If someone told me that a B-36 carried two A-bombs at that time, I would not be surprised," former B-36 crew member Charlie Ronchas observed.[10]

Why was the US Air Force so determined in late 1953 to demolish their B-36 on Mount Kologet? Earlier in 1953, two other Peacemakers had gone down on Canadian soil. These two wrecks, the first in Labrador, the second in Newfoundland, were in similarly isolated terrain but never subject to the same demolition treatment.

The US Air Force had removed all the sensitive, secret equipment from these two other aircraft, though they did not go through all the trouble of blowing up the bombers' remains as with 075. What made the bomber on Mount Kologet different? Was it the deadly cargo it had been carrying, or was the aircraft more intact than the others?

Lost Nuke in Labrador

On February 12, 1953, B-36H Serial 51-5729 from the Seventh Bomb Wing, Carswell AFB, Texas, crashed after running out of fuel while holding for traffic at the SAC base in Goose Bay, Labrador. Two crew members in the rear compartment were killed in the mishap.

Just weeks before the accident, on January 3, 1953, one of the survivors, Colonel George T. Chadwell, assumed command of the Seventh Bomb Wing and was wing commander until June 4, 1954. In this position, Chadwell was privy to information that would never be made public.

Tina Chadwell Weiss remembers the crash. "I was only five years old at the time. I actually do remember the days surrounding the crash. My dad died on active duty when I was in my teens, so I never discussed the crash with him more than briefly. It just became a story I passed on to my children about the grandfather they never knew and that it was the reason we always flew separately as a family."

In 2007 Chadwell Weiss opened the old trunk marked "George Chadwell, Army A.C." at the family home. Inside were a dozen eight-by-ten-inch photos marked "Restricted, Security Information." Chadwell Weiss says the photos clearly show that the B-36 aircraft was in two pieces.

"I was really excited to see them," she says. "It was eerie seeing [a contemporary aerial shot of the crash site] with years of new trees compared to the aerial view taken in 1953. After viewing all of the close-up photos, it is hard to imagine how anyone survived the impact."[11] Today the area cleared of trees by the crash is filled in with younger trees of a lighter green than the surrounding old growth.

Although located about 10 miles off the approach end of Goose Bay's runway 08, the site is virtually accessible only by helicopter. When Blair Rendall visited the wreck in 1978, there were 5,000 rounds of ammo still on board. "I crawled in the tail and there were two boxes there on the fuselage, either side, with printing: 600 rounds 20-mm each. The ammo was still neatly stacked in the boxes as it was 20 years before." For safety reasons the ordnance was removed the following year. The turret and the guns are now gone as well. The Eighth Air Force insignia and registration number are still clearly visible on the tail section.

Lost Nuke in Newfoundland

The second B-36 crash occurred only 34 days after the Labrador incident. Just after midnight on March 18, 1953, RB-36H-25, Serial 51-13721, was en route from Lajes Airdrome in the Portugeuse Azores to its home base, 10 miles northeast of Rapid City, South Dakota. It veered off course in bad weather and crashed on Random Island, Newfoundland. The B-36 struck a 900-foot ridge overlooking Smith Sound, at an elevation of 800 feet. Brigadier General Richard E. Ellsworth and 22 other crew members were killed. In honour of General Ellsworth, Rapid City AFB, South Dakota, was later renamed Ellsworth AFB. An SB-29 search and rescue aircraft involved in the search for this Peacemaker disappeared and none of its 10 airmen were ever found.

Operations to retrieve the remains of the lost crew and salvage sensitive equipment was difficult. Boats were used to cross over to Lower Lance Cove. Today, the site is not quite as remote and can easily be reached by a well-marked trail, about half a mile from the road, to a slate quarry at Nut Cove.

The crash site has remained virtually undisturbed since the US Air Force salvaged certain parts in 1953. Most parts of the bomber's structure are still in place. Over the years, local people have salvaged some of the wreckage, as well as most of the armament. A local youth dragged one of the guns from the scene about a dozen years ago and mounted the electrically operated cannon on a workshop wall. Elsewhere, in nearby towns, there are many parts of the wreck sitting on display in rec rooms or just stored away in basements.[12]

The main wreck is located at the lower end of a small, steep-sided valley. A large piece of the tail section, which has turned 180 degrees relative to the line of fuselage debris, is intact and perfectly upright. A dead tree stump has pierced the starboard stabilizer. The six large pusher engines and one jet pod are still on site. The other three jet pods, however, have gone missing.

Although large sections of wing are scattered around, there is remarkably little of the fuselage. The front section of the fuselage is burned out; the adjacent area is covered in aluminum ash and debris. Nearby are the remains of the cockpit-window frames, pilot seats, nose wheels, turrets and the starboard main bogie. Other wreckage may have gone over the ridge.

At the top of a ridge, a propeller forms a memorial with the names of all the crew members and words taken from Isaiah 40:31: "They shall mount up with wings as eagles; they shall run and not be weary; and they shall walk, and not faint."

A later-declassified document states that the dummy capsule on board Bomber 075 did not contain any radioactive material and that a nuclear detonation had not been a possibility. However, the rest of the document—with headings such as "Weapon Type," "Amount and Type of Radioactive Material," "Amount and Type of HE," "Status of Nuclear Explosive Assembly Components (Los Alamos)," "Status of Fusing and Firing and Ballistic Components (Sandia)" and, finally, "Justification for Investigation Closure"—has been carefully removed.[13]

In the case of the 1953 B-36 crash near the small town of Lacock, Wiltshire, England, the bomber came down in a more densely populated area on foreign soil, so USAF crews there did a thorough cleanup of the area. Local civilians spoke of "hush-hush" operations being carried out to recover sensitive equipment from the wreckage. Surprisingly, the local newspaper carried no news stories of this accident, except for a single letter to the editor.

Mr. W.A. Whittock, the writer of this letter, was clearly not impressed with the pilot and crew abandoning their aircraft over a populated area in England. "I wonder what the pilot and crew were thinking...? Was it—to hell with everybody else...? I sincerely hope that no secrets were taken from the plane before the American Air Force arrived, as we are told some of the plane's equipment is on the secret list."[14]

✪

Lieutenant Richard C. Kirkland, the pilot of a US Air Force helicopter who took part in Operation Brix, has asked many questions about Bomber 075 in *Tales of a War Pilot*, his memoir of his flying career. "For several weeks, we covered every square inch of that area for miles in every direction, without a trace of the aircraft. The B-36 and whatever was in its bomb bay had simply vanished. What had happened to it? Where had it gone?" Kirkland wondered later, "Was there some kind of secret Russian interference involved? Were the two [sic] missing crew members involved in some crazy conspiracy?"[15]

"To this day I don't know what the final SAC report said, because it was classified. Our Air Rescue report simply stated that we hadn't been able to find the aircraft and two [sic] of the crew members. We had no explanation for the mystery. The bomber had been rapidly going down, with tons of ice on its wings. It could only have crashed into the western slopes of those mountains. It was impossible not to have found it but we didn't. End of report.

"An airplane that big would clear out acres of forest when it crashed." Kirkland observed. "And it would probably start one big fire, since it had thousands of gallons of JP-4 and high-octane aviation gas aboard, not to mention what else it carried that might blow up."[16]

Kirkland wrote, "By late afternoon the second day, all the crew was accounted for except two, and still no sight of the big bomber." Kirkland twice mentioned two missing crew members and raised the possibility of them being involved "in some crazy conspiracy."[17]

Barry Borutski does not think that anyone else—for example, Captain Bill Phillips, Bomber 075's navigator—remained on board as well. "I think Schreier was by himself. It wouldn't take much to navigate and fly at the same time."[18]

Authors Peter Corley-Smith and David N. Parker report in their book *Helicopters: The British Columbia Story* that all the missing crew members stayed on board the aircraft. "Five more [crew members] stayed on board. As we learned much later, they had jettisoned a nuclear bomb before attempting to continue the flight."[19]

For Kirkland, the final twist to the mystery did not come until years later. As he wrote in his book:

> I had been transferred to the East Coast and was browsing through the newspaper one morning when I found myself reading a short article about a Canadian prospector who had stumbled onto the wreckage of a giant B-36 bomber, deep in the interior wilderness of British Columbia. The article was sparse and said only that no bodies had been found and the bomber had been identified as one that had disappeared on Valentine's Day of 1950 over Princess Royal Island!
>
> I couldn't believe what I was reading. I was dumbfounded. I read the story over and over, trying to grasp some detail, some point that might provide answers to the swarm of questions that buzzed through my head. How in the world could it have flown that far when, at last report, it had been about

to crash? How could that crippled monster climb over the Cascade Mountains without a crew? What had happened to the missing crewmen? And most intriguing: what had happened to the 10,000-pound atomic bomb? The article made no mention of that.

The whole thing was unbelievable. It didn't make any sense. I was incredulous, and determined to find some answers. Over the next few days I made numerous phone calls, but I might as well have saved myself the time and trouble. I got little additional information. The newspaper didn't know any more than what had been printed and the Air Force Information Office simply said, "Classified." I even called a couple of my old Air-rescue friends, but they didn't know anything about it either.

What puzzled Kirkland most was "how could a faltering aircraft that was about to crash climb over 12,000-foot mountains? The mountains were 10,000 to 12,000 feet high, and the crew had bailed out at 5,000 feet."[20] The answer may be simple: because somebody had been flying the giant bomber!

Somehow the autopilot had been disabled or the aircraft would have flown in a straight line into the ocean. Was this a technical failure or was it caused by human intervention? The Surf Inlet mine caretaker and his wife saw the aircraft circle Princess Royal Island more than once. This means that the automatic pilot setting had been changed almost immediately after Captain Barry bailed out.

Kirkland later tested atomic bombs for the US Air Force on Eniwetok Atoll and flew 69 helicopter rescue missions in the Korean War. Kirkland was awarded the Distinguished Flying Cross, six Air Medals and the Air Force Commendation Medal. After his military career, he became manager and aerospace executive at Hughes, McDonnell Douglas, and HeliSource.

Did the US Air Force locate and visit the wreck soon after the B-36 crashed? Did they just keep a low profile about this to hide the facts about nuclear weapons being involved? Kirkland asked more questions. "What happened when they found the big bomber years later? Was the atomic bomb still in the bomb bay? If the bomb were still there, they would have to bring it out...wouldn't they? And no doubt, in secret. What a gigantic operation would have been required, and the biggest helicopter we had in those days could not have budged it."[21]

Only a few months after the crash of Bomber 075, at the end of May 1950, a chartered helicopter came through the Smithers area on its way to the Meziadin-Stewart area. Since it was only the second helicopter to come through Smithers, it made headlines on the front page of the *Interior News*: "Needless to say the strange looking aircraft caused considerable interest in the community when it landed at the Exhibition Grounds...and many residents took the opportunity to view it at first hand."

The helicopter was reportedly heading to the Meziadin-Stewart area to transfer supplies and personnel "in charting areas of the British Columbia Coast Mountain Range." Could the real mission of this "early" helicopter have been to reach the crash site?

Alternatively, the crash site could have been visited from Annette Island, Alaska, unbeknownst to the Canadian authorities and undetected by any of the few local residents.

Former area resident Dave Kuntz brings forth yet another scenario. "The US Air Force suspected the possibility of the B-36 having come down somewhere in northwestern British Columbia but liked to keep a low profile about it...By keeping a low profile, there was less chance it might be found and fall into the hands of the Soviet archenemy."[22]

Then, three and a half years later, oil millionaire Ellis Hall's missing aircraft finally gave the US Air Force an excuse to search for the missing bomber without causing any suspicion. "As soon as the bomber was located, they seemed to have lost interest in finding Hall's aircraft," Kuntz observed.

Kirkland's last point, about the logistics of flying out a gigantic atomic bomb, is especially interesting and could give the mystery a whole new angle. Was the unarmed nuclear bomb still on board the aircraft when it crashed in the Kispiox Mountains? Bringing it out at the time would indeed have been very difficult, if not impossible. If they did drop the bomb, maybe this was just the "dummy"? If the aircraft carried a second bomb, the "real thing," did it stay on the aircraft? This would also explain why the crash site remained of interest to the US authorities.

"However, because the site was under surveillance," Kuntz theorized, "they were probably worried I would land on it [the bomb] with my chopper, detonate the bomb and blow their cover by blowing the top off Kologet Mountain!"[23]

"I think the 1954 US Air Force guys didn't know it [the nuclear core] was there," Jim Laird speculated in 2003. "It must have been in the box when the 1954 expedition was there, but it doesn't look like they found anything. I think they couldn't get into that part of the aircraft. They look in the bomb bay and find nothing, and say: 'Okay, they threw it out with the bomb.' They figure that either Schreier got rid of it, or that it got thrown out with the bomb."

Why did the demolition team blow up engine No. 2? "Could they have been sent there to erase the cause of the crash," Laird wondered, "because that was a weakness? They could cross-link every fire extinguisher on both wings. He [Captain Schreier] could just keep exhausting bottles of all the other ones. If it wasn't out, there was nothing he could do. It looks like [engine] No. 3 is blown up too and No. 6 is pretty burned."[24]

"I believe they blew up bomb bays Nos. 1 and 2 there because they did not want the dimensions of that particular bomb to be configured into that bomb bay," Borutski noted. "Because Nos. 1 and 2 bomb bay doors do not exist; it's completely blown up. Bomb bays Nos. 3 and 4 are intact as is part of the tail sighting station, which they weren't interested in. Everything is starting to fit. You can't see it from the ground but the aerial shot shows that the fuel that burned, whatever fuel was left in the tanks, caught fire when they blew it up."[25]

As well, what an atomic bomb actually looked like was a secret at the time, and even as late as the 1960s. In those days, it was interesting to see artists' concepts of what a nuke looked like. They were usually portrayed as being very streamlined, with nice fins, whereas the real thing looked more like a blob.[26]

"I can't be sure exactly what happened to the bomb but a great effort was made to destroy bomb bay No. 1 where it was originally held," John Clearwater observed. "Everything was blown up; what wasn't incinerated was melted into tiny pools of metal. Everything is destroyed; the evidence is gone now."[27]

Clearwater later located the birdcage that had been removed from the crash site in 1998. It had been turned in to the US military's Defense Threat Reduction Agency (DTRA). The Connecticut man who had taken this important Cold War artifact had obviously become worried and handed it over to the DTRA. The agency released no official report on the return.[28]

Clearwater's attempt to acquire this relic of the world's first Broken Arrow for the Diefenbunker collection, Canada's Cold War museum in Ontario, failed. Though the DTRA had initially promised to return the birdcage to proper custody, the US Air Force Museum in Dayton, Ohio, had meanwhile asked for the artifact. This museum stalled all of Clearwater's attempts to gain information through legal channels and refused to confirm they had the birdcage. After having been held in Dayton for several months, the birdcage was subsequently transferred to the Department of Energy (DOE) office at Sandia National Labs in Albuquerque, New Mexico. Having originally been the property of the Atomic Energy Commission (now DOE), Sandia would seem to be the appropriate place to keep it. Though it was thought that it eventually would be given to the National Atomic Museum, which is administrated by DOE, the birdcage's current status is unknown.

"If this is just an empty container, why the continued secrecy?" Clearwater wonders. "We may never know if there was a core inside this birdcage because the Air Force and the US government have refused comment and shut the door on this case."[29]

Many questions about what exactly happened during the US's first Broken Arrow incident remain unanswered. "There's a nuclear bomb involved," Doug Craig pointed out. "You have an aircraft that flew hundreds of kilometres, maybe or maybe not on its own. There's just enough here that's tantalizing to keep the questions coming."[30]

CHAPTER 14

What Became of Ted Schreier?

Perhaps the most intriguing unanswered question is: What happened to Captain Ted Schreier? Did Bomber 075's weaponeer/co-pilot actually jump from the aircraft, or did he stay on board, keep it flying for the next three hours and give his life in a heroic effort to save "his" charge, the Mark IV atomic bomb?

Ted Schreier was born on October 3, 1915, in Cashton, Wisconsin, and attended the University of Wisconsin-Madison in 1936. After the Second World War, Schreier left the US Army Air Force for a job in civilian aviation. In 1946 he landed a job with the newly formed American Airlines and settled into domestic life with his wife, Jean, in a home on the north side of Lake Mendota, near Madison, Wisconsin. Less than a year later, Strategic Air Command, facing a pilot shortage, recalled Schreier to active duty. In fact, he was hand-picked to attend the elite Armed Forces Special Weapons Project, where he was trained as a weaponeer.

The fact that the first two crew members to leave the forward position, Captain Phillips and Lieutenant Ascol, and the first two to leave the rear compartment, Staff Sergeants Straley and Pollard, were missing indicates that they ended up in the water before the aircraft passed over land. The fifth missing man, Captain Schreier, does not fit this pattern. If he had jumped next, leaving the forward compartment just ahead of the pilot, he presumably would have landed on Princess Royal Island.

Immediately following the incident there was conflicting information about the status of Schreier and the four other missing airmen. Initially, it was reported that they had been rescued. A headline running right across the front page of the *Fort Worth Star-Telegram* read, "All Men Aboard Missing B-36 Found Alive."[1] Another headline read, "Survivors of 'Ditched' American Craft Found In Queen Charlottes",[2] while a third large-circulation paper reported that three of the men were taken off a rubber life raft some distance from the shore.[3]

During the investigation into the accident, Colonel Flickenger asked Captain Barry if, as far as he knew, everyone had successfully gotten out of the aircraft without injury. Barry confirmed this. He was then asked, "Did the bombardier get out all right?" Captain Barry answered, "Yes, he was the second man out."

Barry was only asked specifically about the bombardier. May there have been confusion about the long-used term bombardier, which historically referred to the crew member who aimed and released bombs, and the newer term, weaponeer, which was used exclusively on nuclear bombers and referred to the man who prepares an atomic bomb for detonation?

Although Barry confirmed that the bombardier was the second man to jump out of the front compartment, further questioning of crew members indicated that Schreier was probably the second-to-last man to bail out. Barry testified he was the last man out, but seemed confused about the sequence of events during bailout. It seems that Barry was not completely sure of Schreier's status when he himself bailed out, and this was reflected in his testimony: "The other man [Captain Schreier] was possibly the *next to the last* [italics are mine] man before me or second ahead of me."[4]

Barry's confirmation that the bombardier was the second man out of the front compartment is consistent with all other testimony. But given the line of questioning, was Flickenger actually referring to the weaponeer, Schreier, as the bombardier in his question, while Barry was confirming that the bombardier, who was actually Lieutenant Holiel Ascol, bailed out in the second position?

Given the clear testimony of Lieutenant Whitfield that Barry and Schreier were both on the airplane when he bailed out, there remains only one apparent contradiction. Barry claims that Schreier bailed out before him, and Whitfield claims that Schreier followed Barry out. In those brief seconds over Princess Royal Island, did Barry simply lose track of Schreier's struggle with his Mae West and parachute while making his own exit?

There was not much time between the moment Barry ordered the crew to jettison the bomb and the moment the crew started jumping from the aircraft. One airman later commented that the crew may not have taken the drill of putting on a life vest in conjunction with a parachute as seriously as they should have. Lieutenant Whitfield's testimony is critical to understanding what really happened. He pointed out to Schreier that he [Schreier] had his floatation vest on over his parachute. Schreier's reaction to this observation and the fact that Schreier was never seen again raises all sorts of possibilities.

Schreier, Barry and Whitfield were the last ones left on board. "Captain Schreier was hurriedly removing his vest [to reposition it under the parachute] when Barry ordered me out," Whitfield recalled. "Barry exited after me. I never saw Schreier jump, and he is one of the missing men. No one knows if he did or did not jump, except Barry, and he is now deceased."[5] If Schreier had jumped as stated by Captain Barry, he should have landed somewhere near Lieutenant Gerhart, Whitfield and Barry.

Jim Roddick speculated on the circumstances regarding Schreier just prior to Whitfield and Barry jumping. "Perhaps Schreier, not Barry, was the last to bail out. Whitfield's recent recollections support this view. Is it possible that his chute never opened and he disappeared in the hilly forest or in one of the small lakes of northwest Princess Royal Island?" Is it possible that Schreier flew the aircraft in this small circle to allow himself a chance to jump over Princess Royal Island in close proximity to the others?

"More likely, it took him a minute or so to readjust his Mae West straps so that they would not interfere with his parachute," Roddick continued. "By the time he would have bailed out, the aircraft under automatic pilot would probably have been back over the water. He may not even have known that Captain Barry had set the automatic pilot to do just that." This raises the possibility that Schreier did jump but either landed in the water or in a spot where he was not found.

Jim Laird suggested yet another intriguing scenario: Captain Schreier kept flying the aircraft, but later was forced to jump prior to the aircraft going down in the Kispiox mountains.

Let's just assume there was somebody on board. We know the last three guys on board were the three pilots. Out of those three pilots, Barry was aircraft commander, but he was not rated for the bomb. Whitfield told us that. Schreier went to Special Weapons School, and he was rated and he had been around for a long time; he was a Captain. Whitfield was also rated but he had the lower rank of Lieutenant. Therefore, Schreier outranked both Barry and Whitfield.

If there was a core on board, they were going to go for a last-ditch effort to save the plane and its cargo. Barry couldn't do it because he wasn't rated. Whitfield was the junior of him and Schreier, so Schreier had to do it. It also makes sense [of] why they sent out Whitfield first. It's now between Barry and Schreier. And in the end, Barry jumped and Schreier didn't. That was by arrangement, I'm sure.

According to Cox's testimony, the plane has gone south. It turned around and came back in from the west and it flies over top of him going east and does a shallow turn and heads north. So it has done a figure eight and it's heading north. The weather station at Cape St. James on the south end of the Queen Charlotte Islands reports the wind blowing at about 50 knots towards the south. So Schreier has only one place to go in his mind, and that's back to base, either Eielson or McChord [AFBs].

The B-36 either went up Skeena River or up Portland Canal and into Aiyansh; they time out about the same. I have actually physically measured the flight line; either way it is 450 miles or about three hours of flight time. There's very little flexibility in that. [By timing it out with a 50-mile headwind, at 12:30 the aircraft is halfway up in the Pitt Island-Banks Island area. One o'clock puts him off the mouth of the Skeena River.] He would be over Terrace at 1:30 a.m. But he might have met an immense fogbank going from Terrace into the mountains like the Seven Sisters.

Laird thought it was less likely that Schreier flew over Terrace, especially since he was not flying high up and no one reported seeing the aircraft.

So he flies up Grenville Channel. That's the logical place for him to go. I think ice [on the wings] is not a factor anymore. But he has two engines shut down while [engine] No. 2 is still sparking. So something is burning in there; it's like a time fuse. He would probably try and pump all the gas out of that wing into the other wing and dry the tanks right around No. 2 so it would not burn through something. Plus you lighten the wing by making the fuel go to the other tank.[6] He's flying north but this thing continues to burn. He monitors it but he can't use the radio because they weren't in contact with the [transmitting] key screwed down. At this point, he's got the detonator box, birdcage and IFI toolkit in front of the aircraft. He flips on the autopilot and goes into the bomb bay and he takes the stuff to a place where he thinks it's safer than where it is now.

It takes something like 10 to 15 minutes. He goes to the rear of the aircraft and ties it down among all the safety gear there. That has got to be the safest place because the tail is usually the one that lasts. And then he goes back to the front. He still has got no radio contact and is flying northwest into a 50-knot gale. That burns up a lot of time and a lot of fuel.

He can see that the wing is actually starting to burn, perhaps toward the No. 3 engine. So he's got a choice here; the last section from Terrace to Woodcock is pretty twisty with big mountains all around. So he flies up as far as Terrace, at the time a small town with lots of low-lying valley fog. He could inconceivably have turned and tried to go up to Woodcock. This airstrip was only a little over five years old; he probably knew about it.

He may have turned north to Aiyansh where the

Postmaster heard him. If he's at Aiyansh at 2:00 AM, he has time to fly out to the Kispiox, circle Hazelton and try to go into Woodcock the back way. But it's fogged out that way, too. So he would have possibly flown from Aiyansh northeast up to the river, and then south down the valley to Hazelton, circled Hazelton at 2:30 AM.

Engine No. 2 is now really burning bad and it has burned its way through about just up to engine No. 3. He's getting worried about it and he knows that the plane is going down. So he turns the plane and points it to a bearing of roughly 075 degrees. He then turns on the autopilot and bails out. Conceivably he could have landed in the Nass River. The only thing is maybe one day a mushroom picker might find a shoe. And of course the US Navy sent a PBY out to check it out the next morning. They flew all around Aiyansh but they didn't go inland from Aiyansh. There's just too many twists and turns with this plane.[7]

John Clearwater calls Laird's theory "interesting and coherent but totally unprovable. Although highly unlikely to be true, Laird's theory is important as it seeks to explain the unexplicable. No one has ever proven how #92075 came to be on a mountain in northern British Columbia. It remains one of the great mysteries of the Cold War."[8]

I think the aircraft took the alternate route, eventually flying up the Nass River, straight toward Aiyansh. The pilot must have spent some time over the Pacific Ocean trying to find his bearings, meanwhile probably discussing or at least contemplating his next course of action. US Air Force officials were reportedly in contact with the airport in Terrace about possibly receiving the stricken bomber there. But with nobody on duty there at night and the runway unsuitable, this left him no choice: either return to Alaska or find a large open snowfield in a remote area of the coastal mountains to attempt to make an emergency landing.

Why would Schreier's exit be singled out in the questioning, and none of the other 16 crew members? Was this just for the record to hide the fact that Schreier actually remained on the aircraft after the rest of the crew bailed out?

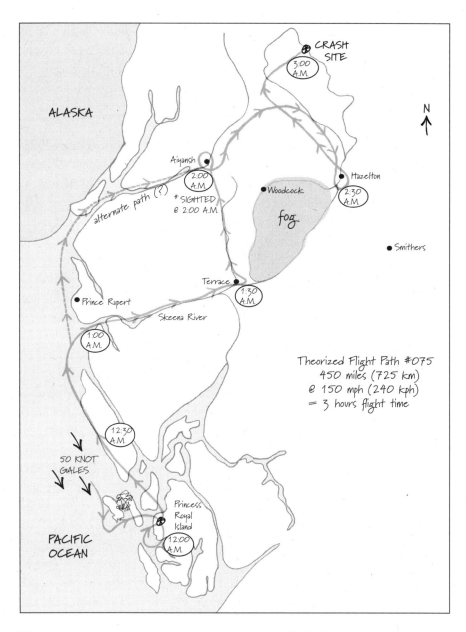

This map shows two potential routes proposed by Jim Laird to explain how Bomber 075 got to its final destination.

MAP BY SANDRA BASKETT BASED ON A ROUGH SKETCH BY J. LAIRD

179

By specifically singling out Captain Schreier, all readers of the report would be made aware that there could be no doubt about anyone staying aboard to fly the aircraft after bailout. Also, by having him bailing out as the second-to-last crew member from the front compartment, it would be easy to explain why he was missing by suggesting that he jumped into the water and drowned like the other four missing men.

The unique treatment of Captain Schreier is found in another interesting location. He is the only missing crew member of Bomber 075 who did not have a street named after him at Carswell AFB. Why was he treated differently than the four other missing airmen? Was a deliberate attempt made to keep Schreier's name out of the public eye?

"I find that subject very interesting," said B-36 historian Don Pyeatt, "and it raises some questions. I don't know the exact dates the streets were named, but perhaps at the time, the Air Force didn't know if he was dead or alive. Or perhaps he was on a super-secret assignment? The imagination can really wander about this."[9]

Doug Craig also remembered the lost adventure magazine article nominally authored by Captain Barry. "The article in the *Man* or *Stag* magazine, which I read in September 1956 and which Dr. Roddick said he kept for several years and probably lost in an office move, was ostensibly written by Capt. H.L. Barry. Maybe it was, but does it not seem strange that Barry was a closet-adventure writer with a day job of B-36 pilot?" Craig asked. "Permit me to doubt it. Further, the time window is rather small. B-36 goes down in 1950. Barry is killed in mid-air collision in Nevada not long after. And we read the article in the trash-magazine pile in the abandoned-mine site where we camped in September 1956. Do military pilots write up their crashes for magazines?"

The article actually posed more questions than it really answered. A US Air Force officer flying an aircraft with numerous secret or classified aspects, including at least the possibility of a nuclear bomb on board, writes an article on losing his aircraft? Craig recollected the article having a phrase something like "the aircraft slanting steeply down toward the sea." Craig figured the US Air Force had an agenda it wanted to make public. "We can only speculate on what that might be: to get into the popular press that the aircraft was definitely gone, not to be discovered."[10]

When a bomb was aboard a bomber, it was in the custody of the weaponeer—in this case, Schreier. As a reservist and weaponeer just for this mission, Schreier was not part of the regular B-36 crew and was probably considered somewhat of an outsider. According to some of his fellow crew members, at the time of the order to jump Schreier had been hiding in the little cubbyhole in which classified material was kept. Apparently, after the bomb was jettisoned and just before bailout, he had become very agitated and upset that the crew had thrown out "his" bomb.[11]

Despite clear evidence that if he *had* jumped, Schreier would have been among the last three to bail out, a 1997 article in the *Fort Worth Star-Telegram* stated that Schreier was one of the first five men to jump. Was this just sloppy reporting, or was it another attempt to deceive readers by making them believe Schreier had drowned like the other four missing airmen?

Roddick rejected the possibility that Schreier did not jump. "Had Schreier, an experienced pilot, decided to stay with the plane, which in hindsight would probably have saved his life, he certainly would not have flown almost due north, but probably would have tried to reach Vancouver," he said.

If Schreier stayed on board, what was he trying to save? What was worth risking his life for? Certainly not the aircraft; there must have been something else. "There is only one reason for Captain Schreier to stay and remain aboard," said Laird. "For whatever reason, he couldn't drop the weapon; so to prevent a radiological disaster, he takes the plane and turns it around and heads back to Alaska."

And then there is the question of whether Schreier in fact could have survived the crash landing of Bomber 075. "The way he came in and the way he picked out the spot, I believe that he survived," said Barry Borutski. "And did Schreier manage to activate his emergency radio after the crash? That would be the first thing, especially if his radio system was intact. The antennas would be intact because they ran on the top of the fuselage. And if he has battery power and the cockpit was intact, he was all set to go. And it is very possible that there was no impact damage at all—if he brought it in nice and just skimmed across the snow, everything would be intact. He could just power up the aircraft's battery to transmit."[12]

"The plane was about 80 to 85 percent intact, [Hunter] Simpson's relative told me," Pierre Cote added. "The nose section was still there; the wing spar, wings; the fuel was still in the fuel tanks. The tail section was still completely intact on the hill behind the engine; they did remove certain bits of material."[13]

Sergeant Harold Harvey, one of the American crew members who flew over the wreck in 1953 and airdropped supplies near it, also noted how much of the aircraft was still intact. He clearly remembered seeing an intact fuselage at the top of a ravine.

Assuming he survived his crash landing, Schreier most likely would have remained with the aircraft. Even if he had survived the crash uninjured, it would have been suicide to try to walk out at that time of the year. The aircraft at least would have given him some protection from the elements. There was lots of survival gear to keep him warm and enough food to keep him alive until he would be rescued. In the back of the fuselage, many empty, rusty tin cans were found.

It could be that the rescuers never came and Schreier eventually perished. The cause of death could have been starvation, exposure or the result of possible injuries. If the US Air Force brought out his remains in 1954, his next of kin were never informed.

Officially, Captain Schreier was said to have died on February 14, 1950, "as the result of an aircraft accident."[14] The letter to his widow stated that he had parachuted into the waters adjacent to Princess Royal Island, but the US Air Force led Schreier's family to believe that he had been flying a transport plane. "We were never told any details about the mission, what it entailed; we found out later he was the third pilot and the weaponeer," his nephew Fred Schreier explained.[15]

Clearly Captain Schreier was a Cold War hero who risked and offered his life to safeguard some highly secret materials. But how could his country celebrate him without giving away secrets and admitting to a near disaster?

PART 4

The Legend Lives On

CHAPTER 15

Heritage Wreck

Fears of the site being plundered expressed by Dr. Doug Craig in his 1997 report were well founded. "There's been a quite a bit of pillaging," he said in 1998 when he returned to the crash site with Jim Roddick. He had speculated that with the inevitable publicity about the artifacts present at the crash site and the ready availability of Global Positioning System (GPS) instruments, the site would become more vulnerable to raiding. Once the accurate location became more widely known, memento seekers removed many of the important heritage items.

On August 1, 1998, during his first return to the crash site since 1956, Jim Roddick noted that all the cannons had already been removed, but the US Air Force star emblem was still there. In addition, many other pieces of interest were gone. "I had hoped the helicopter pilots would have given it more protection than they evidently have."[1]

Because the wreck site of Bomber 075 is so remote and it receives few visitors, the ecological impact of the remaining debris is not of immediate concern. Efforts to get the crash site declared a protected area have never succeeded, though it was hoped that giving the site special status would discourage vandalism.

After a few years of lobbying, Pierre Cote and I had the crash site officially recognized under the British Columbia Heritage Conservation Act (HCA). However, without most of its important artifacts, the site is a far cry from what it was after the US demolition party left in 1954. Originally an almost intact aircraft, it is now no more than a pile of scattered debris.

Though virtually undisturbed for almost 50 years, as soon as the Canadian Armed Forces team left the crash site in 1997, it became a free-for-all for anyone wanting a piece of the B-36. Member of the team themselves removed a number of items, including one of the gun turrets that had torn loose from the tail section. "It's [the vandalism] robbing the plane of its identifiable character," Craig observed in 1998, after two summers of both private and military intrusions had decimated the site.[2]

Even before the wreck site was declared a heritage site, the salvage of military wreckage in general was prohibited without the permission of the Canadian Department of National Defence. This permission is rarely given. In Canada, all military wreckage, including ship and aircraft wreckage, belongs to either the Government of Canada or to foreign governments under the management of the Government of Canada.

After the US Air Force left Smithers in 1954, the United States did not exercise its right of ownership and, for all intents and purposes, abandoned the wreck. The federal government in Canada did not exercise its right of ownership, either. As a result, this meant that the wreckage fell under provincial legislation, through both the Heritage Conservation Act and, because the site is on Crown Land, the Province of British Columbia.[3] It is the business of the Receiver of Wreck, an officer of the Coast Guard, to locate the legal owners of a wreck.

In the late summer of 1997, a chopper belonging to Vancouver Island Helicopters was working in the area under contract for a mining outfit. In their spare time, the crew went to the site to collect artifacts, including at least one of the 20-mm cannons and all loose ammunition. That fall, the explosives case for the Mark IV nuclear bomb detonators had already been removed, although the four detonators that had been in it were reported to have been thrown among the rocks and the case was taken away empty.

Another helicopter crew based about 50 miles to the west of the site at the nearby Ellsworth logging camp along the Cassiar Highway started making regular scavenger trips into the crash site that autumn. Within weeks, many more significant relics were removed.

Highland Helicopters based at Smithers and Meziadin and a privately owned helicopter from Smithers also made trips to the crash site. Other 20-mm cannons were removed—one was slung out complete with the dismantled turret, reappearing across the border in Hyder, Alaska.

Almost a year before the wholesale and unauthorized removal of the artifacts began, Pierre Cote and I expressed concerns about protecting the crash site. On September 30, 1997, Cote sent background information on the B-36 crash to the Archaeology Branch of the British Columbia Ministry of Forests, Lands and Natural Resource Operations in Victoria, pointing out the historical importance of the wreck site. Ian Whitbread, inventory project officer with the branch, stated that he would check out how to make an application to get the B-36 site special reserve status, as had been done at the remote Mount Slesse air-crash site southeast of Chilliwack after the 1956 crash of a Trans-Canada Airlines Northstar CF-TFD, which was accompanied by the loss of 62 lives.[4]

The British Columbia Heritage Conservation Act contains penalties for those who "damage, excavate, dig in or alter, or remove any heritage object from a heritage wreck." Possible penalties for individuals include a fine of up to $50,000, imprisonment for up to two years, or both; for corporations, the penalty is a fine up to $1 million.

Under the Heritage Conservation Act, "heritage wreck" is defined as the remains of a wrecked vessel or aircraft if:

1. two or more years have passed from the date that the vessel or aircraft sank, was washed ashore or crashed, or
2. the vessel or aircraft has been abandoned by its owner and the government has agreed to accept the abandonment for the purposes of this Act.[5]

David Suttill, project officer in the Planning and Assessment Section of the Archeology Branch, promised on October 7, 1997, that he would "put word out to the local helicopter operators regarding the heritage legislation." As soon as the signs were available, he would also have the site posted.

On October 20, 1997, I met Suttill at his office in Victoria. We discussed the possibilities of getting the wreck site declared a protected area, similar to the Mount Slesse site. The site had already been protected since May 25, 1995, under the Forest Act, the Mineral Tenure Act and the Land Act by order in council.

Many of the laws, rules and regulations about wrecks favour the heritage values that the passage of time bestows on artifacts such as the remains of an aircraft. Wrecks also often possess values that are less tangible, but that can still be destroyed by thoughtless or illegal removal by salvagers.

During the late summer of 1998, large-scale pilfering of the crash site occurred. Headlines in the Terrace and Smithers newspapers read, "Downed bird is picked over" and "Group grabs Cold War relics,"[6] after employees of White River Helicopters, a Terrace-based helicopter company using a Bell 206 helicopter, slung out three gun turrets, each holding two 20-mm cannons, a five-foot-by-eight-foot US Air Force star insignia and many other items. Pierre Cote first reported this alleged theft to the provincial Archaeology Branch on September 2, 1998, which in turn immediately contacted the Terrace RCMP detachment. An investigation led by RCMP Corporal Ray Griffith unearthed a large collection of items allegedly taken from the crash site by a group of individuals who would later form the Broken Arrow Aircraft Society (BAAS).

David Suttill confirmed: "They have three complete turret systems each containing two barrels, two burned and rusted and parts of the receiver mechanisms, miscellaneous electrical equipment associated to the turrets and two airplane motor blades [propellers]. Only one of them has rifling left in the barrels and is in any kind of repairable condition."[7]

Griffith, who handled firearms matters in Terrace, said that one of the cannons was in almost-working condition. But he considered the cannons basically inoperable, as they could only be fired by the bomber's destroyed on-board firing systems. However, to be able to display the weapons publicly, they would have to be formally deactivated.

The Archaeology Branch's director, Brian Apland, stated that the artifacts removed from Mount Kologet were "currently in a secure location where they should remain pending a decision on their ultimate fate." Apland mentioned that he would get communications started between interested parties "with a view to determining what should be done with the artifacts in question. While we certainly do not condone unauthorized removal of material from heritage plane wrecks, it is our hope that some satisfactory arrangement can be made through consultation with aviation history and museum interests at the local level for protection and possible disposal of these items."[8]

The Archaeology Branch was then faced with making a decision about what would be the best course of action. The RCMP was primarily concerned about safety, because the guns involved were technically classified as prohibited weapons by the Fire Arms Section at the Vancouver Laboratory.[9] According to the RCMP, subsequent discussions with the parties involved led the RCMP to believe there was no malicious intent and laying charges was not recommended.

Because the almost-seven-foot-long turret systems weigh about 850 pounds, and only one had rifling left in the barrel and was in any kind of repairable condition, it was decided to leave them with the Terrace group for the time being. "Their hangar, where the items are now, is locked and alarmed, but they intend on moving the large parts to a metal boxcar-type storage shed on the property, which will be locked at all times, in the near future."[10]

The RCMP's decision not to lay charges left the Archaeology Branch in a difficult position because they wanted to ensure that heritage objects removed from the wreck site did not disappear into private hands. It seemed their concerns were addressed with the formation of the Broken Arrow Aircraft Society and its endorsement by the City of Terrace.

Spearheaded by the employees of the Terrace-based helicopter company, BAAS was formed to preserve this bit of Cold War history. Barry Borutski, the society's president, claimed that his founding members did not realize the site was protected under the province's Heritage Conservation Act. "To make it right, we formed a society. Our goal is to have these items brought into Terrace to be displayed in an aviation environment. We don't want [these items] to be tucked away in some forgotten spot next to a combine or farm tractor," Borutski said. "We want to give [them] a higher profile than that."[11]

Helicopter pilot and BAAS vice-president Carl Healey agreed and was of the opinion that these artifacts should be preserved under the security of an association for the public to see. The artifacts were not going to be sold for profit to private individuals. "We, however, do stress that we want these items to stay in an aviation environment and not in a dusty museum where you see canoes or tractors or combines. At least there should be some individual on hand to answer questions on a personal basis."

BAAS had ambitious plans to make Terrace the "B-36 capital of Canada." One of the first goals of the not-for-profit society was to seek permission from the BC Ministry of Transportation and Highways to create a roadside pullout on Highway 37, close to the crash site, with interpretive signs and photographs giving the history of the B-36 crash. The group had hoped to place the signs on February 13, 2000, the 50th anniversary of the incident. Borutski explained his group also wanted to set up a permanent display at the Smithers airport of some of the artifacts removed from the site. The bulk of items taken from the crash site would remain in Terrace.

When the society held its first public meeting on November 7, 1998, members of the group tried to generate interest in their plan to build a base of active members. A number of artifacts from the crash site were displayed, including a turret complete with two cannons, the aircraft insignia, a propeller blade, three separate cannons, a number of shell casings, an engine piston assembly and a number of other small objects. In addition they held in storage two more turrets with cannons, another propeller blade, a bomb winch and some parachutes. Pierre Cote, then the society's liaison officer, and Carl Healey chaired the meeting.

After the cannons had been "spiked" to render them inoperable, one turret, complete with cannons, was moved to the Central Mountain Air hangar in Smithers. Borutski, an avionics technician with this airline, started to restore it.

In Victoria, Dave Suttill maintained that Bomber 075 was "clearly a significant heritage wreck. It's from the Cold War era; it's a great curiosity." Taking a wait-and-see attitude, he could only give advice. "Respect its integrity, the same as you would if it were an aboriginal cultural site. As with most things, they're best left as they are."[12] Perhaps referring to the Bulkley Valley Museum in Smithers, he stated, "There are other groups that have an interest in this but didn't go in and take stuff out. I don't think it is really fair for us to make a quick decision saying people who took the stuff out are allowed to keep all of it."[13]

The Bulkley Valley Historical and Museum Society expressed an interest in acquiring one of the three gun turrets, complete with the 20-mm cannons, and the large US Air Force insignia, then held by BAAS. These were the two artifacts the museum society had been looking into acquiring since 1997. As a result of the expressed interest, the Archaeology Branch encouraged BAAS to share access to and interpretation of the artifacts.

Local resident Harry Kruisselbrink's recollections of the B-36 go back to those days. In 1953, he was a student in the Smithers elementary school, and the landing of a US Air Force helicopter in Smithers was the talk of the student body for days. Likewise, as a young student, Joe L'Orsa had become interested in the B-36 crash and had witnessed some of the activities of the salvage and destroy missions that were based out of Smithers.

An article in the *Terrace Standard* described the Bulkley Valley Museum's application as "setting the stage for a northwest turf war over some of the artifacts." The museum was willing to settle for the second turret complete with its 20-mm guns. This turret was not in as good condition as the one BAAS wanted to keep, but was still very suitable for indoor-display purposes. There was a third gun turret that had been exposed to the elements and thus was more suitable for an outdoor display.

Eventually, the disposition of the B-36 artifacts did turn into something of a turf war between the two groups. Despite many promises, BAAS refused to hand over any artifacts to the Bulkley Valley Museum.

Healey claimed the White River Helicopter employees had brought out the artifacts from the B-36 crash site for "safekeeping" and were hoping to keep a good number of them to make a display in their White River Helicopter office on the west side of Terrace along Highway 16.[14] Some items that had been taken from the crash site were later passed on to BAAS. They included a flight helmet, cans of "bug juice," a toothbrush and a shaving kit.

The Archaeology Branch stated in a letter to the Bulkley Valley Historical and Museum Society that "the Archaeology Branch did indicate at the time that the formation of the society (BAAS) would not necessarily lead to exclusive claims over the artifacts that were removed."[15]

It was not long before the Archaeology Branch realized that the Heritage Conservation Act did not have any teeth. It could do very little to protect artifacts removed from the crash site, even though they were protected under the act. "The Ministry has no leverage once the materials are removed from the site," a frustrated Suttill admitted. "The federal legislation overrides the provincial one; ownership is irrelevant."[16]

Two months later, an equally frustrated Apland also admitted that the Archaeology Branch had no enforcement capabilities. "The statute of limitations to lay charges is only six months. It's up to Crown Counsel [prosecutors] to make the call whether charges are laid of commission of the offence."

Apland was not certain about the ownership of the removed artifacts. "BAAS may actually own them," he admitted.[17] Suttill explained that although the Archaeology Branch has control over the artifacts, it has no ownership. He added that it is much like a designated historical building; the Archaeology Branch controls what can and cannot be done by the owner as far as the appearance and structure of the building is concerned.

The Archaeology Branch has always shied away from the ownership question. In the case of BAAS, the ownership of the artifacts removed from the crash site remains a "grey area." Suttill stated that "the Branch is not in a strong legal position to require BAAS to turn over the artifacts to us." The Branch's only and most promising hold on the society was the issuance of future permits.

Meanwhile, BAAS was working on plans to set up a permanent museum in Terrace to display some of the wreckage, photos and other memorabilia from the crash. Rather than acquiring a building to house the displays, the group hoped to obtain an actual, complete B-36 aircraft. Terrace city council backed the idea of a big 160-foot bomber with a wingspan of 230 feet that might slow down American tourists heading north along the Cassiar Highway for Alaska. In the words of councillor David Hull, "There are towns that are on the map because they've got a giant Easter egg, or the world's largest hockey stick or fishing rod. This is a lot more interesting than a lot of those things."[18]

Terrace city council agreed to work with BAAS to develop a protocol for preserving and housing the artifacts. Hull believed a museum or some other form of public display of the aircraft would give "rubber tire traffic" another reason to stop in Terrace. "If you got a full tank of gas and a sandwich in your pocket, there is no reason to stop."[19]

Armed with explanations of how their B-36 would be used as a walk-through display of artifacts removed from Mount Kologet, the society approached Terrace city council seeking property or permanent exhibit space in the Terrace mall. To finance the entire operation, a fundraising effort was planned.

Healey went to Walter Soplata's farm in Newberry, Ohio, to look at a B-36 offered for sale there. He found the derelict fuselage of the second B-36 prototype Serial #42-13571, a YB-36A model later converted to a RB-36E with the four jet pods that had been for sale for some time. The society had hoped to purchase this derelict B-36 and reconstruct it by acquiring a set of wings from another B-36. Healey quickly realized that the aircraft was of no use to his group; the wings had been cut off and dropped, and there was no fuselage and no recognizable tail. "If put together at best it will look like an aircraft crash reconstruction," Healey observed.

It soon became clear that the society would have to scale down their B-36 project, and eventually they put the aviation museum plans on hold. "They [BAAS] had some pretty grandiose ideas, but it has been really quiet since then," commented Jeff Nagel, a reporter with the *Terrace Standard*.

Though it was rumoured that a Terrace developer-businessman had agreed to put up a total of $1.6 million toward the B-36 project, this never materialized. When Nagel was asked who would be willing and able to put up that amount of money, he answered, "Beats me! There's no people here with that kind of money; not anymore."[20]

Though some artifacts ultimately ended up in museums, most of the items removed from the crash site ended up in private collections. In September 2002, RCMP officers seized and exploded a detonator from the private collection of a man from the Meziadin Lake area. Apparently, he did not realize that it was such a dangerous device. Glenn Miller, a former US Navy heavy delivery/nuclear weapons specialist, said the detonators are, in fact, electrical dynamite caps. "They are susceptible to RF radio signals in the 150 MHz low band," he explained. "The lower the frequency, the better the range. All low bottom bands in frequency were allocated to the government. While dynamite caps have leads, detonators do not. They can go off when they form an antenna."

In Stewart, BC, Glenn Miller spotted the bombsight and one of the 20-mm cannons on the balcony of a helicopter company's building. "It's a complete bombsight, an upgraded Norden."[21]

The Bulkley Valley Museum in Smithers eventually did get one of the gun turrets, which became the centrepiece of a small but attractive exhibit that retells the events of the mysterious flight of Bomber 075. Several artifacts from the wreck site, photos of the survivors and an oil painting of the bomber by aviation artist John Rutherford of Kamloops, BC, are now part of a permanent display at this museum.

Another gun turret disappeared to Alberta, while some of the gun barrels and the large cut out Stars and Stripes emblem were last seen rusting away amongst some discarded office equipment behind a building in Terrace.

For many years, Doug Craig had several of the B-36 souvenirs in his possession. "I suppose that I, as finder and possibly as chief scrounger [in] the party, ended up with three items, the kit bag, Geiger counter and a 20-mm projectile." As the 20-mm cartridge still carried its explosive, Craig eventually disposed of it safely. But the kit bag remained part of Craig's family gear for many years. "I last tracked it to my daughter, who, unlike her father, throws stuff away when it gets a bit tatty."[22]

Craig passed the Geiger counter on to a fellow geologist, Leon Price. "We were moving often during the '50s and '60s and had to lighten up a little...One doesn't usually appreciate historical artifacts until they become historical, and by then it is often too late," Craig commented. Price kept the Geiger counter until December 1999, when he donated it to the museum in Smithers.[23]

The Stewart Historical Society Museum received a number of artifacts, which the Canadian Armed Forces donated after their visit to the site in August 1997. The donations included the barrel of a 20-mm cannon, a Gibson Girl emergency-transmission radio, some first-aid supplies, an oxygen mask with a small cylinder and an emergency-survival suit, as well as a pair of US Air Force gloves and a leather flight helmet with goggles. The crank-type radio is in a yellow box with curved sides approximately 30–40 centimetres high and has a 3-inch spool. The Armed Forces took some artifacts back to the Cold Lake base, and some artifacts ended up in the Museum of Transportation in Whitehorse, Yukon.

A bomb-loading manual, a small Alaskan souvenir totem pole and some other personal items, including a hairbrush, a cologne bottle, a small medicine bottle, an engraved mechanical pencil, a first lieutenant's field hat identified with his name on the headband, two standard U.S. military collar pins and a 1950 version of the Seventh Bomb Group insignia pin with its logo *Mors ab alto* (Death from above) were later returned to their owner, Raymond Whitfield.

The British Columbia government was notified of these findings because the wreck is officially considered a historic site under existing legislation.[24]

The whereabouts of the H-1 in-flight-insertion toolkit for the Mark IV bomb are unknown. "This kit was placed for the first time in the aircraft in 1949," said Jim Laird. "In fact, it's in the picture from DND with the birdcage and detonator box. The tool kit is sitting on top of the box."[25]

Given the fact that the crash site is protected by legislation, it is somewhat surprising that Dr. Jim Roddick, who chartered a helicopter to the site in 1998, condoned the removal of the birdcage. It was not only illegal to remove this important atomic artifact, it was also unknown at the time whether the container might still contain a deadly plutonium core. Roddick had retired from the Geological Survey of Canada but maintained a small office at the GSC and a few perks. Accompanying him on the trip, paid for by the GSC, were Dr. Doug Craig, Dick Thrasher and Scott Deaver. The substantial glacier that had filled the glacial cirque was gone, so Roddick scarcely recognized the crash site. "The scene was dramatically different from 1956. The glacier was entirely gone and the cirque was now practically free of snow."[26]

"Probably the greatest moment of our day at the site was when Scott Deaver pulled [out] a pipe framework. It was found partially sticking out from under a slab of talus. He recognized it right away: the plutonium-core container! It was heavy but we were able to manhandle it across the coarse talus to the helicopter landing spot."[27]

The container, or birdcage, consists of a one-inch-thick tubing frame that was bolted to the bomb bay with a half-inch steel plate. This pressurized and desiccated cylinder, about 14 inches high and 8 inches across, with a pressure gauge mounted on top, weighs about 90 pounds. To open it, the pressure had to be released and then the top removed. Protective gear consisting of a rubberized apron, respirator and latex gloves had to be put on prior to opening it. A handling tool was screwed into the base of the capsule support.

"We were a bit worried that the helicopter pilot would question us about our odd-looking freight," Roddick said, "but he wasn't curious." After landing, the helicopter did not shut down. The container was put on the machine without telling the pilot and taken from the crash site to Stewart. "Deaver just put it on without saying anything. The pilot did not ask what it was," Roddick recalled. "Scott [Deaver] had a carpenter in Stewart build a box for the apparatus. Weighing 126 pounds crated, we drove it back to Terrace in the back seat with Dick [Thrasher]."

"We were even more worried about [sending] the box by air to Vancouver and about getting it across the Canada–US border," Roddick continued. Deaver took the cylinder by rental car across the border into the United States, declaring it as a "piece of plane wreckage, destined for a museum." At the time of its removal, no one knew if the container actually held a core. It was not until the container was opened in Connecticut that it was found to be empty. "He reported it to be gleaming and pristine inside, but empty."[28]

Roddick was very much taken by the affable Dick Thrasher, a resident of Cross Plaines, west of Fort Worth. "Thrasher is a charming guy with a very good sense of humour and very mobile for a 78-year-old. It was a very moving experience for him, seeing the very hatch he jumped out of 48 years earlier." That hatch is the only one preserved on the crash site.

For Thrasher, who had flown into Terrace from his Texas home and whose last entrance into Canada had been by parachute from Bomber 075, the visit to the crash site was an occasion of historical significance and almost déjà vu. When his luggage did not appear after his flight, he dryly commented, "How come whenever I land in Canada, I have nothing but what I'm wearing?"[29]

Before leaving the crash site, Thrasher scratched NRTS on one of the larger fragments. When asked what it meant, he replied with a big smile, "Not repairable at this station." Thrasher explained that during routine flights, when the B-36s landed at various US Air Force bases, the flight crews would report any malfunctioning equipment. The list was often long and the maintenance crew would fix what they could. Some of these repairs required special equipment or technicians not available at that particular station. On those still-defective components they would place stickers bearing the letters NRTS.[30]

Deaver later chartered a fixed-wing aircraft and flew with Thrasher over Princess Royal Island to drop a wreath in memory of the five crewmen who died in the accident.[31] Deaver also assisted Doug Davidge with locating Raymond Whitfield, one of the surviving crew members.

Although Whitfield knew that the aircraft had been found years earlier, he was surprised to have his personal effects, collected by Doug Davidge from the wreck, returned to him after 48 years. It brought back memories of his days with Strategic Air Command.

In an interview in 1998 Whitfield noted:

> I am absolutely convinced that our having the B-36 during the years it was in service is the one thing most responsible for there being peace and stability in the world today. Given the attitude of the Soviets then, the fact that they knew that we were prepared and willing to respond to any aggressive act on their part was the only thing that prevented them from carrying out their goal of forcibly controlling all of Europe and other parts of the world as well. We can thank the B-36 for preventing this."[32]

Whitfield's most emotional experience concerning his days in SAC happened long after he had left the service. He had just stepped off a cruise ship onto the dock of a Russian city that had been one of his potential targets. "Seeing that city from the ground, looking into the faces of the people there, totally overwhelmed me. I was immensely thankful that we never had to do what we worked so hard to prepare to do. I could not speak with my wife, who was with me, for quite a while, until I had regained my composure. After thinking about it, I realized that SAC, the B-36 and our flight crews are responsible for those people, and millions of others, being alive today."[33]

Lieutenant Raymond Whitfield

Whitfield had some flying experiences that were potentially more dangerous than the bailout in British Columbia. Once, while landing a B-36 at Carswell AFB, only a few hundred yards from touchdown, Whitfield heard the flight engineer yelling in his headphones, "Take it back up and go around!" Whitfield was not aware of any problem at the time, but he moved the throttles to full power and lifted back up. He turned to the engineer and said to him, "What's the problem? A landing abortion is supposed to be the commander's decision."

The engineer pointed to a wing and told Whitfield that one end of a flap had broken at the hinge and the flap was hanging at a sharp angle by the remaining hinge. By this time, Whitfield was experiencing severe handling problems with the aircraft, which was trying to fly in a high-drag and low-power condition.

The aircraft was almost uncontrollable and would not turn sharply, making a go-around impossible. "We were flying over the densely populated Ridglea area of Fort Worth. I informed the ground to prepare emergency crews for a possible crash somewhere on the airfield and I managed to align the craft for a down-wind landing. Somehow, the slipping turn ended with us on the runway and we managed to stop the plane with the flap dragging the ground."[34]

On another occasion, again while landing at Carswell AFB, two of the propellers reversed pitch while on final approach. Thankfully, they were on opposite sides of the aircraft. After he managed to land the aircraft, Whitfield instructed the flight engineer to do nothing other than kill the engines. "Normally, the props are reversed and full power is applied to help stop the plane. After using the entire length of the runway to stop, using only the brakes, I ordered the plane to be shut down and we just left it there."

The follow-up investigation revealed that some cadmium plating on the limit switches that sensed the propellers' position had flaked off and had shorted the wires attached to the switches. This had caused the propellers' control system to erroneously reverse the pitch. This incident led to maintenance procedures that prevented future occurrences of the problem.

Following this incident, Lieutenant Whitfield flew many more missions until he left SAC in 1951 to become chief pilot of Air Force flight testing at Convair in Fort Worth. He learned to love this work and it proved to be the most pleasurable time of his flying career. It also enabled Whitfield to enter what became a long business career as an engineer and marketer of computer systems. In 1976, the former B-36 commander entered a seminary to become a clergyman.

CHAPTER 16

Lost Nuke on Film

Douglas Dickson, one of the rescuers aboard the *Cayuga*, once observed that the story of 075 "would make a hell of a documentary movie." Indeed, at the beginning of the new millenium, moviemakers on both sides of the border started to show interest in producing documentaries on the mystery surrounding Bomber 075's demise, and on nuclear weapon accidents, known as Broken Arrows, in general.

Eric Longabardi, a California producer and investigative journalist researched and produced a detailed television program that outlines the history of nuclear accidents, *America's Lost Bombs: The True Story of Broken Arrows*. The two-hour documentary first aired on November 12, 2001, on the History Channel. Veterans who survived America's nuclear weapon accidents share their experiences in the program. One of the points Longabardi's documentary makes is that while the US military insists that the nuclear deterrent ensures peace, there are those within the military who disagree, including former US Secretary of Defense Robert S. McNamara.

Emmy Award-winning producer Michael Jorgensen of Myth Merchant Films came next with his production of a one-hour program on the Bomber 075 incident for the Discovery Channel. In his documentary *Lost Nuke*, which first aired in 2004, the Edmonton-based producer told the story of Bomber 075 and the mystery that surrounds its last flight.

Between August 27 and September 3, 2003, a Myth Merchant film crew spent a week at the Bomber 075 crash site. Jorgensen followed researcher Jim Laird, historian John Clearwater and me to the crash site. During seven days spent on the mountainside, the team photographed the geography of the site and the wreckage itself, measuring and recording the details of the items found.

Besides taking part in the attempt to unravel some of the site's secrets, Clearwater had a second mandate. On behalf of the Diefenbunker, Canada's Cold War Museum in Carp, Ontario, he fully documented the crash site. "We did find conclusive evidence of the atomic bomb," Clearwater said. "I was able to pick up specific items related to the bomb."[1]

This was the first known visit to the crash site by a professional Cold War academic and museum researcher. Having received permission under the British Columbia Heritage Conservation Act to carry out a "site alteration," Clearwater recovered 36 artifacts and took them to Carp to the museum for research and display. Both the Bulkley Valley Historical and Museum Society and Broken Arrow Aircraft Society voiced their reservations about this.

To coincide with the Discovery Channel's premiere of *Lost Nuke*, on November 18, 2004, a companion exhibit opened at the Vancouver Museum. Besides the artifacts recovered from the crash site during the filming the previous year, the exhibit also included full-scale mock-ups of the Mark IV bomb and the bomb's "birdcage," built for the filming of *Lost Nuke*. This travelling exhibit, organized by the Alberta Aviation Museum, was scheduled to finally end up at the Diefenbunker in Ottawa.

The news conference that was to be held at the Vancouver Museum was unexpectedly cancelled—unexpected to all except Clearwater, who had pre-empted the event by prematurely talking to the press. In the November 18 editions of the *National Post*, the *Vancouver Sun*, *Edmonton Journal* and *Ottawa Citizen*, Clearwater suddenly denied the team's findings.

With a headline reading "No missing A-bomb in northern B.C., expert says," Clearwater took the wind out of *Lost Nuke*'s sails. He asserted, "I think the theory about a nuke being lost in BC is discredited. If there was a five-tonne object on board and it smashed into the side of a mountain, you would have expected some kind of damage."[2]

Clearwater acknowledged that, despite his findings, there were still researchers who believed the theory that weaponeer Captain Schreier stayed on board. "I recognize the possibility, which I find remote, that a person stayed with the airplane," he said. Clearwater admitted he could not explain how an aircraft without a pilot changed direction 180 degrees and flew over several mountain ranges for another two to three hours with no one at the controls. He suggested that possibly the ice that had clogged up the engines and covered the wings had broken up, allowing the aircraft to gain altitude and keep flying.[3]

Clearwater's statements caused a lot of confusion. A headline the next day in the *Edmonton Journal* on November 19 read "US plane carrying nuclear bomb may have crashed in BC," directly contradicting the previous day's headline.[4]

One can only speculate on the reason for Clearwater's unexpected comments after years of close co-operation. His statements drastically conflicted with earlier conclusions and were made public without first informing Jorgensen and the other members of the *Lost Nuke* expedition.

Did somebody "lean" on the nuclear weapons expert, who also maintained a residence in Texas? Did someone say, "Listen, Dr. Clearwater, if you want to secure future research contracts with us, you'd better change your tune about this Lost Nuke deal"?

On January 27, 1997, Clearwater had claimed during the CBC program *As It Happens* that the B-36 wreckage had been found on Vancouver Island that time. I can only hope this was the result of poor research rather than a deliberate effort to fool the Canadian public coast to coast.

Jorgensen, who was caught off guard by Clearwater's suddenly conflicting statements, simply said, "What we do is put all the evidence on the table and we let the viewer decide who they believe."[5]

Since the program first aired in Canada on November 19, 2004, viewers have had ample chance to watch it. The UK History Channel carried it in Europe as well but the program didn't air in the US until several years later. Eventually, National Geographic purchased the documentary for broadcast in the US and its territories. For its version of the film, National Geographic used a different narrator and added a scene explaining how a nuclear core being on the flight was an impossibility.

Another B-36 Peacemaker Makes It to the Silver Screen

Bomber 075 was not the only B-36 Peacemaker that made it to movie screens in recent years. The History Channel's Deep Sea Detectives TV series featured the story of the crash of No. 49-2661A, the 121st B-36 built by Convair at Fort Worth.

Originally a B model, it had been returned to San Diego for conversion to a D model, which included the addition of jet pods on each wing. On August 5, 1952, as the aircraft was heading south along the coast near La Jolla, en route to San Diego's Lindbergh Field, an engine on the right wing caught fire. After the crew bailed out and as flames engulfed the aircraft, pilot Dave Franks banked out to the sea to keep it from crashing into homes. All eight crew members were civilians, delivering the aircraft for the US Air Force. Six of the men who jumped from the burning aircraft survived. The seventh, first flight engineer Walt Hoffman, drowned. The body of Franks was never found.

The wing burned "like tissue paper" and an engine fell off north of Tourmaline Canyon in the city of La Jolla. When the bomber hit the water, there was a large ball of fire that burned for a few minutes, then disappeared. The cause of the fire was never proven, but the most likely culprit was an engine alternator that overheated and ignited its magnesium alloy housing. Military divers retrieved parts of the B-36 from a wide debris field, but halted salvage efforts because of the dangerous diving depth.

Nearly 50 years after the aircraft crashed, and after many hours of research and interviews with eyewitnesses, Steve Donathan, a dive instructor from the Loma Portal area of San Diego, found the wreck. Donathan's first find was a jet engine that had fallen off the bomber and sunk in 57 feet of water near La Jolla's Bird Rock. After combing an area three miles from shore with sonar and underwater drop cameras, Donathan spotted the wreckage at 260 feet. Despite the depth, the ghostly outline of the B-36 was unmistakable. After charting the exact location, Donathan returned several times to explore the wreck. What he found was a pile of crumpled, twisted metal encrusted with marine life. To verify what he found, he cut off a small section of the aircraft's skin.

For fear that scavengers would desecrate what was left of the wreck, he kept its location secret. Finally, on June 13, 2004, Donathan broke his silence and led Dan Crowell of the History Channel to the wreck. Along with veteran underwater explorer Joel Silverstein, they filmed the remains of the B-36 on the ocean floor. Sharing his findings with the military and the Scripps Institution of Oceanography, Donathan hoped that publicity generated by the show would inspire protection of the wreckage.[6]

Although Jorgensen's *Lost Nuke*, narrated by the American-born Canadian actor Colm Feore, got rave reviews in Canada and won several awards, its reception in the United States was lukewarm at best. A popular US-based B-36 forum posted the day before the altered version of *Lost Nuke* aired in the US for the first time, "Supposedly the US National Geographic TV channel has purged the film of its conspiratorial bullsh*t regarding the B-36 crash. It's time for an accurate telling of the story."[7]

"Unfortunately, the film is more of an effort to [impugn] the US Air Force than to be a documentary," Don Pyeatt noted. "It tries to prove that a 'live' nuke was lost from a B-36 in Canada, even though that would have been an historic impossibility. I regret having been involved with its production."[8]

Was Pyeatt, the official researcher of the Seventh Bomb Wing B-36 Association and webmaster of the B36 Era and Cold War Forum (Delphi Forums) unaware that in February 1950 the US Air Force actually had received two nuclear bombs on loan from the AEC?[9] Or was this an attempt to deceive visitors to the popular B-36 forum and everybody else for that matter?

It took the AEC almost a month of demanding answers about what had happened to their nuclear bomb before Major General Thomas White finally admitted that the US Air Force had lost it: "Jettisoned, *presumably over the sea* [italics are mine], and it exploded while in the air."[10]

Epilogue

"Never fired a shot in anger," the phrase associated with the B-36, is a valid one. But just because the aircraft was never used in real combat and was only held in reserve as a deterrent, its importance should not be diminished. Rather, it should be emphasized. The general public never knew the role the B-36 played in preventing global nuclear war because during its operational life in the early Cold War years, the aircraft was operated under the tightest secrecy and security. General Harry Goldsworthy said it well: "Technology passed the honest B-36 by and left it outperformed, but never outclassed."[1]

Without a combat record, it will never be known how effective the B-36 might have been in an actual war situation. Though available in limited numbers at the beginning of the Korean conflict in June 1950, B-36s were not used there because plenty of B-29s were available and sufficient for the purpose. Also, because the B-36s were still fairly new, engineers were still working on eliminating the bugs. The only time the B-36 flew in Korean airspace was when three RB-36s from Guam over-flew the Korean peace talks in a hometown formation.

The Peacemaker was only good for bombing at altitudes higher than 35,000 feet. Because they flew slower than the B-29s at lower altitudes, they would have been sitting ducks. Even with their faster speeds at those lower altitudes, many B-29s were shot down.

Too late for the Second World War, unused in Korea and retired just prior to the Vietnam conflict, the B-36 was not too late for deterrence. It also gave SAC an aircraft that could conduct extreme long-range, high-altitude simulated combat missions, thus pioneering many training and operational procedures still in use by SAC today.

In the late 1950s, a new era in strategic bombardment began with the US Air Force's transition from the B-36 to the all-jet B-52 Stratofortress.

With the introduction of the B-52, there was no more need for the B-36: it had become a "white elephant." The aircraft's complexity and high cost of maintenance probably kept it from being used for any further flying purpose. The Peacemaker was gone, but not its legend.

There is very little to memorialize this historic era and the men who designed, built, maintained and flew the B-36 Peacemaker. The tragedy of the B-36 program is that it has been mostly ignored in recent years. Today, there are only four surviving B-36s on public display. The most complete one is a "J" model housed at Dayton, Ohio, in the National Museum of the US Air Force.

Another B-36J is on display at the Strategic Air and Space Museum, at Mahoney State Park, 25 miles west of Offutt AFB in Ashland, Nebraska, and close to the Platte River. The facility, which opened to the public in November 1997, allows all aircraft to be displayed under cover. It replaced the former Strategic Air Command Museum next to Offutt AFB, where the B-36 was originally on display outdoors.

The third B-36, an RB-36H, is a reconnaissance version of the aircraft and is on display outside of the Castle Air Museum at a former air force base near Atwater, California. This aircraft was previously on display at Chanute AFB in Illinois.

For years, supporters of the B-36 Peacemaker Museum group at Fort Worth worked on restoring their B-36, *The City of Fort Worth*. In 2005, however, the US Air Force decided to move this aircraft to the Pima Air and Space Museum in Tucson, Arizona. The B-36 had been built at Fort Worth and remained there for decades. Restored from near-ruin by a group of volunteers in the mid-1990s, the aircraft was going to be the centrepiece of a museum dedicated to the rich history of Fort Worth. But the US Air Force decided otherwise. Although the Cold War–era bomber had been decommissioned many years earlier, the USAF retained ownership. In May 2005, the B-36 Peacemaker Museum's request to display the aircraft at Meacham Airport in Fort Worth was rejected.

The decision touched off a public outcry, similar to one in the early 1990s when the Air Force wanted to move the aircraft to South Dakota. That time, the public-relations campaign worked and Fort Worth was given another chance. Sadly, fundraising by two aviation-related groups, the Peacemaker Museum group and the Aviation Heritage Association, never gained enough momentum. The bomber remained at the Lockheed Martin plant in Fort Worth, largely hidden from public view.

It took 22 truckloads to move *The City of Fort Worth* to Tucson. The first shipment, the forward fuselage, wing tips and a couple of engine nacelles, arrived on July 22, 2005. The last shipment, the main wing section with all 230 feet of it on a special truck that was 150 feet long, arrived September 29. When the nose section arrived, Tucson's mayor was there to welcome it and two TV stations covered the event.

Before the move, the aircraft had been used to film part of the Myth Merchant Films' *Lost Nuke*. Whether the Canadian-made documentary influenced the US Air Force to take the B-36 Peacemaker Museum group's bomber away from Fort Worth is unknown. The group had allegedly assisted "a Canadian filmmaker in using the B-36 for filming without permission from the Air Force Museum [now the National Museum of the US Air Force in Dayton, Ohio]."

According to a museum spokesman, the museum requires groups to get approval for the use of military aircraft in movies, in part to make sure that the film "benefits the Air Force." According to retired brigadier general Bill Guy, Jorgensen did receive prior authorization from Air Force Public Affairs. However, as it turned out, the documentary *Lost Nuke*, "about a training accident in 1950 that involved a nuclear weapon, implicated the Air Force in a cover-up of the incident."[2]

✪

In December 1999, the Seventh Wing B-36 Association dedicated a memorial plaque at the Arlington National Cemetery in Virginia, adjacent to grave 4483-G on Grant Avenue, Section 3. The plaque eulogizes all B-36 personnel:

> *The Peacemaker: In memory of the outstanding contributions of air crews and ground personnel who supported the B-36 Peacemaker, nuclear force deterrent of the Strategic Air Command from 1948 to 1958. Their sacrifice, dedication, readiness and vigilance significantly impacted on the successful*

and peaceful outcome of the Cold War. Peace was their profession; and, they did their job well.[3]

The families of Bomber 075's crew are left with only memories and some vexing unanswered questions. Will their questions about this first lost nuke ever get answered?

Fred Schreier was only six when his uncle Theodore (Ted) was put in charge of Bomber 075's atomic bomb. "I don't know why all the secrecy," he said. "What could be so important? It seems like a cover-up when the families are not told what happened. What harm would it do to open the books, supply us with answers to the questions of what really happened 50 years ago?"[4]

Doug Craig summed the whole thing up with one simple question: "Why can we not get an official statement which would clear up the whole issue?"[5]

As for Bomber 075, television producer Michael Jorgensen does not think that the US military will ever come clean and tell the full story. "If Dirk [Septer] is right about what happened, it will never see the light of day—ever!"[6]

The official files will most likely remain closed, and the few surviving crew members will remain silent as well. "I think what they know will go to their grave[s] with them," Jorgensen concluded.[7]

To Jim Laird, the years of secrecy and misdirection can mean only one thing: "Something happened that night," he said. "There's some dark secret they don't want anyone to know."[8]

The mystery surrounding Bomber 075's final flight may never be unravelled. The real truth may remain forever hidden in a shroud of deceit, misinformation and myth.

Notes

Prologue

1   For consistency with historical accounts, Imperial measurements have been used throughout this book.
2   US Department of Defense/ Department of Energy, *The Histories of Nuclear Weapon Accidents 1950–1980.*

Chapter 1: Dawn of the Nuclear Era and Cold War

1   *Strait of Georgia Island Tides,* July 31, 2003.
2   Ibid., original source: Hiroshima: Harry Truman's Diary and Papers, 8/9/45, excerpt from public statement by President Truman.
3   Gar Alperovitz, *The Decision to Use the Atomic Bomb.* Part 1, 3, quoting memoirs of Admiral Leahy.
4   Ibid., 334, quoting 1949 memoirs of General Arnold.
5   Letter, from Herbert H. Hoover to *Army and Navy Journal* publisher Col. John Callan O'Laughlin, August 8, 1945.
6   Meyers K. Jacobsen, "Names and the B-36," *American Aviation Historical Society Journal* (Fall 1971): 186–188.
7   Raleigh Watson, B36 Era and Cold War Aviation Forum (Delphi Forums), April 9, 2003.
8   Walter Mitchell, B36 Era and Cold War Aviation Forum (Delphi Forums), April 5, 2003.
9   David Pugliese, "The downing of US bomber 2075," *The Citizen's Weekly* (Ottawa), February 13, 2000, C3.
10 Ibid.

Chapter 2: Birth of a Peacemaker

1   The newly created US Air Force became a separate military service on September 18, 1947, with the implementation of the National Security Act of 1947. Prior to 1947, the responsibility for military aviation was shared between the army for land-based operations and the navy for sea-based operations.
2   Meyers K. Jacobsen, "Peacemaker," *Airpower* 4, no. 6 (November 1974): 8–27, 50–55.
3   Richard C. Kirkland, *Tales of a War Pilot,* 75.

4   On October 20, 1950, the Fairfield-Suisun AFB was officially renamed Travis AFB after Brigadier General Robert F. Travis, Commander, 5th Strategic Reconnaissance and 9th Bombardment Wings. On August 5, 1950, General Travis died in the crash of a B-29 Superfortress that was transporting a nuclear weapon.
5   Meyers K. Jacobsen, "Peacemaker," *Airpower* 4, no. 6 (November 1974): 8–27, 50–55.
6   Ibid.
7   Steve H. Henderson, pers. comm., November 2, 2003.
8   Stewart, in real life, was a Second World War B-17 pilot. He flew 20 combat missions and served in the Air Force Reserve for several years after the war.
9   Meyers K. Jacobsen, "The red-tailed beauties of the 7th Bomb Wing," *American Aviation Historical Society Journal,* 24, no. 1 (Spring 1979): 35–36.
10 Ibid., 32.
11 *Maclean's,* 24, November 1, 1999, pp. 46–47.

Chapter 3: The Mark IV Nuclear Bomb

1   ScannerL22, B36 Era and Cold War Aviation Forum (Delphi Forums), July 6, 2003.
2   Retap2, B36 Era and Cold war Aviation Forum (Delphi Forums), July 24, 2004.
3   Walt Mitchell, B36 Era and Cold War Aviation Forum (Delphi Forums), July 24, 2004.
4   ScannerL22, B36 Era and Cold War Aviation Forum (Delphi Forums), July 6, 2003.
5   Jim Laird, pers. comm., March 8, 2004.
6   Jim Oskins, *Nuclear Weapons Maintenance—The Early Years,* 4.

Chapter 4: "Abandon Ship!"

1   R.P. Whitfield, interview by Don Pyeatt, July 31, 1998.
2   Charlie Ronchas, B36 Era and Cold War Aviation Forum (Delphi Forums), July 28, 2003; Jerry Fenton, B36 Era and Cold War Aviation Forum (Delphi Forums), August 2, 2003.
3   Dick Thrasher, *Lost Nuke* documentary, 2004.
4   Report on Operation Brix, 12 Group RCC, 1.

5   Major Aircraft Accident, Aircraft 44-92075, B-3738-A, March 1, 1950, interview Col. Bartlett, 12.

6   Major Ralph R. Taylor, Crew Capabilities of Aircraft #075. Memorandum for Commanding General, February 14, 1950, 2.

7   Major Aircraft Accident, Aircraft 44-92075, B-3738-A, March 1, 1950, report on 075, February 17, 1950, 1.

8   *Fort Worth Star-Telegram*, February 16, 1997.

9   Major Aircraft Accident, Aircraft 44-92075, B-3738-A, March 1, 1950, testimony of crew of B-36 A/P 44-92083. The earth's time zones were once divided among the letters of the alphabet. Zulu (Z) Time is the international code word for Universal Coordinated Time, formerly known as Greenwich Mean Time (GMT). Universal Time Corrected (UTC) is maintained by the National Bureau of Standards and is used in navigation and communication.

10 Major Aircraft Accident, Aircraft 44-92075, B-3738-A, March 1, 1950, testimony Lt. Cox, February 22, 1950.

11 In the case of engine fires or failures, the propeller blades can be rotated parallel to the airflow to reduce the drag, a process called feathering.

12 *New York Times*, February 15, 1950; *Daily Colonist* (Victoria, BC), February 15, 1950.

13 In 1958, the CAA was reorganized as the Federal Aviation Agency (FAA). Originally created as the Civil Aeronautics Authority in 1938, it was divided in 1940 into the Civil Aeronautics Administration and the Civil Aeronautics Board.

14 Mission report (Suspended) (RCS:ARS-CPS-C2A), April 11, 1950, 1.

15 Major Aircraft Accident, Aircraft 44-92075, B-3738-A, March 1, 1950, testimony of crew of B-36 airplane No. 44-92083 (Capt. Cooper) on February 20, 1950, 1–2.

16 R.P. Whitfield, interview by Don Pyeatt, July 31, 1998.

17 Roddick, *Gentle Giant*, 5.

18 Bob Preising, pers. comm., January 31, 2004.

19 Major Aircraft Accident, Aircraft 44-92075, B-3738-A, March 1, 1950, report on 075, February 17, 1950, 2.

Chapter 5: Operation Brix

1   Early in 1946, the RCAF had been instructed to establish a national search and rescue (SAR) organization. The plan called for the creation of SAR flights (not squadrons) in most regions of the country. Each unit was to be equipped with a variety of aircraft to handle different kind of missions.

2   *Vancouver Sun*, March 11, 1987. Soon after Operation Brix, *Cayuga*, which had only been commissioned in 1947, would go on to serve in the Korean War. Sailors serving on her described her as a "happy ship."

3   Dirk Septer, "A Mystery Never Solved," *Canadian Aviator* 19, no. 1 (January-February 2009): 16–17.

4   Doug Dickson, pers. comm., 2001.

5   Ibid.

6   Percy Lotzer, pers. comm., July 24, 2001.

7   The Sikorsky H-5, the military version of the S-51 helicopter, evolved from the wartime R-5 and was powered by a vertically mounted Pratt & Whitney R-985 Wasp Jr. engine. The RCAF introduced its first Sikorsky S-51 helicopter in 1947. In May 1949, RCAF Station Sea Island near Vancouver received two S-51s, 9606 and 9607. Vancouver retained 9606 for search and rescue on the west coast. Aircraft 9607 was assigned to the Army Survey Establishment to support mapping work between Fort Nelson and Fort St. John. The S-51 served with the RCAF from 1947 to 1965. After the larger and more capable Piasecki H-21A arrived in 1955, the S-51 was largely relegated to training.

8   *Daily Colonist* (Victoria, BC), February 17, 1950; Peter Corley-Smith and David N. Parker, *Helicopters: The British Columbia Story*, 138.

9   Operation Brix, "Daily Search Summary," February 14, 1950.

10 *Daily News* (Prince Rupert, BC), February 16, 1950; *Daily Colonist*, February 16, 1950.

11 *Daily Colonist*, February 16, 1950.

12 Ibid.

13 Ibid.

14 Percy Lotzer, pers. comm., July 25, 1999.

15 *Daily News*, February 17, 1950.

16 Doug Dickson, pers. comm., 2001.

17 Kirkland, *Tales of a War Pilot*, 72.
18 Ibid., 77–79.
19 Ibid., 82.
20 Ibid.
21 Ibid., 83–84.
22 "Well done Cayuga," *Crowsnest*, April 1950, 4.
23 *Fort Worth Star-Telegram*, February 16, 1997.
24 Percy Lotzer, pers. comm., December 2000.
25 Ibid., July 24, 2001.
26 Ibid.
27 Report on Operation Brix, 12 Group RCC, Appendix "A," 2.
28 *Daily News*, February 16, 1950.
29 Ibid., February 17, 1950.
30 Ibid., February 16, 1950; *Time*, February 27, 1950, 25.
31 *New York Times*, February 18, 1950.
32 *Daily Colonist*, February 23, 1950.
33 *Nanaimo Free Press*, February 17, 1950.
34 "Well done Cayuga," *Crowsnest*, April 1950, 4.
35 *Nanaimo Free Press*, February 20, 1950.
36 "Well done Cayuga," *Crowsnest*, April 1950, 4.
37 R.P. Whitfield, interview by Don Pyeatt, July 31, 1998.
38 Naval message, February 21, 1950, from *Cayuga* to Canflagpac 12 Grp. Hq.
39 Naval message, February 16, 1950, Aircraft 1526 to Commander 17th Air Facility Annette.
40 *Nanaimo Free Press*, February 21, 1950; *Daily Colonist*, February 22, 1950.
41 Report on Operation Brix, 12 Group RCC, Appendix "B."
42 Report on Operation Brix, 12 Group RCC, 4.
43 Meeting minutes on Operation Brix, *Cayuga*, February 27, 1950.
44 "Well done Cayuga," *Crowsnest*, April 1950, 4.
45 Clearwater, *Broken Arrow #1: the World's First Lost Atomic Bomb*, 122.
46 Percy Lotzer, pers. comm. December 2000.
47 Percy Lotzer, pers. comm., n/d.
48 Percy Lotzer, pers. comm., December 2000.
49 Peter Corley-Smith and David N. Parker, *Helicopters: The British Columbia Story*, 139.

50 Letter, from Roger M. Ramey, Major Gen. USAF, to Group Capt. J. A. Easton, Headquarters 12 Group RCAF, March 6, 1950.
51 Letter, from General Hoyt S. Vandenberg to Admiral H.T.W. Grant, Chief of Naval Staff, March 28, 1950.
52 "Well done Cayuga," *Crowsnest*, April 1950, 4.
53 Meyers K. Jacobsen, "The red-tailed beauties of the Seventh Bomb Wing," *AAHS Journal* 24, no. 1 (Spring 1979): 35.
54 Cedric Mah, pers. comm., August 20, 2001.
55 Letter, from Brig. Gen. H.H. Underhill, USAF Acting Director of Military Personnel, to Mrs. Jean C. Schreier, May 25, 1950.
56 *Daily News*, March 20, 1950.
57 Ibid., May 23 and 28, 1952.
58 Eric Longabardi, pers. comm., August 2001.
59 Dick Thrasher, *Lost Nuke* documentary, 2004.
60 Letter, Lt. Col. Jas. F. Watt, QMC Memorial Division, to Mrs. Jean C. Schreier, February 20, 1953.
61 Jim Roddick, pers. comm., November 1, 2000.
62 Report of AF Aircraft Accident 10 mi. south of Perkins, Okla. between B-36 No. 49-2658A and F-51 No. 44-84973A.
63 Roddick, *Gentle Giant*, 15.

Chapter 6: Survival Stories of the Crew
1 R.P. Whitfield, interview by Don Pyeatt, July 31, 1998.
2 The Eighth Air Force history for January-June 1950, V. 3, accident report No. 50-2-14-12.
3 *Nanaimo Free Press*, February 16, 1950.
4 Jim Roddick, *Gentle Giant*, p. 12.
5 *Fort Worth Star-Telegram*, February 16, 1997.
6 *Nanaimo Free Press*, February 16, 1950.
7 *Fort Worth Star-Telegram*, February 16, 1997.
8 Percy Lotzer, pers. comm., July 25, 1999.

Chapter 7: The Official Story
1 Meyers K. Jacobsen, "The red-tailed beauties of the 7th Bomb Wing," *AAHS Journal* 24, no. 1 (Spring 1979): 34.

2   Major Aircraft Accident, Aircraft
    44-92075, B-3738-A, March 1, 1950,
    interview Capt. Payne,
    February 20, 1950, 5.
3   Memorandum from Major Ralph R.
    Taylor, crew capabilities of aircraft
    #075, February 14, 1950.
4   Major Aircraft Accident, Aircraft 44-
    92075, B-3738-A, March 1, 1950,
    Interview S/Sgt. Fox, February 20,
    1950, 5.
5   Major Aircraft Accident, Aircraft 44-
    92075, B-3738-A, March 1, 1950,
    testimony Col. Bartlett, 1–4.
6   Memorandum Major Ralph R. Taylor,
    crew capabilities of aircraft #075,
    February 14, 1950.
7   Major Aircraft Accident, Aircraft 44-
    92075, B-3738-A, March 1, 1950,
    testimony Lt. Cox, February 22, 1950.
8   Ibid.
9   Major Aircraft Accident, Aircraft 44-
    92075, B-3738-A, March 1, 1950,
    testimony of crew on aircraft No. 44-
    92081 (Lt. Stacker),1, 3, 9.
10 R.P. Whitfield, interview by Don
    Pyeatt, July 31, 1998.
11 Major Aircraft Accident, Aircraft 44-
    92075, B-3738-A, March 1, 1950,
    testimony Lt. Cox, February 22, 1950,
    12.
12 Meyers K. Jacobsen, "The red-tailed
    beauties of the 7th Bomb Wing,"
    AAHS Journal 24, no. 1 (Spring 1979):
    34.
13 *New York Times*, February 15, 1950.
14 David Pugliese, *Citizen's Weekly*,
    February 13, 2000, C4.
15 Letter, from Col. K.F. Hertford, CE,
    to Carroll L. Tyler, Manager, Santa
    Fe Operations Office, US Atomic
    Energy Commission, Los Alamos, New
    Mexico, April 5, 1950, 1.
16 R.P. Whitfield, interview by Don
    Pyeatt, July 31, 1998.
17 Bob Preising, B36 Era and Cold War
    Forum (Delphi Forums), January 18,
    2005.
18 R.P. Whitfield, interview by Don
    Pyeatt, July 31, 1998.
19 Paul E. Gerhart, *Fort Worth Star-
    Telegram*, February 16, 1997.
20 *Edmonton Journal*, June 9, 1989.
21 US Department of Defense/
    Department of Energy. *The Histories of
    Nuclear Weapon Accidents 1950–1980.*
22 *Vancouver Sun*, November 19, 1981.
23 *Maclean's*, November 1, 1999, 46.
24 *Defense Monitor* X, no. 5 (1981): 4.
25 *Globe and Mail* (Toronto, ON), January
    27, 1997.
26 John Clearwater, interview with *As It
    Happens*, January 27, 1997.
27 SAB200304050000 Secret/Restricted
    Data, A Compendium of US Nuclear
    Weapon Accidents (U) 3.1 Accident;
    B-36, off the coast of British Columbia,
    Canada (February 13, 1950).
28 *Nanaimo Free Press*, February 15, 1950.

Chapter 8: Surprise Discovery

1   Between August 17 and September 5,
    1953, both US and Canadian aircraft
    participating in SAR Operation Hall
    flew a total of 2,048 hours trying
    to locate the missing de Havilland
    Dove, registration NC4272C, and its
    occupants.
2   Edward Hoagland, *Notes from the
    Century Before: A Journal from British
    Columbia*, 9–12.
3   Harold Harvey, pers. comm., 1992, via
    Scott Deaver.
4   Scott Deaver, pers. comm.,
    January 7, 1993; April 29, 1993.
5   *Prince Rupert Today*,
    December 15, 1991.
6   Pierre Cote, pers. comm.,
    August 16, 2003.
7   Kim Lee, pers. comm.,
    February 19, 1998.
8   Percy Lotzer, pers. comm.,
    March 6, 1992.
9   Roddick, *Gentle Giant*, 7.
10 Percy Lotzer, pers. comm.,
    October 24, 1999.
11 Cedric Mah, pers. comm.,
    April 9, 2000; August 20, 2001.
12 Joe L'Orsa, pers. comm., July 13, 1994;
    Interior News (Smithers, BC), July 22,
    1992.
13 Harry Kruisselbrink, pers. comm.,
    July 18, 2001.
14 Marcella Love, pers. comm.,
    July 9, 2001.
15 Harry Kruisselbrink, pers. comm.,
    January 21, 1999.
16 Scott Deaver, pers. comm.,
    August 24, 2002.
17 *Interior News*, August 19, 1954;
    Omineca Herald (Terrace, BC), August
    26, 1954.
18 *Interior News*, July 22, 1992.
19 *Vancouver Sun*, March 11, 1987.

20 Dave Coverdale, pers. comm., October 16, 2002.
21 The Silver Hilton on the Babine River is locally known as the "Babine Hilton."
22 Harry Kruisselbrink, pers. comm., October 9, 2002.
23 SAB200304050000 Secret/Restricted Data, A Compendium of US Nuclear Weapon Accidents (U) 3.1 Accident: B-36, off the coast of British Columbia, Canada (February 13, 1950).

Chapter 9: What Was Known About the Incident?

1 *AAHS Journal* (Spring 1979): 34.
2 Major Aircraft Accident, Aircraft 44-92075, B-3738-A, March 1, 1950, testimony Lt. Cox, 21, and February 22, 8.
3 Roddick, *Gentle Giant,* 14.
4 Kirkland, *Tales of a War Pilot,* 85.
5 Ibid., 83.
6 *Nanaimo Free Press,* February 15, 1950.
7 Barry Borutski, pers. comm., December 17, 2002.
8 David Pugliese, *Citizen's Weekly,* February 13, 2000, C4.
9 *Vancouver Province,* February 15, 1950.
10 Naval message, from *Cayuga* to Canflagpac 12 Grp. Hq., n/d.
11 Naval message, from Canflagpac to *Cayuga* Info 12 Grp.
12 Roddick, *Gentle Giant,* 15.
13 R.P. Whitfield, interview by Don Pyeatt, July 31, 1998.
14 Kirkland, *Tales of a War Pilot,* 86.
15 Pierre Cote, pers. comm., October 30, 2000; August 16, 2003.
16 Barry Borutski, pers. comm., October 5, 2002.
17 Joe L'Orsa, pers. comm., December 15, 1998.
18 *British Columbian,* February 7, 1953; Goleta Air and Space Museum. *Convair B-36 Wrecks,* pamphlet.
19 *Omineca Herald* (Terrace, BC), February 15, 1950; *Daily News* (Prince Rupert, BC), February 14, 1950.
20 Barry Borutski, pers. comm., via Joe L'Orsa, December 15, 1998.
21 Dave Kuntz, pers. comm., September 23, 2002.
22 Barry Borutski, pers. comm., March 30, 2000; June 26, 2001.

23 Brian Lockett, pers. comm., November 30, 2003.
24 Don Pyeatt, pers. comm., November 30, 2003.
25 Barry Borutski, pers. comm., October 5, 2002.
26 Ibid., October 12, 2002.
27 Ibid., October 5 and 12, 2002.
28 Operation Brix, "Daily Search Summary," February 14, 1950
29 Aircraft Accident, Aircraft 44-92075, B-3738-A, March 1, 1950, testimony Lt. Cox, 21.
30 Mark Munzel, pers. comm., January 7, 1996.
31 Brian Lockett, pers. comm., November 30, 2003.

Chapter 10: What Did the Government Know?

1 Operation Brix, "Daily Search Summary," February 14, 1950.
2 Kirkland, *Tales of a War Pilot,* 74.
3 Ibid., 73.
4 Flight C, 4th Rescue Sqn. Mission report (Suspended) (RCS:ARS-CPS-C2A), 4.
5 Ibid., 10.
6 Historical record, 12 Group Headquarters, Vancouver, December 1, 1949–May 31, 1950, 2.
7 Letter, Maj. Gen. Thomas D. White to William L. Borden, Executive Director Joint Committee on Atomic Energy, March 17, 1950.
8 Naval message, from Canflagpac to *Cayuga* Info 12 Grp.
9 Flight C, 4th Rescue Sqn. Mission report (Suspended) (RCS:ARS-CPS-C2A), 9–10.
10 Historical Record, 12 Group Headquarters, Vancouver, December 1, 1949–May 31, 1950, 2.
11 Doug Craig, pers. comm., March 5, 1997.
12 Roddick, *Gentle Giant,* 2.
13 Jim Laird, pers. comm., n/d.
14 Cedric Mah, pers. comm., April 9, 2000; August 20, 2001.
15 Ibid.
16 Marcella Love, pers. comm., July 9, 2001.
17 *Interior News* (Smithers, BC), October 2, 1968.
18 Harry Kruisselbrink, pers. comm., December 30, 1998.

19 Pierre Cote, pers. comm., January 31, 1999.
20 Joe L'Orsa, pers. comm., January 31, 1999.
21 Pierre Cote, pers. comm., January 31, 1999.
22 Dave Kuntz, pers. comm., January 25, 1999.
23 Kim Lee, pers. comm., February 19, 1998.
24 SAB200304060000 Summary of Air Force Accidents Involving Nuclear Weapons (U): February 28, 1969, 1.
25 Nuclear Weapon Accidents (Secret), US Department of Energy, Albuquerque Operations Office, Office of Emergency Plans and Operations, January 14, 1992.
26 *Fort Worth Star-Telegram*, February 16, 1997.
27 Roddick, *Gentle Giant*, 11.
28 The crash site is visible on 1:31,680-scale air photo stereo pair BC1147 No. 4-5 (taken on September 8, 1950) and also on scale 1:15,840 BC4342 Nos. 101-102 (taken on August 14, 1965).
29 Doug Craig, pers. comm., September 5, 2001.
30 Ibid.
31 Dave Kuntz, pers. comm., September 23, 2002.
32 Scott Deaver, pers. comm., February 25, 1992.
33 *Yukon News*, October 1, 1997.
34 Barry Borutski, pers. comm., October 30, 2000.
35 Dick Thrasher, *Lost Nuke* documentary, 2004.
36 Pierre Cote, pers. comm., January 31, 1999.

Chapter 11: What Did the Crash Site Reveal?

1 Roddick, *Gentle Giant*, 1–2.
2 Doug Craig, pers. comm., September 5, 2001.
3 Ibid.
4 Ibid., October 9, 2002.
5 Ibid., September 5, 2001.
6 Letter from Doug Craig to John Clearwater, March 2, 1997; Doug Craig, pers. comm., September 5, 2001.
7 Roddick, *Gentle Giant*, 2.
8 Ibid.
9 Doug Craig, pers. comm., April 17, 1997.
10 *Vancouver Province*, November 19, 1981.
11 *Vancouver Sun*, November 20, 1981.
12 Letter, from Jim Roddick to Doug Craig, August 8, 1996.
13 David Pugliese, *Citizen's Weekly*, February 13, 2000, C4.
14 Doug Craig, pers. comm., September 18, 1997.
15 Scree, also called talus, is a geological term given to an accumulation of broken rock at the base of mountain cliffs or valley slopes.
16 Jim Laird, pers. comm., March 8, 2004.
17 United States Air Force, Tactical Weight Form F.
18 Scott Deaver, pers. comm., n/d.
19 *Yukon News*, October 1, 1997.
20 Doug Davidge, pers. comm., 1997.
21 A radome is a structure or enclosure that protects a microwave radar or antenna and is transparent to radar or radio waves.
22 Barry Borutski, pers. comm., October 12, 2002.
23 Ibid.
24 Barry Borutski, *Flight Journal* (December 2000): 32–36.
25 Glenn Miller, pers. comm., September 26, 1997.
26 Ibid., February 17, 2004.
27 Corporal Sims, August 24, 1999, Stewart Detachment RCMP File 97-384, 116.
28 Constable McArthur, November 16, 1999, Stewart Detachment RCMP File 97-384, 128.
29 Constable McArthur, April 13, 2000, Stewart Detachment RCMP File 97-384, 140.
30 Dave Coverdale, pers. comm., September 13, 2000; October 16, 2002.
31 Jim Roddick, pers. comm., November 1, 2000.
32 Corporal P. Blanch, March 31, 2000, Stewart RCMP Detachment File 97-384, 129.
33 Dave Coverdale, pers. comm., May 8, 2000; October 16, 2002.
34 Ibid., October 16, 2002.
35 Thomas D. Holland, pers. comm., February 12, 2004.
36 The members of 4 CRPG are the successors of the Pacific Coast Militia Rangers, formed in 1942 and considered the model for the modern Canadian Rangers program that has since expanded to other parts of

Canada. A high percentage of the 3,600 Canadian Rangers are of Aboriginal ancestry. Their official motto, *Vigilans* (the guardians), summarizes their mandate and underscores the scope of their activities. With the fundamental responsibility of providing a military presence to protect Canada's sovereignty, they also contribute to the activities of the Canadian Forces by providing expertise about the local area and volunteering in rescue missions.

37 *Terrace Standard*, October 2, 2002.
38 Pierre Cote, pers. comm., August 16, 2003.

Chapter 12: What Was Known About the Bomb?

1 *Edmonton Journal*, June 9, 1989.
2 Glenn Miller, pers. comm., February 17, 2004.
3 David Pugliese, *Citizen's Weekly*, February 13, 2000.
4 Doug Craig, pers. comm., October 9, 2002;
5 Jim Laird, pers. comm., October 17, 2002.
6 Doug Craig, pers. comm., October 9, 2002.
7 Over a period of 30 years, Chuck Hansen compiled a very large collection of documents on how the US developed the atomic bomb. His book, first released in 1988, caused quite a stir. Prior to that, little was known about many of the weapons he wrote about, not to mention the atmospheric test series. All of his material was obtained through the Freedom of Information Act; it sometimes took months or years for Hansen to receive a response to his requests. In 1995, Hansen released an updated and expanded 2,500-page, 8-volume version, *Swords of Armageddon: U.S. Nuclear Weapons Development Since 1945*.
8 Scott Deaver, pers. comm., August 1, 1996.
9 In April 1951, President Harry S. Truman assigned nine Mark IV atomic bombs to the custody of US Air Force Chief of Staff General Hoyt Vandenberg.
10 Scott Deaver, pers. comm., August 24, 2002.
11 *Vancouver Sun*, April 17, 2004.
12 Clearwater, *Broken Arrow #1: The World's First Lost Atomic Bomb*, 9.

13 David Pugliese, *Citizen's Weekly*, February 13, 2000, p. C 4.

Chapter 13: What Happened to the Bomb?

1 Glenn Miller, pers. comm., February 17, 2004.
2 The Mark V, which had a yield of 40 to 50 kilotons, was developed from 1946 onward and was operationally deployed between 1949 and 1955. The weapon weighed 3,175 pounds, was 10 feet 8.5 inches long and had a diameter of 3 feet 7.75 inches.
3 Bob Baragar, pers. comm., November 27, 2000, via Jim Roddick.
4 Scott Deaver, pers. comm., March 3, 2001.
5 Doug Craig, pers. comm., October 9, 2002.
6 Ibid.
7 Jim Laird, pers. comm., January 19, 2004.
8 Glenn Miller, pers. comm., February 17, 2004.
9 Clearwater, *Broken Arrow #1: The World's First Lost Atomic Bomb*, 11, 34.
10 Charlie Ronchas, pers. comm., July 22, 2004.
11 Tina Chadwell Weiss, pers. comm., n/d.
12 Goleta Air and Space Museum, "Convair B-36 Crash Report and Wreck Sites," www.air-and-space. com/b-36%20wrecks.htm
13 SAB200304050000 Secret/ Restricted Data, A Compendium of US Nuclear Weapon Accidents (U) 3.1 Accident: B-36, off the coast of British Columbia, Canada (February 13, 1950).
14 *Wiltshire Times* (Trowbridge, Wiltshire, England), February 14, 1953.
15 Kirkland, *Tales of a War Pilot*, 84.
16 Ibid.
17 Ibid.
18 Barry Borutski, pers. comm., October 12, 2002.
19 Peter Corley-Smith and David N. Parker, *Helicopters: The British Columbia Story*, 41.
20 Kirkland, *Tales of a War Pilot*, 86.
21 Ibid.
22 Dave Kuntz, pers. comm., September 15, 1999.
23 Ibid., September 23, 2002.
24 Jim Laird, pers. comm., September 25, 2003.

25 Barry Borutski, B36 Era and Cold War Aviation Forum (Delphi Forums), October 5, 2002.
26 Scott Deaver, pers. comm., January 19, 2005; Bob Preising, pers. comm., January 18, 2005.
27 John Clearwater, *Lost Nuke* documentary, 2004.
28 Michael Jorgensen, *Lost Nuke* documentary, 2004.
29 John Clearwater, *Lost Nuke* documentary, 2004.
30 David Pugliese, *Citizen's Weekly*, February 13, 2000, C4.

Chapter 14: What Became of Ted Schreier?
1 *Fort Worth Star-Telegram*, February 16, 1950.
2 *Nanaimo Free Press*, February 15, 1950.
3 *New York Times*, February 16, 1950.
4 Major Aircraft Accident, Aircraft 44-92075, B-3738-A, March 1, 1950, testimony Capt. Barry, 19.
5 R.P. Whitfield, interview by Don Pyeatt, July 31, 1998.
6 The B-36 used its fuel in this order: inboard tank, centre tank, outboard tank. The weight left near the tip prevented the wing from bouncing.
7 Jim Laird, pers. comm., September 25, 2003; January 19, 2004.
8 Clearwater, *Broken Arrow #1. The World's First Lost Atomic Bomb*, 99
9 Don Pyeatt, pers. comm., December 10, 2003.
10 Doug Craig, pers. comm., April 17, 1997.
11 Scott Deaver, pers. comm., 1992.
12 Barry Borutski, pers. comm., October 5 and 12, 2002.
13 Pierre Cote, pers. comm., August 16, 2003.
14 Letter, Brigadier General H.H. Underhill, USAF Acting Director of Personnel, to Mrs. Jean C. Schreier, May 25, 1950.
15 Fred Schreier, *Lost Nuke* documentary, 2004.

Chapter 15: Heritage Wreck
1 Jim Roddick, pers. comm., February 1, 1999.
2 *Terrace Standard*, October 14, 1998.
3 Dave Suttill, pers. comm., February 12, 1999.

4 On December 9, 1956, a Trans-Canada Airlines North Star aircraft with 62 people aboard crashed on Mt. Slesse, southeast of Chilliwack, BC, about three miles north of the international boundary. Since May 25, 1995, the crash site has been protected under the provincial Forest Act, the Mineral Tenure Act and the Land Act by BC cabinet order.
5 Heritage Conservation Act [RSBC 1996], Chapter 187.
6 *Terrace Standard*, October 14, 1998; *Interior News* (Smithers, BC), October 21, 1998.
7 David Suttill, pers. comm., January 6, 1999.
8 Letter, Brian Apland to Lillian Weedmark, Curator Bulkley Valley Historical and Museum Society, October 8, 1998.
9 Terrace RCMP File 98-4974, 15.
10 Fax, from Ray Griffith to Ministry of Small Business, Tourism and Culture, Terrace RCMP File 98-4974, 30, September 25, 1998.
11 *Terrace Standard*, October 21, 1998.
12 Ibid., October 14, 1998.
13 Ibid., October 21, 1998.
14 Carl Healey, pers. comm., October 19, 1998, via Lillian Weedmark.
15 Letter, Archaeology Branch to Bulkley Valley Historical and Museum Society, March 31, 1999.
16 Dave Suttill, pers. comm., December 11, 1998.
17 Brian Apland, pers. comm., February 15, 1999.
18 *Terrace Standard*, November 18, 1998
19 *Terrace Times*, November 18, 1998.
20 Jeff Nagel, pers. comm. November 29, 2000.
21 Glenn Miller, pers. comm., February 17, 2004.
22 Doug Craig, pers. comm., March 5, 1997.
23 Ibid., October 24, 1999; March 5, 1997.
24 Doug Davidge, Environmental Impact Study of USAF Bomber, unpublished report.
25 Jim Laird, pers. comm., September 25, 2003.
26 Roddick, *Gentle Giant*, 12.
27 Ibid., 13.
28 Ibid., 15.

29 Jim Roddick, pers. comm., November 1, 2000.
30 Roddick, *Gentle Giant*, 13.
31 Jim Roddick, pers. comm., December 16, 1998.
32 R.P. Whitfield, interview by Don Pyeatt, July 31, 1998.
33 Ibid.
34 Ibid.

Chapter 16: Lost Nuke on Film
1 *Terrace Standard*, December 17, 2003. The Diefenbunker, nicknamed after former Prime Minister John Diefenbaker, was designed and built in secrecy between 1959 and 1961, during the height of the Cold War. This huge four-story bunker, buried deep under a hillside near Ottawa, Ontario, was meant to house crucial elements of the Canadian government during a nuclear war. Should the unthinkable have happened, the Diefenbunker would have been a haven for those providing the thin thread of continuity of government. With the Cold War having officially ended in 1991, the Department of National Defence closed the bunker in 1994. After the Government of Canada designated the structure a National Historic Site of Canada, the bunker now fulfills a new role as Canada's Cold War Museum.
2 *Vancouver Sun*, November 18, 2004.
3 Ibid.
4 *Edmonton Journal*, November 19, 2004.
5 Ibid.
6 *Scanner*, 7th Bomb Wing B-36 Association, Vol. XXV, No. 3, October 2004.
7 Don Pyeatt, B36 Era and Cold War Aviation Forum (Delphi Forums), February 24, 2009.
8 Don Pyeatt, B36 Era and Cold War Aviation Forum (Delphi Forums), December 29, 2006.
9 Delphi Forums's B36 Era and Cold War Forum is a public forum for B-36 and SAC Cold War veterans.
10 Letter, Maj. Gen. Thomas D. White to William L. Borden, Executive Director Joint Committee on Atomic Energy, March 17, 1950.

Epilogue
1 Roddick, *Gentle Giant*, 16.
2 USAF *Aim Points*, June 10, 2005.
3 Dedicated December 1999 by the 7th Bomb Wing, B-36 Association.
4 Fred Schreier, *Lost Nuke* documentary, 2004.
5 Doug Craig, pers. comm., December 2000.
6 *Terrace Standard*, March 16, 2004.
7 *Edmonton Examiner*, September 1, 2004.
8 Jim Laird, *Lost Nuke* documentary, 2004.

Selected
Bibliography

Alperovitz, Gar. *The Decision to Use the Atomic Bomb and the Architecture of an American Myth.* New York: Knopf, 1995.

Backer, J.H. *The Decision to Divide Berlin.* Durham, NC: Duke University Press, 1978.

Bertell, Dr. Rosalie. *No Immediate Danger: Prognosis for a Radioactive Earth.* Toronto, ON: The Women's Educational Press, 1985.

Borutski, Barry. "Cold War Relic B-36-B. The final destination of the USAF's first Broken Arrow." *Flight Journal* (December 2000): 32–36.

Center for Defense Information. "US nuclear weapons accidents: Danger in our midst." *The Defense Monitor* X, no. 5(1981): 3.

Clearwater, John. *Broken Arrow #1: The World's First Lost Atomic Bomb.* Surrey, BC: Hancock House, 2008.

Corley-Smith, Peter, and David N. Parker. *Helicopters: The British Columbia Story.* Victoria, BC: Sono Nis Press, 1998.

Craig, D.B. "Crash site investigation of USAF aircraft No. 2075." Unpublished report, 1997.

Davidge, Doug. *Environmental Impact Study of Crash Site of USAF Bomber.* www.cowtown.net/proweb/brokenarrow2.htm

Eldridge, Morley, et al. "Mt. Slesse air crash site archaeological investigation." Unpublished report prepared for Chilliwack Forest District by Millennia Research, Sidney, BC, 1994.

Hansen, Chuck. *U.S. Nuclear Weapons: The Secret History.* San Antonio, TX: Aerofax, 1988.

———. *The Swords of Armageddon: U.S. Nuclear Weapon Developments since 1945.* CD-ROM. Sunnyvale, CA: Chukelea Publications, 1995.

Hoagland, Edward. *Notes from the Century Before: A Journal from British Columbia.* San Francisco: North Point Press, 1982.

Jacobsen, Meyers K. "Peacemaker." *Airpower* 4, no. 6 (November 1974): 8–27, 50–55.

———. *Convair B-36: A Comprehensive History of America's "Big Stick."* Schiffer Publishing Ltd., 1998.

Johnsen, Frederick A. *Thundering Peacemaker: The B-36 Story in Words and Pictures.* Tacoma, WA: Bomber Books, 1978.

Kirkland, Richard C. *Tales of a War Pilot.* Washington, DC: Smithsonian Institution Press, 1999.

LeMay, Curtis, with MacKinley Kantor. *Mission with LeMay: My Story.* New York: Doubleday & Company, 1965.

Oskins, Jim. *Nuclear Weapons Maintenance—The Early Years.* 35th Munitions Maintenance Squadron, Biggs AFB, Texas, March 1956 – July 1969.

Pyeatt, Don. "Re: B-36 crash on Mt. Kologet 13 Feb 1950." Interview on July 31, 1998, with Ray Whitfield. www.cowtown.net/proweb/brokenarrow3.htm

Roddick, Jim A. "*The Gentle Giant. A Peacemaker at Peace. Annals of the Cold War.*" (unpublished) 2000.

Septer, Dirk. "A Mystery Never Solved." *Canadian Aviator* 19, no. 1 (January–February 2009): 16–17.

———. "Broken Arrow." *BC Aviator* 3, no. 2 (October-November 1993): 23–27.

———. "Broken Arrow: Many questions remain." *West Coast Aviator* 7, no. 6 (July-August 1998): 10–15.

———. "Broken Arrow." *Airforce Magazine* 21, no. 4 (Winter 1998): 12–16.

Tucker, Robert C. (ed.) *Stalinism: Essays in Historical Interpretation.* New York: W.W. Norton, 1977.

United States Department of Defense/Department of Energy. *The Histories of Nuclear Weapon Accidents 1950–1980,* 1981.

———. *Summaries of Accidents Involving US Nuclear Weapons 1950–1980.* (Accident) No. 2, April 11, 1950/B-29/Manzano Base, New Mexico.

Index

DIRK SEPTER is an aviation historian and photographer who focuses on British Columbia and the Canadian Arctic. He was the lead investigator in the television documentary *Lost Nuke*, which first aired on the Discovery Channel in 2004. He has continued to research the story of the first Broken Arrow, which he began doing in the late 1980s.

Dirk has published over 100 articles in aviation magazines in Canada and the UK. For several years he wrote a regular column called "North of Sixty" in *Canadian Aviator*. He was born and raised in the Netherlands, where he served in the Royal Netherlands Air Force. He moved to Canada in 1973 and currently lives on Cortes Island in British Columbia.